ONIONS IN THE WASHING MACHINE

By

Jane Readfern-Gray

Published in 2016 by FeedARead.com Publishing – Arts Council funded

Copyright © Jane Readfern-Gray

First Edition

A CIP catalogue record for this title is available from the British Library.

ACKNOWLEDGEMENTS

A huge thank you to Maria and to my dad for helping with the editing of this book. Thank you to Debbie, because without your help, this book would still be sitting on my laptop; you've been brilliant! Thank you Adrian for your amazing photography skills and to Linda for your help too. Much love and hugs to my husband and best friend Gaz for all your support and to mum and dad. You have been tremendously supportive throughout the years whether good or difficult times; you are both amazing. Lastly, thanks to everyone who gave their permission to appear in the book it would be tremendously boring without you.

CONTENTS

1. Early Years

Lancashire is where I was born, and Lancashire will always be my home no matter where I live. Recently, I was walking down a street, when an elderly gentleman walked past me and expressed his admiration for my guide dog. I recognised his accent immediately, and enquired to where he was from. He stopped, paused, and proudly announced, "Lancashire!" Although, like me, he had not lived there for a number of years, the pride and affection which emanated from that single word all goes to prove that you can take someone away from Lancashire, but they will always carry a piece of that beautiful county with them wherever they go.

I certainly gave my family a shock one snowy evening in December 1968 when I arrived into the world, 11 weeks earlier than expected, and weighing just 2 pounds and 5 ounces. My parents were told that it was unlikely I would make it through the night, and one nurse even asked my Mother if she had ordered a pram, because she would need to cancel it. My weight dropped further to 1 pound and 14 ounces. It was clearly an extremely traumatic time for my close family, but I'm glad to say that God had a plan, and I pulled through.

I was only a few months old when my parents started to notice that there was something wrong with my eyesight. I was taken to many doctors and consultants, and it was presumed that too much oxygen at birth had caused the problem. The prognosis for the future, however, was varied, with some predicting that my sight would be so poor I would be unable to read or write, and others concluding that the only thing I would be unable to do was drive a car. I admire my Mum and Dad for the way they negotiated their way through the difficult times ahead of them. It is fair to say that a family in the same situation today would receive much more help and support from relevant sources, than during the 1960s. Thankfully, changing attitudes, and advancing technology have greatly improved the lives of people with disabilities in recent years but, at that time, it was very hard for them.

Some of my earliest recollections are of living in Great Harwood. My Mother ran her own business, and we lived in the flat above the premises. It's really strange some of the things one does remember. I have a vivid memory of walking to the chip shop on the corner of our street and asking for some chips. I craned my neck and watched as the polystyrene tray descended to my level thanks to a kind member of the public, and I thought how high up that counter seemed. I remember there being a confectioner's across the road from my Mum's shop, but

7

I was too scared to cross that busy road. Those fast noisy cars frightened me. Looking back, that's probably a good thing. I recall being bought a brown leather coat with a matching cap. One Christmas, I accidentally broke a bauble from the Christmas tree. Nobody saw me, but I felt so bad, I hid the broken pieces inside my leather cap and hid it under the settee. When my Mum found it, she was only concerned about whether I'd cut my hands. I also remember Thursdays, Every Thursday evening my Nanna and Granddad would visit, and Granddad would always bring me a special present. Sometimes it was a toy, sometimes a jigsaw, sometimes a teddy bear.

On one of these occasions my Granddad came up to the flat wearing a surprised expression, and exclaimed, "What the b****y hell is going on in the shop?" Perplexed, Mum and Dad ran downstairs to find that I had discovered a box of tampons, unwrapped them, and hung them over the window display in the shop for the whole town to see. I have absolutely no recollection of this event, and still maintain that it's just a story invented to blackmail me at various points in our family life. Well it won't work any more people! Now everyone knows.

Music has been one of my greatest pleasures in life, from an early age. We had a small square record player with a speaker grill on the front. I must have been around four years old as I sang along to songs such as "Claire" by Gilbert O'Sullivan; and "Johnny Rege" by the Piglets. It was around this time that I began attending a local primary school. I remember playing games in the hall, climbing the rope ladders during PE, and enjoying making pictures with lots of cotton wool, glue and brightly coloured pieces of paper. At the end of each day, before we were allowed to collect our coats and meet our parents, we had to sit and listen to a piece of classical music. There was one in particular that I liked so much, that my Mum had to ask my teacher where it was from. Consequently, the first record purchased for me was Tchaikowski's "Swan Lake". I am convinced that this daily requirement greatly contributed to establishing my love of music covering many different genres.

When I was five years old, we moved to a small town called Clitheroe, where my grandparents lived. In fact, we went to live with them for a few months, while my Father and various other people renovated the house to which we were moving. My grandparents lived on a small council estate. The people were very friendly, and my Nanna's brother lived opposite us. My Great Grandmother, whom we called Granny, also lived there, which made for quite a busy household. It was a happy place. We played outside on long summer evenings until it went dark. Hide and seek was one of our favourites. All the children would play happily together, and, on one occasion, some of us hid in our coal shed and it took some time for us to be found.

My Dad came home from work one day and took me out to the garden to show me something very exciting. In reality, it was an octagonal shaped cylinder, around five feet tall and made from thick cardboard. Dad had created a door and we made it into a pretend rocket. I put a blanket in the bottom, threw some books and comics in there together with some sweets, and I was content. At the time, I thought that my rocket was so cool. I was quite miffed years later, when I found out that it was actually just a large bin.

In contrast with those warm summer evenings, I remember snuggling up in front of a lovely coal fire and watching the TV on cold, dark winter nights. This would often be accompanied by the smell of freshly baked cakes or biscuits, made by Granny.

A particular favourite of mine, were something Granny called "Goosnargh Cakes". These were very thin shortbread style circular biscuits that tasted wonderful. Nobody since has been able to make them, although they have tried. I don't know where Granny got the recipe, but I'm convinced that even if we did have it we wouldn't be able to match hers. My Granny was a lady with a great sense of humour. My Nanna told me the story of when she had gone to the theatre but was disappointed to find that the woman sitting in front of her was wearing a particularly large hat which was obstructing Granny's view. Granny politely asked the lady to please remove her hat so that she could see. The woman ignored her, so moments later, Gran asked again. When the lady ignored her request a third time, she simply put out her hand and flicked off the hat, much to the woman's surprise.

Unfortunately, we hadn't been staying at Nan and Granddad's house for more than a few months when we were confronted with some very sad events. Granny died, and within six months, Granddad died suddenly. It was a very difficult time for everyone, especially my Nanna, who lost her mother and her husband in such a short period of time. I still remember the night of Grandad's death quite clearly, even though I was only five. My sister, who is three years younger than me, and I, were sleeping in our bedroom, when Granddad came home. I woke when I heard some activity. Someone was walking up and down the stairs. Granddad wasn't feeling well, and Nanna was going downstairs to get him various remedies to make him feel better. I heard conversations, and neighbours visiting to help, the doctor calling, and hearing the news that Granddad had died. I lay in my bed feeling sad and frightened. I heard my Mum come home, after spending the evening with friends. The news was devastating for her, and I clearly recall her cries of distress from downstairs in the kitchen. I remember my Mum driving me to school the following morning, and some days later, being sent with my sister to play with our neighbour's children while everyone went to the funeral. It was a strange, sad time. I didn't tell my parents about what I had heard that night until I was an adult. I don't know why I chose to keep that secret; I guess I just thought it might make them more upset. We have spoken about the event in recent years, and I think they were surprised that I had remembered it so clearly.

Nanna came to live with us, in our new house. It seemed rather large when we moved in there. The property was originally five small cottages, which had been made into one house with my Mum's shop next door. Two of the rooms upstairs were so large I could ride my small bike around in there. Adjacent to the house was a large field where my sister and I would play. Saturday mornings were always fun. Unfortunately, Mum had to work, so Dad used to sit and watch TV with us. Barnaby the Bear was our favourite. Then we would play board games or, if it was a nice day, we'd go outside and play football or Frisbee.

I was always quite a tomboy. I enjoyed playing in the mud, and riding my bike, or the go-cart that Dad made for me. I had a friend named Jack, with whom I liked to play. One of Jack's neighbours had a back yard with a metal pole in it, which was cemented into the ground. Why it was there was a mystery, but it provided fun for us. We used to wait until the householder had gone out, and then climb up the wall, lean forward and grab on to the pole, and slide down. It was brilliant, until one day when we were caught in the act. Just down the road from our house was a pub. I had been playing in our field, when I noticed a huge pile of soil in the corner of the small car park. I thought it would be great to go hunting for worms, so off I went. I got stuck in, and minutes after, while I was searching, knee deep in the soil, I heard a fierce voice behind me.

10

"What the bl***y h*ll do you think you're doing in that soil, get out!" I'd never been a fast runner, but on that day I made an exception.

My sister and I have always got on very well, but there have been occasions when relations wavered. She won't be happy with me for spilling the beans, but she was only about three at the time. Once she hit me on the head with a glass and, another time, with a poker. Compared to the glass that really did hurt. I suppose we were around the ages of ten and seven, on a fateful day when we got into deep trouble. We were fighting over an inside door, the type found in a hallway, a couple of feet away from the front door with a glass panel. Kirsten wanted to come in, and I wanted her to stay out. We both pushed and pulled on the door with all our strength. This wasn't about the door, it was about who was the boss. As we each fought to establish our authority, Kirsten decided to throw all her weight against the middle of the door. She was determined to go through that door, no matter what my wishes were. Her entrance, however, was made through the middle of the door, where the large glass panel had once been. Luckily, neither of us was hurt, but the loud smash alerted Nanna, and she was furious. She cleared up the glass while chanting, "Just you wait till your Dad gets home!" That was a phrase to strike fear in to the very depths of our being, and we retreated to our bedroom with much trepidation. We didn't realise, that that particular day, was Mum and Dad's wedding anniversary, but instead of celebrating, they were searching for a glazier.

Whilst living in Clitheroe, my sister and I attended Edisford County Primary School. I managed quite well, even though my sight was poor. If I sat at the front of the class, I could see enough to read the board. There were occasional incidents where I would be subjected to some name calling, but on the whole, it was a happy time. The staff were very understanding with me, but I have to admit that I always did feel different to everyone else. I hated playing sports outside, because I couldn't see the ball well enough if we played rounders. If we were split into teams, I would always be one of the last to be picked by my peers. I've always been quite good about just getting on with things, and that's exactly what I did. I enjoyed helping my sister with her reading. Most afternoons when we returned from school, we would sit part way up the stairs and put our books on the windowsill, where the light was good, and there I would listen to Kirsten read and help when she struggled. She has always been a very good reader, and Dad constantly reminded me that it was down to my diligent help.

Mum and Dad worked very hard, sometimes for extremely long hours. Nanna became our primary carer during the week. In the morning, she would wake us, get us ready, and walk us to school. I used to look forward to her collecting us at the end of the day. I would always leave my coat on the end peg in the cloakroom, next to the window. When it was home time, I'd run for my coat, look out of the window and there would be my Nan's smiling face, beaming at me. She would wave her hand as if to say "Come on" and I'd rush out to meet her. Frequently, she would have a chocolate bar for us, which we would eat on the way home. Nanna would then make dinner for everyone while we watched TV or played together.

When I was about seven years old, I was allowed to walk my sister to school. During one trip, something unfortunate happened. Each morning, we would walk past a field with a large gate. It was usually empty but, one day, we noticed two horses – a small black one and a rather large white one. From then on, each morning we would take an apple and feed them. I always fed the white horse, and Kirsten the black one. However, on this occasion, my sister decided that we should swap. Kirsten gave her apple to the white horse and, while I proceeded to give mine to the black one, the other took issue. He leaned forward and sunk his teeth into my shoulder. The pain seemed intense, and I cried, peeling away my jumper and looking down at my shoulder, now arrayed with a variety of colours including black and purple. I made a tearful journey home, and Nanna took me to the doctor, who added insult to injury by administering a tetanus injection.

Unfortunately for me, this wasn't an isolated incident. I visited a park with Dad while Mum was shopping one afternoon. We went to feed the ducks and swans, and I must have become over-confident because, as I leaned forward to offer a piece of bread, a swan bit my finger. As I screamed, my Dad laughed, and I was extremely unimpressed.

It's very common for children to pester their parents for a pet, and we were no exception. We wanted a dog, so one day Dad came home with - two gerbils. It wasn't quite what we were expecting, but, nevertheless, we were quite excited. We filled up the water bottle, and put down fresh bedding in the cage. Then we sat for ages, watching them scuttle round. When it was time for bed, we insisted on taking our new found friends with us. However, the novelty soon wore off. You have probably guessed what the problem was. That wretched wheel kept us awake all night. After that, the cage remained in the living room. It was while I was removing one of the aforementioned creatures from its cage that I was subjected to more pain from an animal. Any sensible gerbil would be grateful for being lifted from its confined surroundings and duly make a break for freedom, but not this one. It bit the skin between my index and middle fingers, and just wouldn't let go. This feisty creature hung on with his tiny needle-sharp gnashers, despite the deafening decibels I delivered in to his ears. As the blood streamed down my arm, I shook my hand until eventually, he let go and dropped to the floor, taking with him, a piece of my flesh, and every shred of affection I had for the gerbil population.

I mentioned earlier that I used to be quite a tomboy. In contrast to our Saturday morning football, Sunday afternoon meant the country run! Kirsten and I would be dressed in our Sunday best, and the family would take a drive into the country in Dad's car. Mum would usually have to drag me off the street, and prise me out of my jeans and jumper, while I protested and resisted as much as I could. I hated getting dressed up. At the time of writing this book, the last time I wore a dress was when I got married, and that was twenty years ago. As a child, I used to get car sick, so you can appreciate my dislike for this ritual. While lots of little girls were delighting in dressing up like princesses, I was playing with my bow and arrow. What's the point of a doll, when you can make a spaceship out of Meccano, which will fire rockets, and why bother with a boring sparkly pink bag, when you can have a cool cap gun. Caps were great: they only cost two pence a pack and lasted ages. Sometimes we'd put them in our guns, and sometimes we'd sit on the ground and scrape them with stones, and watch those little sparks. I also liked to visit the joke shop, investing in whoopee cushions, and finger traps, not to mention the fake dog pooh, and the pretend rats. You could really have some fun with those. So there I was, getting on with life, doing most of the stuff that eight year old kids do, not having any notion of what I was about to be confronted with, and how my life would suddenly change.

2. Troubled Times

I had just begun year five of my primary education when things started to get tough. At regular intervals, I had visited a low vision clinic, and been issued with glasses, and various different magnifiers, but they never helped a great deal. Now, however, I noticed that the print size on work sheets and textbooks was getting smaller, and I was struggling. Through my right eye, I had always only been able to tell the difference between light and dark, but my left eye was the good eye. Admittedly it wasn't a huge amount of vision, but it was extremely precious to me. I was given a monocular. The easiest way to describe it is like having half a pair of binoculars, a single cylinder shaped magnifier, which I held up to my good eye. I can vividly remember the hours of frustration, as I grappled, to get the stupid thing into focus. The skin around my eye became red and sore, and I just wanted to throw it across the room. I became increasingly despondent, but felt too embarrassed to tell anyone. I didn't want to make a fuss, and I didn't want anyone fussing over me. I wanted to be like everyone else, to blend in with everyone else. I'm glad to say that a child facing the same circumstances today, would benefit from having a teaching assistant, and helpful resources such as enlarged photocopied work sheets, but during the 1970's, this support was not offered to me. At that time, my vision, though severely impaired, was stable. I could still read large print books, watch TV, and get around outside without the need for any help. It was clear though, that I had reached a point in my education where I now could no longer manage independently, and would require extra help. As I sat at my desk in the classroom, I used to wonder how I could confront the problem.

It was during this time of uncertainty that I awoke one morning to find that my problems had just become a whole lot worse. I opened my eyes and looked around the bedroom. I closed them and opened them again. I yawned, rubbed my eyes, and looked around. I closed my eyes and dived under the covers. This was just a bad dream. When I plucked up the courage to emerge and look around again, anxiety and fear were beginning to set in. The cheerful pink walls were faded and pale. I turned to look at the poster over my bed, and it was dim and blurred. In fact, everything was pale in colour and very blurred. I don't know how long I lay there, while my sister lay asleep in her bed beside me, but at the time, it seemed forever. I can recall very few details of the following couple of hours, except to say that somehow, I got up, washed and dressed and walked my sister to school without telling anyone. A short time later, I found myself once again, sitting at my desk worrying about what I was going to do about my problems.

The previous day, we had been busy doing a school project focusing on "holes, gaps, and cavities". Looking back, it seems strange that I would remember those three seemingly insignificant words, but the reason is that this piece of work required an extensive amount of drawing and colouring, and the task that day was to complete it. I will never forget the horror, the frustration, and the helplessness I felt as I stared down at the desk in front of me. The room was filled with around thirty other noisy children who were getting on with their day, busily colouring and chatting as normal. The sound seemed to wash over me as I gazed towards the windows, and then up at the ceiling, every second wishing that things could go back to the way they were the previous day. Before me was a large sheet of paper containing my unfinished work. The colours that had seemed so bright were now faded. Next to the paper was a pot of colouring pencils. I wearily took one, and desperately tried to continue, but my best efforts were futile. My ability to see any definition was gone. All I could see, with a struggle, was a large mass of merged pale colour. I made several attempts to try again, before just giving up and simply staring down, with the weight of defeat hanging over me, and a growing sense of isolation. I was plagued by the reality of the fact that what I was able to do yesterday I could no longer do today. I must have stayed there for around an hour, until the children were clearing away, ready for break time. I reached the point where I could contain my emotions no longer and, as I sat there, the tears began to fall. Finally, I made a tentative approach to my teacher's desk, and told her that I didn't feel well.

I was taken to the library, where I was given a large beanbag to sit on, and told to rest, and maybe read a book. Read a book! Read a book? If only she knew; and yet, I didn't want her to know. I didn't want anyone to know, I wasn't ready to tell anyone yet. As she left, I flopped down on the beanbag and cried. I was alone, but I didn't feel anymore alone than I had already felt in that crowded classroom. After a while, I made a brave attempt to walk across the room and selected the first book I touched. I sat down and flicked through the pages, and with each turn of the page, wished and hoped that my sight would return as quickly as it had left. Disappointed, I returned the book, and grabbed another, repeating this ritual several times, before returning to my beanbag and falling into a tearful heap. At regular intervals, staff members would come to check on me. They would asked what was wrong, and each time, I would tell them that I just didn't feel well. No one ever asked me anything to do with my vision, so I suspect they had no idea what was really wrong. It was during my times alone, that I began to ponder how I was going to tell my parents what had happened. I was anxious, being aware that my Mum especially had experienced a tremendous amount of stress and sadness in recent times. I don't know why I felt a sense of responsibility, but I did. For myself, I felt that telling someone would be giving up. If I waited just a while longer, things might change, and then there would be no need to have told anyone in the first place. If I did tell them, it would cause so much upset, and it would be so final. I was scared about how much my life, and theirs, would radically change forever.

Shortly before lunch, the headmaster came to tell me that he was going to take me home. The corridors were quiet because everyone was busy in the classrooms. I followed him out of the front door, and can remember very well what happened next. It seemed so dull and dark outside. As I squinted to look around, it didn't seem as if I was in full daylight, but more like the end of a day, when there is still some daylight left, but you know that very soon it will be dark. We needed to walk along a straight path, lined by raised flowerbeds on either side with grassy areas behind them. I had walked this path so many times without a care, but today I made my way very slowly, tentatively, gingerly, frightened of falling or tripping. I kept zigzagging my way along, bumping and scraping my feet on the concrete edging which protected the flower beds. Each step was like moving forward in to the unknown. I felt very vulnerable and powerless to do anything about it. I strained to see the headmaster who strode out for what seemed a long way ahead of me. At one point, he turned, and called to me, the irritation clear in his voice, requiring me to get a move on. When we arrived home, he knocked on our front door, but nobody answered. So I was promptly taken back to the library, to ponder a while longer.

During the afternoon, I told my teacher that my Nanna would now probably be at her brother's house. Uncle Horace lived only a few steps away from the rear of the school field. He lived alone, as his wife had sadly died a number of years previously. Every day, Nanna would walk to his home to take a meal she had made for him, and to help out with any cleaning which needed to be done. I was taken there, and when she opened the door, my teacher told her that I was unwell and left me with Nanna. I had not considered that this would be my last day at school for a while. I sat on the small settee in the back room, while Nan knelt on the floor in front of me, cleaning out the coal fire. Still feeling dazed, I listened as she busied herself with her jobs, occasionally checking to see if I was ok, and talking or humming to herself. The sound of her voice was comforting, and when she had finished, I held her hand tightly as we walked home. I don't know if she noticed anything different about me as we walked, but she never mentioned anything. Back in my bedroom that afternoon, I played with some toys, still anxious about how I was going to tell my family. When my parents arrived from work, they enquired whether I was feeling better, and I can recall feeling very awkward. The defining moment of that day was when we were all sitting in the living room. I faced further enquiries as to what was wrong with me, and I tried to avoid the issue. That was, until my Mum confronted me with the question, "Is there something wrong with your eyes?" I sat silently as the tears fell again. At that point, it felt like my world was imploding and I could do nothing to stop it.

Our G.P. was called immediately, and it was considered to be such an emergency, we were required to make a trip to his house where he examined me. I can remember a very tense car journey, and then being led into a darkened room, lit only by a bright desk lamp in one corner. I sat feeling numb as everyone talked about me and discussed what could be done. At one point, my Mum asked me to tell everyone what colour her jacket was. She held out her forearm under the light. I looked down at her sleeve. I hadn't really noticed her jacket on the journey, and the light was so bright that to me it seemed to be white and that is what I said. There was an immediate negative reaction. When we left, I strained to see the jacket as we got into the car, and perceived that it was green. It had been so dark in that room apart from that one light. Now I had made matters worse, and I felt so bad. The next few days are quite a blur. I remember spending a great deal of time just playing in my bedroom. I do, however, have a recollection of Mum taking me back to school. I'm not entirely sure whether it was to see if there was any way I could return, or if it was simply to collect some of my belongings. While she chatted to staff members, ironically, I was taken to the library, to sit on that same beanbag to wait for her. The library was situated next to the large hall, and I could hear the children in assembly. It felt very strange. I think I knew by then that it would be the last time I would be attending that school. As we walked home, I held on tight to Mum's arm, still feeling very tentative, and nervous about tripping down kerbs.

Another very poignant moment occurred soon after, whilst standing in the street with Nanna. Across from our house, lived my Nanna's cousin, Aunty Mildred. We were returning from a short trip to a local shop, when she stopped to talk with us. It was very strange standing there. I could hear two voices I knew very well, but I could no longer see the familiar faces synonymous with those voices. As I stood listening, I experienced a deepening sense of isolation. It felt as if I was living in a familiar world, but I was no longer as in touch with that world as I had been before, kind of distant and uncomfortable. If someone with full sight was required to wear a blindfold for the day then still try to get on with their daily routine, they would feel very different both mentally and physically. The difference between that situation and mine would be that the blindfold could be removed at any point, and normal life resumed immediately.

Up to this point, I had weathered the storm of mixed emotions, but had not been confronted by anger until the day I found something that took me back to my last day of school. I was clearing out my school bag, when my fingers wrapped around my monocular. Anger and resentment started to well up. The memory of all those hours grappling to read with that thing seemed to close in on me. I've never admitted this to anyone, but I blamed that piece of equipment for my loss of vision. I felt that all the stress and strain, had caused the sudden deterioration of my sight and I hated it. I really hated that useless hunk of junk, sitting there smugly in its pretentious leather case. I threw it down in total disgust, wishing I could stamp on it and completely destroy it. I'm sure that countless people have used the same magnifier, and found it to be greatly advantageous, but I never wanted to find it again.

In the weeks that followed, life slowly stabilised. I stayed at home with Nan, playing, watching the TV which I could still see if I sat directly in front of the screen, and listening to the radio. Each day we would walk down to take a meal for Uncle Horace, and I would try my best to assist with the cleaning duties. I visited Leeds infirmary several times to see a consultant, but did not return to school. It was decided that I required eye surgery which needed to take place as soon as possible. The procedure was to be carried out on my right eye to see if the sight could be improved. I didn't enjoy my stays in hospital very much. There was nothing wrong with the ward or the staff. I suppose the experience of sudden loss of vision had left me feeling very vulnerable. During my first visit, Mum stayed with me. The operation was a new procedure, and would take some time to perform. I was taken to the theatre in the morning and, I am told, didn't return until lunch time. I have a vague recollection of waking up in my hospital bed, but feeling so groggy, I simply turned over and went back to sleep, and this continued until the following day. During this time, Mum bought me a light sabre, (from the film "Star Wars"), but it wasn't until a few days after the operation that I began to appreciate it. One evening, I woke and asked if I could go to the toilet, a nurse came over and helped me. When I returned to bed, I asked if I could look at my light sabre. Everyone else was asleep, and the ward was quiet and very dark. The nurse took it from under my bed and switched it on. I stared at the contrast between the darkened ward, and the orange glow of the light. That told me I was still in touch with my world and I went back to sleep. I didn't like it when Mum had to leave in the evening. I felt lonely and a little scared. During the day, when I had recovered from my operation, we would spend the time listening to music, and Mum would read to me. On one occasion, a staff member approached us, and asked if I would like to make something. We were taken into another ward, and to a room with a large table in the centre. On there, was a huge box full of arts and crafts materials. We had great fun that afternoon, constructing silly hats, masks, and pictures.

At the same time, there was a young boy in my ward who had been involved in an explosion. His eyes had been damaged, and he had suffered terrible pain. I can remember his agonising screams filling the ward at regular intervals, as the nurses put medication in his eyes. Eye drops can sting, when treating just a minor problem, but in his situation, the pain must have been intense. My Mum described how he would lie on the bed, and grasp his soft toy tightly as if he was strangling it and scream out in pain as the nurses administered the eye drops. I felt so sorry for him. We spent time playing together in the playroom, and I thought he was very brave. During my second stay in hospital, which closely followed the first, we had bonfire night. It was great, because the staff wheeled our beds in long lines to corridors where we watched a firework display, and we ate gingerbread and treacle toffees. The atmosphere was cheery and loads of fun. Nanna stayed with me that time, but thankfully it was only a short stay. One day, my Aunty Jenny came to visit me. The surgeon arrived to examine me and announced that I could go home a day early. I

19

remember feeling so glad that she had come, and she helped us pack and took us straight home. It took a few weeks until I noticed and appreciated the benefits of those two operations, but it's something I'm still very grateful for today.

3. "Boo To You Too!"

Following my return from hospital, I was visited by a representative from the local education department, to be given an assessment. The test seemed to go on for ever, and I wondered why I had to have them. I was informed that a teacher would be visiting me several times per week to tutor me at home. I found this quite exciting as I had started to get rather bored. My teacher was very understanding. I could work at my own pace, using large print, without feeling rushed or under pressure. As well as covering the basics; reading, writing and maths, we would also play word games, or have a quiz. I eased back in to my education quite well and looked forward to those sessions. Every morning I would get up early to arrange the kitchen table with my learning resources when everyone had finished breakfast. A kitchen that turned in to a classroom seemed a fun idea.

Around that time, Kirsten and I had a big surprise. Mum and Dad arrived home one evening carrying a very scruffy looking dog. I didn't know that my parents had friends who owned their own boarding kennels. For quite some time, my Mum had wanted a Yorkshire terrier and they had been contacted because a stray dog had been taken in to the kennels. He was quite large for a Yorkshire terrier. He had a tan coloured head, and a dark brown body, with steely grey markings across his back. I felt so sorry for him as I stretched out my hand and felt his terribly matted coat, the poor dog was shaking with fear. Once we had seen him, he was taken to the local vet to be cleaned and vaccinated. When he returned 24 hours later, he looked like a vastly different dog. His fur was smooth and fluffy, and he smelled much better. We all fell in love with him immediately. He was definitely a hit. Kirsten and I took him for a short walk that evening, where we enthusiastically discussed prospective names. We had many suggestions, but were exasperated when we returned home. My Mum started calling him "Boo!" and we thought it was silly. The unfortunate thing was that he responded to that name and so it stuck. It caused countless embarrassing situations for my Dad, especially when walking him last thing at night. Whilst strolling through the park one evening, Boo disappeared and had to be called. At the time, a young couple were walking a few yards in front, and the gentleman turned round and shouted, "Boo to you too!"

Boo was definitely an eccentric character. He seemed to need lots of exercise for a small dog. Even though the vet told us he didn't have any mobility problems, he would lift his left front paw and run on three legs. It was quite comical. One of my happiest memories of Boo was taking him to walk up Pendle hill. It was a steep climb for my sister and me, and would take quite some time. As we made our way, me holding tight on to Dad's arm, I would hear Boo running around. It always happened that as we were roughly half way up, that I would hear him barking high above up ahead. He would look down as if to say, "What are you doing? I've been up and down this hill several times, and you're still down there!" We would always laugh and shout, "You may be smaller, but you've got four legs and we've only got two!" It simply didn't matter how long we walked him, he never seemed to tire. He also had a very independent streak. He insisted on going out for a walk by himself, making his return known by barking and scratching at the back door. We also found this trait very comical. On one occasion, he went missing. We were so upset, that an appeal was put out on local radio. It turned out that he had been adopted by a family only a few streets away. When my Dad went to collect him he found that Boo had been bought a very expensive lead and collar, and around a month's supply of dog food, which my Dad felt obliged to buy. I seem to remember eating plenty of beans on toast and soup that month. In fact, Boo probably ate better than we did!

Boo was a dog who loved to travel in the car. He would often stand on the back seat, stretch his two front paws up on to the edge of the window frame, and look out of the window. He loved it if you opened the window a little, but not too much, just in case he decided he liked the look of somewhere, and jumped out to explore. None of us would have put it past him, so the window only ever went down a tiny bit. Boo had an orange rubber bone that he would proudly carry around the house. Sometimes Nanna would play with him, holding the bone high in the air too high up for him to jump up and grab it. He would sit there looking up and whine until it was dropped and he would grab it and run. One sad day, Boo went out and didn't return. We all waited and hoped and wished he would. When the days turned to weeks, and our appeals for his return were fruitless, it slowly and painfully dawned on us that we would probably never see him again. Kirsten and I really missed him and were at times quite tearful. Dad sat us down one day and explained that Boo was a very clever dog who loved to explore. He related how he thought that Boo was probably now sitting on a deckchair on a sunny beach somewhere, wearing a pair of sunglasses and eating a large ice-cream. The image made us laugh and did help to cheer us up. I've never forgotten that story. I hoped for so long that it was true.

Shortly before Christmas 1977, we moved from Clitheroe to a small village just outside Accrington. The house was much smaller than our previous one, but we soon got used to it. During a couple of winters living there, it snowed so heavily, that it came over my knees. I'd never seen snow that deep before, and thought it was fantastic. It did however, make very hard work of going to our local shop to get milk or bread. A journey which normally took only five minutes, now took at least fifteen. It seemed a long hard trek, and I was glad when we arrived home. We did however, have great fun making snowmen, and having snowball fights. We were always quite sad when it melted away, not to mention Kirsten's disappointment at no longer having the prospect of extra days off school.

Talking of school, because we had moved to a different part of the county, I no longer had my home tutor, and was completely unaware of the heartache I was about to be confronted with concerning my education. One evening, I was told that I would be attending a new school. I was apprehensive, as the school was in a different town, and for the first week, I would have to travel by taxi, arranged by the local education authority. From the second week onwards, I would be traveling by school bus with many other children. I am not going to make known the location or the name of the school for reasons which will become apparent. I wish to stress that there was nothing wrong with the establishment; it just wasn't right for me and my personal circumstances.

On my first day, I was a little nervous about starting a new school, but so are most children. I was introduced to a girl called Kerry, who showed me around, and sat next to me. I observed that there were many pupils with other disabilities. Some were in wheelchairs and others using walking frames. I know that it sounds rather silly, but it was something I hadn't been informed about, and took me by surprise. In class, my teacher was called Mrs. Fields, and she was to teach me for most of my lessons. We spent the first day learning the difference between small and capital letters, and how to write them. In the afternoon, we had a maths lesson, where we were instructed how to add together two digit numbers. I am definitely no super brain, but it didn't take long for me to ascertain that my peers were the same age as me, but doing work that I had done when I was much younger, What was going on? The following morning, we continued with small and capital letters. Shortly before lunch, we watched a TV programme. It was called "Words and Pictures." I was surprised at the time, because it was a programme I had watched regularly during infant school. In the afternoon, we were taught about vowels. The teacher gave us a special phrase to commit to memory, A, E, I O, U ten pounds. I will never understand why the decision was made to send me to a school for children with complex needs, but it caused a period of trauma, which was one of the worst times I can remember.

Initially, I felt rather confused, because I don't recall at any time, meeting another pupil with a visual impairment. After the first couple of days, I tried to explain to my family that I wasn't enjoying school because they were doing "baby work". That's not meant to sound insulting, just the view of a mystified nine-year-old. It was perceived that I was simply finding it hard to settle into a school routine again, and the days rolled on. My Mum bought me a well-known brand of sports bag, in the hope that I would cheer up. It was a kind thought, but my problems were not that easy to solve. Kerry was a good friend to me and, for most of the time, stayed close by my side. One day, we sat on a bench talking in a corridor just before lunch, when a much older boy walked past us. He shouted something, and as I strained to look over towards him there was a silent pause, and then suddenly he slapped me across my face very hard. I'd never seen stars in my life, even when I had better vision, but that day was the closest I got. It was certainly a shock; and yes, it hurt.

To add insult to injury, lunch times made me feel distinctly uncomfortable. I always had to sit between the headmaster and Mrs. Fields. As they chatted to each other, every day without fail, the conversation would switch over to the subject of the new blind girl. My teacher would constantly express her discomfort about teaching someone who couldn't see. I will never forget one phrase she uttered day after day, "You see, I've never had any experience of this type of thing before!" You don't have to be an adult to feel completely humiliated and demoralised. I just sat in silence, and ate, wishing all the time I could be anywhere else but there. Looking back, it's ironic and comical. I hadn't had the experience of being in a school for children with complex educational needs, and I was as reluctant to be with certain staff members, as they seemed to be with me. After a few days, I was moved from Mrs. Field's class into a different one. The children were a couple of years older than me and the work a little more advanced. I continued to protest at home, and only a few days later was moved up to another class again. I was at this point beginning to feel slightly happier, as the academic level was more suitable. However, my class mates were all much older than me, around fifteen and sixteen. It was during my time in this class that I experienced a degree of bullying. They wanted to know why a nine-year-old was in their class and began making snide comments. I worked alone most of the time, and those old feelings of isolation returned.

On one memorable day, I spent the morning doing English exercises. My teacher Mr. Mann had read out some comprehension exercises on to cassette tape. I was to listen and then write down my answers. I can remember feeling glad that at last I was doing some work that made me think. This would be in stark contrast with the afternoon. It was time for an art session. We were issued with a large sheet of thick paper and told to trace a pattern on there with a fine pencil and then paint it. Because the paper was a dark colour, I was unable to see the contrast between it and the pencil lines. I was, therefore, issued with three paint pots, and a paint brush and given the following instructions. "Just dip the brush in the paint and splurge it on to the paper like this!" For me, it was simply the last straw. I felt like I had been subjected to more frustration than I could take. I did exactly what I was told, dipping my brush in to the paint and randomly splurging it on to the paper. As I reflect upon that day, it brings a wry smile to my face. In a way, I suppose, it was quite artistic, because it actually did reflect the way I was feeling at the time.

I always dreaded the coach journey home, because I was scared that the driver would forget to tell me when it was my stop. I tried to get a seat near a window, and strained to look at the buildings to see if I could recognise my house. When I arrived home that evening, I continued to express my frustrations. I appreciate that it must have been an awful time for Mum and Dad too. They were still convinced that I needed time to settle in to a daily routine, but I felt I just couldn't take it any longer. I seem to remember that the discussions got rather heated that night and when I had reached a point where I felt that no one wanted to listen, or would understand, I knew I had to do something radical. We only had one bathroom in the house, and I went in there, locked the door, and cried, like I'd never cried before. I felt like I was fighting an unwinnable battle all alone. In a way, it felt worse than the day I lost my sight, because at this point, I genuinely thought that nobody cared or understood me anymore. My family

25

begged me to open the door but I refused. If they didn't care, then what was the point? What would that achieve? That night was really the lowest point I can remember. I am aware that I have used the word frustration several times, but that's just the way it was. Frustration, isolation, anger, sadness, and increasing anxiety – I felt completely miserable, and now it seemed that nobody was prepared to help me. I'm sure that most people reading this book, have at some point in their life found themselves in a situation where they feel that they have cried so much, they simply can't cry anymore. Well I finally reached that point, and eventually emerged from the bathroom and went to bed.

The following morning, Nanna woke us as usual, and asked us to get ready for school. As my sister busied herself, I lay there not wanting to move. I was called several times, but I just wanted the day to wash over me. I didn't care anymore. The world could get on with its business, as long as it left me alone. I didn't want to fight any longer. My head hurt, the world was an unhappy place, and I wished it would all go away. When Mum and Nanna couldn't manage to get me out of bed, Dad was called. He was just about to leave for work and wasn't happy. The coach arrived to collect me, but I wasn't ready, and so it left without me. Dad was clearly frustrated as he was forced into physically lifting me out of bed. I refused to respond or interact with anyone. All the time, I was crying out for someone to listen to me, to hear the reasons behind my behaviour, and to try to understand how I was feeling.

It was decided that Dad would drive me to school that day, and find out what all the fuss was about. On arrival we were taken to the headmaster's office, where he explained that the staff were very pleased with me. I was working well and fulfilling their expectations. At that point there was a knock on the door. A boy of around fifteen entered and chatted with the head. It turned out to be someone who had been in my art class the previous day. My Dad was shown some of the work I had completed, and then the head teacher asked me and the other boy to go and get the art work we had done. He added that I had done some fantastic art work and my Dad should see it. On the way back to the office, I remember carrying that large piece of paper and feeling very ashamed of my effort. However, I was also aware of the fact that Dad knew I could achieve better things, and hoped he would feel as mystified as I did. I will never forget the moments that followed. As the teacher asked us to proudly display our work, I held it high in front of me. There was a moment of stunned silence, and then I heard some priceless words from my Dad, in his broad Lancashire accent, "Yer not bloody stoppin' 'ere!!!"

Life can be very strange sometimes. Splurgy portrait had been the last straw that dragged me down to the depths of despair, yet less than twenty-four hours later it had been instrumental in causing my moment of triumph. I heard Dad say, "Come on, we're going." As we walked out of the school, I was elated. A huge weight had been lifted from my shoulders, and the feeling of desperation slowly ebbed away. In general terms, there was absolutely nothing wrong with the school. I'm sure that many students loved it and achieved great things. It's probably fair to say that someone in the education department made an ill informed decision. I am confident that the same mistake would not occur today.

In the days that followed, Mum and Dad felt angry and upset about the distress I had gone through. I don't blame them at all, it had not been their decision, and times were as difficult for them as they were for me. I didn't realise it then, but they were determined that the same mistake wouldn't re-occur, and so took it upon themselves to find me a suitable school. Remember, this is in the days long before the wealth of information available on the internet, and so must have been a massively difficult task. Before I knew anything about it, they were forced to contemplate the possibility of my having to attend a boarding school, and therefore spend much less time at home. That's not an easy decision for any parent to make, and, bearing in mind my recent history, it must have been a worrying prospect. Apparently, Mum spent hours going through the phone book, and talking on the telephone. Eventually they found a prospective school, and a visit was arranged.

4. The Road to Recovery

It was a cold evening in December 1978, when I made my first visit to St. Vincent's School for Blind and Partially Sighted Children, in Liverpool. On our arrival, we were taken into the entrance hall, and asked to wait in the parlour where Sister Josephine would join us shortly. Sister Josephine was the head teacher. In fact, many of the teaching and care staff were nuns. I sat quietly as my parents talked at length with her, before she gave us a tour of the school. I can remember thinking it was a massive place, and wondered how I would ever be able to find my way around. As we walked down the long corridors, we noticed that they were filled with photographs of the pupils; examples of their work; and tactile diagrams and maps. Sister Josephine was very warm and friendly, including me in the conversation, and taking many opportunities to gently place my hand upon pictures and models that she thought may have been of interest to me. I also recall very clearly the first time she placed my hand upon a page of Braille. It felt overwhelmingly complex, and I was intrigued as to how anyone could possibly make any sense of it.

During the evening, we were also joined by the teacher in charge of the junior school, Mrs. Pope. She sat with me, asking lots of questions, including when it was my birthday. When she realised that I had just turned ten, she enquired as to what I had done, and what presents I had received. She showed me the machine used to write Braille, and wrote some out for me to take home. We then walked to the junior girls group, where I was introduced to Miss Josie. She was in charge of looking after around 20 junior girls, and was responsible for their pastoral care. At that time, the girls were playing on a large soft play area, and Miss Josie asked if I would like to join them. I refused, feeling quite shy, and also a little scared. The girls sounded like they were having a great time, but I was frightened of falling over, or banging into someone. Miss Josie took my hand and helped me around the soft play. I felt very vulnerable, and I think she sensed that. She held my hand tightly, talking with me as we walked around. Her manner was very reassuring, and I felt safe with her. She encouraged me to jump off a high area, but I was reluctant, and made a feeble attempt to jump of a much lower part. The atmosphere was so warm and friendly and, secretly, I hoped that Mum and Dad would choose this school for me.

I'm pleased to say that my parents did choose St. Vincent's, and so, in January 1979, once again we made a journey to Liverpool. We arrived on a Monday evening. Miss Josie helped me carry my case to my bedroom which I would be sharing with three other girls and, together, we put a poster above my bed. The previous week, Nanna had bought me a puppet show which had several finger puppets, and a large cardboard stage. We carried it down to the playroom, where I opened it, and showed it to some of the girls. My Mum was very tearful as they left, but I was so engrossed in meeting my new friends, that I simply turned, gave them a wave and got on with what I was doing. When it was bed time, we all walked down a long corridor and up three flights of stairs, to the area where our bedrooms were. We had two sinks in our room, and at the end of the hall, was a bathroom with two toilets and two baths. . As Miss Josie showed me round and helped me run a bath, She asked me if I knew how to test the water to make sure it was the right temperature. I informed her that the best way was to use your elbow. I think she was very impressed at my knowledge. What I didn't tell her, was that I had been watching "Blue Peter" the week before, where I had gleaned this nugget of information. When we were all ready, we knelt round my bed to say prayers before getting into bed. Miss Josie was one of the warmest people you could meet, but was also very strict in certain areas. She set boundaries, and that was a line you really didn't want to cross! Once you were in bed, and the lights turned out, there was to be no talking, *absolutely no talking*, and that was final.

Miss Josie also exercised strict protocol with regard to bed making. I remember her teaching me how to do this, and thinking it was an awful lot of fuss just for making a bed. Firstly, the sheet was to be placed on the bed and opened out. Then you had to ensure it was on straight by checking the length on each side at the top and the bottom, measuring it against the bed frame. Adjustments had to be made accordingly until it was straight. The sheet was then tucked in at the top, and then the bottom, making absolutely sure that there were no creases. Then came the completely new concept of "the envelope corner". I had never heard of this before. There I was, standing at the top side of the bed, lifting the sheet and tucking it in forming the envelope which I would pull gently with one hand while tucking the sheet at the side with the other. This procedure would then be repeated at the bottom end and then round the other side, all the while making sure there were *no creases*! A similar procedure would then need to be repeated with two blankets, before the rules pertaining to the counterpane. I have fond memories of Miss Josie chatting with other staff members, but all the time keeping a close eye on us as we made our beds. She could notice a crease from a mile away, and would call over to us, "Smooth out those creases please." One particular time I was tucking in my sheet, not realising that I had tangled it in the middle. Miss Josie shouted, "Jane, I know you've made a lovely cross in the middle of your bed but please adjust it." At the time I thought that she was quite obsessed with envelope corners and creases. After all, we were going to sleep in the bed, not exhibit it at the Tate Gallery! She was also very strict concerning table manners. However, underneath it all, I was happy to respect her authority. She was, and still is, one of the warmest, kindest, fairest, and consistent people I have ever met.

On that first night, I fell asleep quite contentedly, not feeling at all anxious or homesick. Later that evening I awoke, to hear someone moving around. I turned and saw torchlight, and heard the whisper of a familiar voice, then turned over and fell asleep again. The next morning, I asked "Miss, did you shine that light on me last night?" Miss Josie laughed and told me that she had wanted to check that I was ok. After breakfast we made our beds, and then I was shown to my classroom. I vividly recall walking down the long corridor past the dining room, and then turning right up a slope and on to Queen's Wing, where my classroom was located. I was introduced to my teacher, and sat at a desk opposite another girl who I had not met before. We began talking and I remember thinking she was very gentle and friendly. My teacher was a young gentleman who appeared to be welcoming and reassuring. He brought me a magnetic board containing a variety of shapes. My task was to place some small shapes on top of larger shapes and fit them correctly. As I busied myself with the task, my friend opposite was writing Braille and I thought she must be extremely clever to be able to do that. Each time I completed a task, I would be given a more difficult one. I was enjoying myself, and didn't realise how quickly the time was going, until suddenly Miss Josie arrived to take me back to her group for break. We were given juice or milk and biscuits and time to play for a short while before returning to the classroom until lunch.

At lunchtime the whole school would eat together in the large, high ceilinged dining room. We sat at long rectangular tables, and it was always very noisy. Grace was said both before and after each meal, although sometimes, I wondered why we'd bothered giving thanks. I'm sorry to say that the food wasn't great. The meal I hated most was spam fritters. I cannot possibly describe my displeasure at being presented with that completely disgusting dish. Others included, plates of ham with boiled cabbage and powdery boiled potatoes and somewhat sticky mince with mashed potatoes and peas. The food I hate most is liver. Just the smell of it turns my stomach, so when it was served up one day, I had a sudden sense of dread. I was so relieved when I tentatively informed Miss Josie that I really didn't like it, she simply took it away and brought me a fresh plate of sausages, mash and vegetables without the liver. If Miss Josie knew we genuinely didn't like a particular type of food, she would never make us eat it. She would also never make anyone eat anything she didn't like if they didn't want it. She always made sure we ate a balanced diet, but was extremely fair and didn't force us to eat absolutely everything. I soon grew to respect her greatly for her fairness and consistency. Sometimes we would sit at the table to find that we were going to have soup for starters. This gave me rather a deflated sinking feeling, for two reasons. The soup was always thin and never particularly appetising, but, worst of all, if we had soup to start with, it meant there was not going to be any pudding.

Feast days were always something to look forward to. These were days when we would celebrate the lives of certain saints. At lunch time, we normally had chips, and I remember having a particularly tasty trifle. Our favourite dessert was "instant whip". The staff would come around and give us rich tea biscuits to accompany it, which we would put into our bowls and crush with our spoons to mix them in. On one occasion, I was required to have my lunch early before the rest of the school because I had an eye appointment at the hospital. Miss Josie was to take me and so she had to eat early too. I was presented with a plate of cheese pie, boiled potatoes and grilled tomatoes, which didn't provoke much of an appetite. The staff had steak. It turned out that Josie didn't like steak, and I wasn't keen on the cheese pie, so she suggested that we swap. I felt very privileged. I was eating a staff meal, which was quite good, and not yucky cheese pie; now that was cool. Miss Josie told me not to tell anyone—sorry, if you're reading this, I managed to keep that secret for the last thirty-three years!

Breakfast and evening meals were eaten in smaller dining rooms, situated in our groups. In the junior girls, we had a lady named Mrs. Nicholson, who used to arrive early each weekday morning to prepare our breakfast. She would then assist Miss Josie with our supervision during break, lunch, and afternoon play-time. Once, at lunch, she approached me, telling me that I hadn't quite finished, and told me to open my mouth. My face was a picture as I munched on a Brussels sprout, Yuck!! She fell into hysterical laughter, and from then on, always referred to me as her little Brussels sprout. Hmmm! Each Friday, we finished school at lunchtime, and ate a meal before going home. Around midmorning the waft of fish fingers would fill the corridors. One day I was particularly hungry and ate several of them but, on the way home, I regretted my act of indulgence as I felt rather sick. Following that event, I never ate lunch on Friday ever again, instead choosing to collect my bag and simply wait for my transport. Whenever that distinct smell hit my nostrils, I felt nauseous. It took many years for me to regain my taste for the aforementioned food.

Each Monday morning, I would travel to school by taxi. The journey took around forty-five minutes, and I had to be accompanied by an adult, so Nanna travelled with me. I usually had the same driver whose name was George. He was a man in his early sixties who was very cheerful and talkative. During one journey, we found out that we both played the organ, and this gave us lots to talk about. One day, Nanna asked George if we could possibly stop at the shop so she could buy me some batteries for my cassette recorder. The shop was en route and around five minutes away from school. George got out of the car and joined us in the shop. While Nanna bought the batteries, George went across to the counter and chose a variety of sweets and chocolate bars. When we got back to the car, he handed me the large paper bag. My face lit up, and I thanked him. From that day onwards, every Monday morning George would stop the car at the same shop and say, "Come on Jane!" He would take my hand and lead me into the shop and ask me to choose a variety of sweets and chocolates. He noticed that at the time I liked Smarties, and so bought me a box of them. I couldn't believe it. I had never had a whole big box of Smarties before. He added more chocolate bars, before once again presenting me with that large paper bag and leading me back to the car. Each week would be the same, a large box of Smarties and loads of chocolate bars.

On arrival at school, we would put our bags upstairs in our bedrooms. The first task of the day was to go straight to our classrooms where we were required to write our news. This took the form of a written account of the things we had done over the weekend at home. Each one of these offerings would be marked by the teacher, and then stored in our personal news folders. It would be interesting if I could read those stories now. I think I would probably laugh, cringe, and be rather embarrassed all at the same time. When I first joined the school, I had enough sight to be able to write using a thick black felt tip pen. I had a large bright red plastic folder in which I kept all my maths work. I could also see to read using a closed circuit TV. A book could be placed on a flat tray directly under a camera, which would display the words in very large letters on a TV screen. There was always the possibility of my sight deteriorating further, and so the decision was made that I should begin learning Braille.

Mrs. Orpen gave me my first Braille lesson. I learned the letters A, B, K and L. This may seem rather random, but it was for a good reason. There is a wealth of information available about Braille, so I will refrain from boring you with the details. At the end of the lesson, she commented that I was a fast learner, and asked if I was enjoying my experience. My reply was that I thought it was really good, and could we do some more. I think it took me around eighteen months to learn the full code, because there is a wealth of abbreviations and word signs to commit to memory.

On the afternoon of my first day, we all went down to the music department. We sat on plastic chairs set out in a semi-circle around the room. In front of us, stood a gentleman next to a piano and he began asking us questions. My classmates began shouting out the answers, and I thought it seemed rather rude. If I had done that at my previous schools I would have been in trouble, so I put my hand up. Luckily, my teacher had stayed for the beginning of the lesson. He sidled over to me, and whispered in my ear, "Jane it's ok, you can shout out the answers because Mr. Wilson is blind and won't be able to see your hand." I was quite surprised, but now I understood the situation.

Mr. Wilson was a great teacher, with a good sense of humour. When we were eating our evening meal, he would often join us in our little dining room for a cup of tea. He would set us riddles or word puzzles to solve, and sometimes we would muse for days over the answers. He never would tell us straight away, and seemed to like keeping us in suspense. He could be quite a tease, deliberately calling me every girl's name beginning with J, except for Jane. Around that time, Dad expressed his wish for me to begin piano lessons, although I didn't feel particularly enthusiastic about the prospect. Mr. Wilson began teaching me, but I'm sorry to say that I was very poorly motivated. This may have had something to do with the fact that my best friend had just begun learning to play the flute. I liked the sound and wanted to do the same. I persevered for a few months with the piano, but after making very slow progress, I was finally allowed to give it up and begin flute lessons.

So, all-in-all, I settled into my new routine very quickly. I was very happy, and established a good circle of friends. The one and only time I got homesick was during my first week there. The other girls were playing murder in the dark, but I didn't want to join in. I was a little tearful. Miss Josie noticed, and took me in to the dining room. She sat me on her knee and gave me a hug. I can remember telling her that I missed my dog. In the conversation that followed, we began to laugh about something, and that was suddenly the end of my sadness. It never bothered me again, and I continued to settle in very well.

5. My Liverpool Home

As part of the junior girls group, we each had to take on individual daily chores. In our bedrooms, we took turns in emptying the bins, cleaning the sinks, tidying the wardrobes, and dusting the dressing tables. The age range of the group was between eight and twelve years. Downstairs, the older girls would be asked to set the tables each evening ready for breakfast the following morning. Others would be responsible for doing the dusting, tidying the toy cupboard, and the bookcase amongst other things. My task was to collect the bread. Every afternoon straight after school had ended, I would walk along the corridor to the main dining room and open a huge cupboard door. The cupboard was stacked from top to bottom with bread. I selected two loaves, and carried them to our kitchen ready for our evening meal, and breakfast the next day.

Back in the classroom I was growing in confidence with regards to my Braille reading and writing skills. Those of you familiar with Braille might remember reading stories from the set of blue and green books known as "Wide Range Readers". My sister was very cross with me one evening at home when Mum told us to turn off the light and go to sleep. We were both reading at the time. Kirsten could no longer read, but I hid the book under the covers, and carried on. As she lay there moaning about it not being fair, I realised there were at least some advantages in not being able to see. . My sight continued to deteriorate slowly, and I was using print less and Braille much more. I did however have opportunities which had not been available to me previously, such as pottery lessons, cookery lessons, and a variety of sports. I enjoyed bashing the clay before creating a thumb pot, a coil pot, or a tile containing a tactile picture. Cookery was great because we were able to eat cakes, and even take a box of our creations back to our group to share with our friends. Most weeks, whilst we waited for our cakes to cook, we would make Angel Delight and then cover it in sprinkles and eat it even though it hadn't had time to set.

The sports facilities were excellent. We had a gym and an indoor swimming pool. I was never really much of a gymnast, but I did enjoy swimming. As a young child, Dad had regularly taken Kirsten and myself to our local swimming pool, so by the time I arrived at St. Vincent's, I could swim. I wasn't a brilliant swimmer, but was never afraid of water. Our P.E. Teacher Mrs. Errington, was a lovely lady, with a fantastic sense of humour. She was always extremely encouraging, and during that first year I gained several swimming certificates. Each year, a special swimming gala would be held at Worcester College for the Blind. Pupils from schools for the visually impaired around the UK would have to compete for a chance to take part. . I wasn't involved in my first year, but I was later to become aware of something which made me determined to improve my skills and be able to compete. The day after their triumphant return from the gala, all the juniors who took part were called to Mrs. Pope's classroom and each person was presented with a large bar of chocolate.

I loved going home on Friday, and felt sorry for those children who only went to see their families every other weekend. Following the fish finger incident, Nanna would usually bring me a packed lunch to eat in the taxi on the way home. When we arrived, we would unpack my bag, and then take Boo out for a walk, to meet my sister from school. On Saturday afternoons I had my organ lesson, and Sunday was usually a quiet day. That was until I began to nag my Mum to take us swimming. Around that time, the family began to notice that my accent was changing. They would often exclaim, "Ooh, you've got that Liverpool twang!" I love the Liverpool accent, and for many years later, I could speak with the accent, and often fool others into thinking it was where I was originally from. We did eventually go swimming, and the whole family enjoyed it so much It became a regular Sunday morning event. After a few weeks, my Dad's auntie and uncle decided to join us, and it was a brilliant social occasion. A few times, Miss Josie came to join the party. So, inevitably, my swimming skills improved, and I was elated when I was chosen to take part in the Liverpool swimming gala, and then the Worcester gala.

Being selected for this event meant that you would miss a full day of school. We assembled in the front hall, before piling on to the coach. Pupils from both the junior and senior departments took part, so there were quite a lot of us. One teacher would take his guitar, and we would sing songs on the journey. I was to take part in the under thirteens girls' breaststroke. While we waited to compete, we cheered our friends on. After my race, I was told I had come fourth, and wouldn't need to swim in the final. Shortly after, I took the opportunity to get changed and return to the side of the pool. A while later, a rather flustered PE teacher rushed over to me asking why I had done this, I had come third and needed to race in the final which was due to start in a few moments. I had to rush back in to the changing room, and put on my wet swimming costume, which was cold and uncomfortable. I did, however, think it was quite funny, as the teacher ran in to race me over to my place ready to take part. Many of the staff laughed about that one for weeks. I finally got my reward, as we were called in to the classroom the next day, and felt very proud when I was handed a large bar of chocolate.

Mrs. Pope, the head of the junior School also had another tradition. On your birthday, you would knock on her classroom door and announce your news. She would then proceed to open a cupboard and remove a large jar of sweets. She would warmly wish you a happy birthday, and enquire how old you were. We always received a sweet for each year. On my eleventh Birthday, I was very pleased to find that the sweets were sizeable, and, even cooler, they were shaped like skateboards. Now that's got to be much better than eleven midget gems!

The junior sports day was always a big event. Our parents were invited to attend if they were able, and there were many different races. As well as running, there was the sack race, the flipper race, in which we had to run while wearing a pair of flippers, the egg and spoon race and the three legged race. At the end of the afternoon, everyone would gather in the activity room or the junior boys playground where we would be given ice cream and receive our prizes. The winner of each race won ten pence, second prize was five pence and third prize two pence. I don't know why this system was chosen, but nobody complained. It was always a great day, and everyone was encouraged to compete no matter what your degree of ability. During my first year, my Mum and Auntie Jenny attended. They were very moved by the warm atmosphere. All the parents stood enthusiastically shouting their words of support across the field. We certainly felt spurred on. My family was touched by seeing totally blind and partially sighted kids participating together. Even those children who had additional disabilities were helped to take part by members of staff and encouraged to feel part of the event.

Unfortunately, on my last sports day I fell over during the flipper race and sprained my wrist. Miss Josie had to take me to the children's hospital to have an x-ray. I'm not quite sure, but it probably wouldn't be far from the truth in saying that the people responsible for building the hospital foresaw that I would need their services on many occasions and thought it best to build close to the school. On the first occasion, I sprained my ankle while running around on the soft play. We seemed to wait for hours before going to x-ray and then being bandaged up before returning to school. For the next few days, I had to be pushed around the building in a wheelchair. I got very bored and frustrated at not being able to get around freely.

The second time, I was making my way to the flight of stairs that led to our bedrooms, when I overshot the entrance off the corridor, tripped over a mat, and fell down three steep stone steps. I didn't fall very far, but landed awkwardly. My ankle hurt, and I struggled to get up. Luckily one of the staff, Mr. Lambton, was not far away and came running to my assistance. When I told him my ankle hurt he carried me up the stairs to Miss Josie. As I sat on the bed, feeling quite sorry for myself, she checked my ankle and after a while, the pain receded. It wasn't long, however, before I noticed the pain in my wrist, which had started to swell. The school nurse, Sister Ita, was called, and she advised us that we needed to go to the hospital. Poor Miss Josie had to endure the long wait once more in the accident and emergency department. It was around nine PM when we arrived, and as we waited I remember feeling rather tired. My wrist was put in a sling and we were asked to return in the morning. It continued to be very painful, and as we sat in the waiting room the following day, Miss Josie told me that she thought I may have to be very brave. Josie was always very entertaining during those times. She would tell me funny stories, and play word games with me to while away the hours. Eventually we were called in to a side room and I had a metal plate put around my wrist and hand to keep it secure and then covered with a large bandage.

I travelled home as usual on the Friday afternoon, but, that evening, my wrist grew increasingly painful. As I lay in bed, I couldn't sleep. I had a very restless night, and the next day, Mum took me to our local hospital. I'm not sure if I had caused further damage in the previous couple of days, but after another x-ray, the Doctor announced that I had fractured my wrist and needed to have a cast. I returned to school on Monday, feeling rather proud of it, but the novelty soon wore off. My fresh white plaster cast was soon covered in pictures and messages written by staff members and friends. I was definitely unimpressed one morning when a teacher decided to read some of the messages out during a school assembly. I was unaware that my Dad had written "Jane loves Stephen" inside a little heart. After around six weeks, the cast was removed, but I had to have another one fitted for a further two weeks. As this left me feeling rather despondent, Dad came up with an idea to cheer me up. One of our favourite TV programmes was "Swap

Shop". Dad suggested that he and Kirsten would colour my cast in multi-coloured hoops, and then write "Swap Shop" in bright, bold letters across the front. The cast, once it was removed at the hospital, would be sent into the programme. Kirsten thought it was a great idea and I agreed. That was until I realised how long I would have to sit still while they carried out their artistic endeavours. Furthermore, Mr. Lambton, who had carried me up three flights of stairs because I had initially complained of a painful ankle, would take great pleasure, whenever he saw me around the building, in taking hold of my wrist and exclaiming, "Hi Jane, how's your ankle?"

I can't tell you how relieved I was to get rid of that cast, but I don't remember whether we actually did send it to the BBC. My third visit to the hospital was after sports day, and the fourth occurred as a result of a back problem. This time Josie and I spent the day walking from one department to another. I had numerous x-rays, and several consultations with different doctors. Miss Josie did her very best to keep me amused, but towards late afternoon, it was clear that I had had enough. I was frustrated by the amount of times I was required to go behind the screen, get undressed, have an examination, and then dress again. My patience reached breaking point, and during another request for me to remove my clothes, I attempted to lighten the atmosphere by giving a rendition of the stripper music while removing my blouse. Josie fell into uncontrollable fits of laughter, and I joined in. Shortly after, we returned to school. I'm not sure if they concluded their examinations, or I was simply thrown out in disgust! I know I was never sent a further appointment, so maybe the latter is true.

Interspersed with these inopportune visits to the A and E department, were regular appointments at St. Paul's Eye Hospital. These also meant hours in a waiting room. Miss Josie and I enjoyed them as much as a headache! When she approached me one evening in the playroom to deliver the dreaded news, I rather dramatically faked sudden illness and dropped to the floor in rather exaggerated turmoil. Miss Josie laughed, and said there was absolutely no getting out of it. It was wet and cold outside when we left school and boarded a bus into town, and very wet, cold and dark when we returned. I never enjoyed those occasions, because during every appointment, several student doctors would be ushered in to my examination room to discuss my eye condition, and see the evidence for themselves. One by one, they would sit opposite me and gaze in to my eyes. If I'd been a few years older, and had a little more sight, then I suppose the experience could have been quite pleasurable, bearing in mind the doctors were usually young and male. However, only being between the age of ten and twelve at the time, it wasn't the case. Gasps of "amazing!", "fascinating!", and "very interesting!" would fill the room. All the time I sat patiently, thinking, "It may be to you mate, but it's not exactly a picnic for me! Maybe next time I should sell tickets at a price, and really make it worth my while, if it's that entertaining!"

I think I inherited my sense of humour from Dad. I have always marvelled at his ability to be so blatantly cheeky and get away with it. I was once invited to have tea at my friend Maureen's house. She lived very close to the school and went home every evening. Four girls from the group were invited, and we were excited at the prospect. My parents had become involved in the Parent-Teachers Association, and knew Maureen's parents quite well. The previous weekend, Dad gave me an empty ice-cream carton and told me to take it with me and tell Maureen's Mum to fill it with her home-made trifle for him. On another occasion, I asked if I could make Miss Josie a birthday present. Dad wasn't satisfied with simply wrapping the gift and sending it back with me, but decided we should construct a surprise pass the parcel present. The gift was wrapped in several layers of paper, interspersed with other surprises and messages. As Josie removed the first layer of paper, a deluge of biscuit crumbs fell on to the floor and on her lap. A note read "Oh crumbs!" After removing further layers, she found a packet of crushed cheese and onion crisps and a note which said "Don't get cheesed off, carry on." Several sheets of paper followed before revealing an empty cigarette packet, and an empty lighter with the caption, "Bet you're fuming!" Eventually, she found a bottle of perfume, all the time saying, "I bet this was your Dad's idea.

It wasn't just my Dad who tested Miss Josie's patience. After all, not only did I cause her to endure endless hours of boredom in Liverpool hospitals, but I gave her cause for concern at other times. At the end of one lesson, I was tidying my things away, when I heard a noise over by the classroom door. As I was about to leave to go for my morning break, I went to investigate. I stretched out my hand to open the door, but found that it had been locked. I wasn't that bothered at the time. I knew the door would be unlocked when the children returned in twenty minutes, and I had plenty of work to keep me busy. I was however surprised because I had been unaware until then, that the doors were normally locked each break time. Around ten minutes later,

I heard a very flustered but familiar voice ringing down the corridor. "Jane, where are you?" I shouted through the door, and moments later, Miss Josie reappeared with the caretaker to set me free. She ran over, hugged me tightly, and took me back to our little dining room. I also tested her patience with my dislike of skirts and dresses. I had to wear a skirt all week as part of the uniform, so why in the world would I choose to wear one in the evenings, even if I was going out somewhere? I can't remember what the occasion was, but Josie repeatedly asked me to get changed, and I told her I couldn't find a skirt in my wardrobe. Shortly after, she approached me saying, "Jane, what's this ghost I've found in your wardrobe? It looks very much like a nice skirt." I didn't answer, just scowled, and stomped off to get changed.

I was normally a well behaved pupil, but did stray occasionally. On my return to school following my recovery from chicken pox, I was told about a new member of staff who had been appointed to give some of us singing lessons. I found my new teacher to be quite eccentric, and sometimes didn't know quite how to react to her. She gave me a wealth of singing exercises, and was adamant I should sing with a broad Lancashire accent. Unfortunately, I didn't like her choice of songs for me. I first learned the jazz standard, "Summer Time," and then was asked to sing "Climb Every Mountain" from the film "The Sound of Music". It really did feel like I'd climbed Ben Nevis by the time I'd finished. The song was quite long, and the high note at the end felt like I was just about to split my kipper! The last straw, months later, was when she proceeded to teach me "Greensleeves". At the end of the lesson, she asked me if I liked the song. She was not at all happy with my retort, "Not really Miss, it's far too mushy for my liking". She immediately burst into tears, and promptly escorted me back to my classroom to inform my teacher. I did make one small achievement as a result of the lessons. I was entered in a singing competition at Liverpool's Bluecoat Chambers where, much to my displeasure, I had to sing a song entitled "The Kangaroo". So, as instructed, in the broadest Lancashire accent I could muster I stood in the middle of the stage and sang. I was more shocked than surprised, when it was announced that I had won third prize, and went home proudly clutching my certificate.

The last lesson on Monday afternoon was known as "speech". In reality, it was similar to an elocution lesson. Our teacher was also blind, and had a guide dog. This particular member of staff was quite strict, both in manner, and concerning the content of the lesson. Our pronunciation always had to be very precise, and I have to admit, this irritated me. During one lesson, a new boy who had joined our class sat next to me on one of the bean bags in the activity room and whispered that he had some sweets. He told me that we would have to eat them with the paper on so that our teacher wouldn't hear us unwrapping them. Hmmm! A chance to get away with something naughty: pass the sweets mate. As we sat there defiantly munching, and they did take quite a lot of munching, I thought to myself, that the sweets were not achieving the buzz I had craved, but the act of getting away with it was worth the endurance of dental problems and eating sweet wrappers. She never did notice, but if this book is ever produced in alternative formats, then the secret is well and truly out.

I really enjoyed the craft lessons we used to have in the activity room with Mrs Orpen and Mrs Armstrong. We made various different raffia baskets, pompom animals, and I wonder if anyone remembers making a scarf on a circular peg frame? Another weekly event I remember very clearly was the junior assembly in the hall every Wednesday morning. Mrs. Pope would give out to two people from each class, the merit badge, and the courtesy badge. The worthy recipients would have the badge pinned on their school jumper for the week until the next assembly.

There was one particular week when I certainly wouldn't have been considered for either of those awards. Yes folks, its confession time. I once arrived at school on Monday morning and went upstairs to unpack. As I did so, my best friend also arrived. We chatted about what we had done over the weekend, and I told her that I had visited a joke shop and brought some things back to school to have some fun. Suddenly, we heard a door open and footsteps. As she walked past us, one of the teachers said "Good morning." We said "Hello", and had a short conversation together. During our conversation, I offered her a sweet. She said, "Thank you Jane, that's very kind, and took the sweet. The smile on my face was sweet too, because it was a joke pepper sweet.

We continued with our day, and didn't think anything else about the matter until we were due to go for an R.E. lesson the following afternoon. As we went to leave our classroom, our class teacher told us that there would be no lesson because the teacher who had eaten my sweet was off school feeling sick. Immediately, I knew what my friend and I were thinking: "Oh no, what if that's because of the pepper sweet?" We never said anything, and I don't know whether I caused her illness or not.

6. Out and About

As part of the school curriculum, those children who had very little or no sight at all were given mobility lessons. This involved orientation firstly inside the school and later outdoors using a white cane. A special technique to use the cane effectively is required, and takes a great deal of practice. As we became more competent in our technique, we would be taken outside around a quiet housing estate nearby to practise our skills. At first I didn't mind those lessons, but there came a point when I really dreaded them. At the most advanced level of the training, we were required to undergo something called "drop offs". Once the teacher assessed that you had become fully familiar with a specific area covering a block of roughly eight streets, a test would be arranged. You would travel in the car with your teacher, and then be dropped off with your cane on to a street. Obviously, the teacher knew where you were, but you didn't. The idea was for the individual to detect clues about their surroundings in order to ascertain where they were. These could be detected if there was a grass verge with your cane, and that would locate you in a specific street. I think that was Alvanley Road. It may be that you could hear traffic and this would give a further clue. All the while your tutor would be watching a safe distance away to make sure you were safe. When you were dropped off, you would be told which street to walk to in order to be met by the teacher. If I was asked to do that now, it wouldn't bother me, but at the age of eleven or twelve, it really filled me with dread.

On one occasion, I was dropped off at a busy location. I stood contemplating the best route to take to meet my teacher when a member of the public approached me. She was adamant that I needed to cross the road, and before I could get the words out, had done her supposed good deed and dragged me across the road to the other side. This was a road we had clearly been told not to cross. I had to stand for ages, waiting for someone else to take me back so I could begin my journey. When I reached my destination safely, the teacher was beginning to get worried, because I had taken longer to arrive than expected. I was very relieved when I no longer had to continue with those lessons. I must mention though, we were never at risk, as there was always a staff member close by, and it helped to give me the confidence I have today with regard to mobility. If I ever do get lost, I never panic. I know plenty of people who find this type of situations extremely distressing, and I fully sympathise with them.

Shortly after joining St. Vincent's, I began attending Mass. I had no previous knowledge concerning Catholicism, and my family have never regularly attended church, so this was a new experience for me. We were however made to feel welcome in the services, except for taking Communion. I loved the songs, and acquired a genuine belief in a good God, who cares for and responds to those who communicate with him. Even at the age of eleven, it was my opinion that this basis of faith in a loving God created the warm and friendly atmosphere within the school. Occasionally, Mass would be held for the whole school during the afternoon, and we would be pleased because it meant no lessons. On St. Vincent's day, we had Mass and a party afterwards. The senior pupils were not generally allowed to use the soft play, but on that day, an exception was made.

Trips out were a regular part of our learning. We visited the local police station, Liverpool's cathedrals, and the Tate Gallery to name a few. The biggest outing of the year however was to New Brighton. The outing took place every June, and we looked forward to it with growing excitement and anticipation. In the course of the year, taxi drivers from across Wirral would busy themselves raising money at numerous events to fund the day. In preparation, we would visit the sewing room to be fitted with a St. Vincent's blazer. Additionally a list was read out giving information about the pupils and staff with whom we would be travelling, and the number of our taxi. The trip was for junior and senior pupils, and really was a day to remember. On the day, around eleven thirty, we would all line up along the long front corridor with the friends/staff member we were to travel with. Our names were called, and we would make our way to our taxi outside. I cannot possibly describe the level of excitement we felt.

On my first trip, I travelled with my best friend Annie, and we were so pleased when we found out we were travelling together. Even better, was the fact that Mrs. Errington, our P.E. Teacher would be travelling with us. She was so much fun, this day just got better and better, and we hadn't even left school! Because there were so many cars, we had a number of police escorts on motorbikes, to help us negotiate our way across the city. We thought it was so cool, as the police stopped the traffic on several occasions to let us through. We certainly felt like little celebrities. En route, we went through the Mersey Tunnel. We looked forward to this part because the police had given the taxi drivers permission to be able to sound the car horns all the way through, and we laughed at the noise everyone made. The day always took the same format, and so the first place we visited was the Riverside Restaurant for lunch.

We were always given fish and chips with peas, followed by ice-cream. After a thoroughly enjoyable meal came the next highly anticipated event: pressie time! The range of gifts for the juniors included, vanity cases for the girls and large soft toys or radios shaped like a car for the boys. Pupils from the senior department were given gift vouchers. When we were all ready, we made our way back to the cars. The next part of our day was a trip down the river Mersey aboard the ferry, the Royal Iris. While on board, we were treated to a disco hosted by a DJ from Radio City. There were competitions where we won prizes, and copious amounts of crisps, fizzy drinks, and iced lollies. I really don't know how we managed to eat so much in one day. At the end of the disco, we would all stand, join hands and sing along as the DJ played "Ferry Across the Mersey" by Gerry and the Pacemakers. Ever since then, it has been a song that's always been very special to me. Whenever I hear it, all those happy memories come flooding back.

Around four PM it was time to get back into our taxi, to be taken over to the fairground. We screamed on the ghost train, and spun on the satellite ride, before taking a more sedate ride on the merry-go-round. It was fantastic fun, and, what's more, it was all free to us. After approximately an hour on the fair, we were taken to our last destination of the day, The Golden Guinea club, where we were given a meal and treated to another disco. We returned back to school around eight thirty, tired, but having enjoyed a brilliant day.

Christmas was always something to look forward to at St. Vincent's. A month before the end of term, we had a weekly disco on a Monday evening. There would be stalls selling trinkets and sweets. I always tried to save my money and use these opportunities to buy small gifts for my family for Christmas. We had a junior girls group carol service, and a main carol service in the chapel, for the whole school, which families would be invited to attend. The services were always very beautiful, with some pupils singing solos and Mr. Wilson playing the organ. Even after I had left the school, I would return for the Christmas service. We always had a Christmas party in the junior department, which would last all afternoon. We played games, had a disco, and sometimes had a fancy dress competition.

In school, we had two dogs whom we would regularly hear trotting around the building. Sheba was an old and very placid dog. I say placid because many of us would trip over her as she lay sprawled out in the middle of the main corridor. Following the event, she would sometimes move, but on most occasions, she would continue to assume her position, and simply go back to sleep. This behaviour was in complete contrast to that of the other dog. She was named Beauty, and was owned by the school nurse. Most of us were very scared of Beauty. Her fearsome barks would often echo down the corridors. We were always frightened that she would bite us, but I don't think she ever did. It wasn't just pupils though, who were uneasy in her presence. One member of staff, if she was anywhere near our playroom, and heard Beauty, would immediately call for Miss Josie's help. I always admired Miss Josie's complete lack of fear of this dog. She would simply call to Beauty in a low, confident and firm voice. Beauty would then be quiet and stand still until the staff member had walked past safely. One day I had accompanied Miss Josie to help her with taking the meal trolley back to the kitchen. I stood outside by the school's gong, while she took the trolley in the kitchen, but then froze as I heard the sound of Beauty. She barked fiercely and proceeded to walk slowly around me. I didn't dare move a muscle, and stayed rooted to the spot until Miss Josie returned.

Talking of fear, it reminds me of one of the most embarrassing moments of my life. I was chosen to play the part of the princess in a production of "Aladdin". The whole experience was a nightmare from start to finish. A boy who was in the year above me was chosen to play Aladdin, and seemingly never ending rehearsals meant we saw quite a lot of each other. One member of staff used to take great pleasure in teasing us about being boyfriend and girlfriend. This carried on for weeks, as rehearsals continued. At one point in the production, I was required to sing a solo which wasn't a particular problem to me until the day of the performance. Everything was going fine, and I remembered all my lines, but then came the time for the big solo! I stood centre stage, and as I opened my mouth to sing, fear suddenly gripped me. The notes that proceeded from my mouth were out of tune, and all I can say is I made a complete dog's dinner of all three verses. No one really said anything to me following the event but I did hear snippets of conversations. I was so angry with myself for messing up, and I was never asked to take part in a play again. I can laugh about it now, but at the time, I really wanted to just hide away.

Unfortunately for me, this wasn't the only event during that year to cause some unhappiness. On the run up to Easter, we were encouraged to give up something for Lent. I decided that the thing I enjoyed most was watching TV and I would give that up because it would be quite a sacrifice for me. Up until that point, I could see the television if I sat up close to the screen. When the six week period was over, I dashed to the TV to resume the activity I had missed so much, only to find that I could no longer see it. My vision had obviously been very slowly and gradually deteriorating and once again I was hit by the reality of having to adjust to something I could no longer do. I distinctly remember my family encouraging me to sit down in front of the TV instead of sitting on the sofa and just listening. Slowly, I think they realised what had happened.

In the summer of that year, I went with my best friend Annie on a trip to Lourdes in France. This was arranged and paid for by a charity which raised money for disabled children to visit the famous shrine. Our parents didn't travel with us, so it was quite an adventure. A number of weeks beforehand, we were introduced to the carers who would be looking after us, so we could get to know them. The group consisted of around twenty children between the ages of eight and sixteen, with disabilities ranging from diabetes to those requiring a wheelchair. Annie and I were the only two blind people. We had a wonderful time. Our sighted carers were great fun, and the hotel where we stayed was excellent. We visited the holy baths, had Mass in the basilica, and took part in several torchlight processions in the evenings. Even though I could see very little, the sight of all those candles in the dark night sky was amazing to me. We went pony trekking in the mountains, and running in the meadows, where there was so much space, we could run freely without the need for sighted assistance. There were many humorous moments, including the time when I was running in the meadows and someone saw me and shouted, "You've been healed!" On another day, Annie and I were given a ride down the road in wheelchairs, and a priest stopped us to bless us. I felt rather guilty, because I thought it felt a bit like telling a lie at the time, but we did laugh about it later.

My final year at St. Vincent's was quite eventful. At Christmas, I won a competition. Firstly, I won front row tickets to see a pantomime in Blackburn where we lived. The main celebrities taking part were "Brian and Michael" who had had a number one hit in the pop charts with "Match Stalk Men." Before the show, I was taken to meet them in their dressing room, where Michael signed the cap he had worn on "Top of the Pops" and gave it to me. I had my picture taken with them by the local newspaper, before going to see the panto. After the performance, we were invited to join the party with all the cast to collect other autographs and to chat with them.

The second part of the prize was a VIP day out at Blackpool Tower, and seats in the Royal Box, for the circus in the evening. Mum, Dad, and Kirsten were invited, too, and we had a brilliant time. The funniest part was visiting the animals backstage before the circus. As I patted a huge elephant in complete awe of its size and stature, my Dad stood beside me holding a bag which contained some discarded food. Suddenly the elephant wrapped its trunk around my Dad's waist and lifted him from the ground. I don't know if he was trying to retrieve the food, but it certainly gave Dad a huge shock. As Dad's feet dangled in mid-air, the ringmaster suddenly shouted "Down Zimba!" and the elephant obeyed. My Mum, sister and I, couldn't stop laughing, and it took a while for us to compose ourselves in order to continue the tour. I don't know what Dad thinks of elephants today, but I don't remember him ever suggesting a trip to a zoo or safari park.

The following January, I have a vivid memory of a Saturday afternoon at home. I walked through the dining room, and in to the kitchen to go outside to the car to travel to my weekly music lesson. As I walked through the kitchen, Mum suddenly said, "How do you fancy going to a new school, Jane?" As I walked out through the back door, feeling surprised, I retorted with a firm and completely uninterested "No thanks." As I sat in the car waiting for Dad, I thought the idea was completely preposterous. Leave St. Vincent's-- NEVER!! I forgot about that brief exchange over the days that followed, but was irritated on my return home from school, to find that Mum wanted to read a book to me all about a school in the south of England. Mum tried to tempt me with the prospect of dual controlled driving lessons, but it didn't matter what facilities they offered, I didn't want to go. The school was Chorleywood College for girls in Hertfordshire; the only grammar school for visually impaired girls in the country. Mum and Dad were keen for me to attend and, regardless of my views, arrangements were put into place.

Each prospective pupil was required to attend an assessment which included an overnight stay at the college. So in March 1981, my parents drove me over to Hertfordshire. To make matters worse, I was bought a dress which I had to wear over the two days. On our arrival, we were shown to the sickbay area of the school, where we were to sleep that night. I was sharing a room with one other girl, and Mum helped me unpack my overnight things while we chatted. Not long after, our parents were asked to leave, and we spent the afternoon and early evening having presentations, and individual interviews with different members of staff. After supper, we were taken to wash and get in to bed.

My roommate and I were very different in personality. She was definitely a girly girl, and I definitely wasn't. I remember thinking she had a very posh accent, and I felt quite out of place in her presence. She was however friendly and we chatted briefly. The one thing we did have in common was that as we got in to bed, we both had books to read. I asked my new friend what she was reading, and she replied "Charlie and the Chocolate Factory." She asked me the same question, and I replied, "A Bomb in a Submarine." I don't think she was very impressed.

The following morning, after breakfast, we attended the college assembly, before beginning the written part of the assessment. This covered English, maths, and Braille reading. I found some of the work quite easy, but some of it difficult. As we drew close to lunch time, my Brailler broke. A teacher had to bring me a replacement machine, and to my horror, minutes later, that one broke too. Another one was brought for me, and luckily, that lasted for the rest of the day. We had a break for lunch, but continued afterwards until around three o'clock. By the end of the afternoon, my head was spinning. It had seemed like a very long day. We were taken into the common room, and given a packed lunch for the journey home. We waited for our parents to collect us, and I was very glad when mine arrived.

I got in to the car to find that I had been treated to a gift, the latest album by my favourite band, Adam and the Ants. I was very pleased, and couldn't wait to get back to school to show my friends.

It was late that evening when I arrived in Liverpool, and I remember going straight to bed. As I snuggled down, Annie whispered, "How did you get on?" I replied that I was ok, but inside I was feeling quite strange. I wanted to pass the assessment, because I wanted to achieve that goal and not to fail, but I didn't want to pass, because that meant I would have to leave the school I loved - and so began the first of many nights during which I would lie awake worrying about Chorleywood, and what would happen. Apart from that life returned to normal. I got on with my daily routine until, one day in May, Sister Josephine came in to my classroom, and asked if she could speak with me. She took me out in to the corridor and told me the news that I had passed the assessment, and congratulated me. She then proceeded to tell all my teachers in the junior department, and the next thing I knew we were all congregating in the activity room. Mrs. Pope asked me to stand in front of everyone and announced my good news. Indeed, it was viewed around the school as being quite an achievement. When I returned home at the weekend, I received a deluge of cards and presents congratulating me. I became quite swept up in the euphoria, but when it came to night time, and I lay in bed thinking, I felt very different.

My parents wanted me to have the best possible opportunities, and now I fully respect their decision, although I didn't at the time. Following the news, many people would enquire as to how I was feeling, and every time I would reply that I was fine and looking forward to it, but it was a complete lie. I was just putting a brave face on and secretly fretting about the move to a new school. I didn't want to leave my friends. I was also used to going home every weekend, but moving much farther away from home meant I would be visiting much less than I was used to. During that final term, I noticed that my best friend was spending much less time with me and more with others. I figured it was because I wouldn't be around the following school year, and this made me feel uncomfortable. I don't blame her. It just felt very strange. On my last trip to New Brighton, I didn't travel with Annie, I don't know who made that decision, but that felt very strange too. I never mentioned anything to anyone, least of all Annie, I knew I had to toughen up and just deal with the situation. In the junior girls playground, we had two normal swings, a large tyre swing and a climbing frame, which had a ladder on one side leading up to a crow's nest. I remember climbing up there one day, and just standing there listening to my friends below having fun, and wishing I could stay. How I wished there was some way I could stay.

During my last week at St. Vincent's, Mum and Dad organised a leaving party for me. My uncle had a friend who was in a local band, and he came to be the DJ for the disco. We had a great time. I had a huge cake made which said "St. Vincent's rules OK!" and everyone from the junior school was invited. During the course of the evening we did the rowing boat dance, only you eighties kids will be familiar with that, and even Sister Josephine joined in. We have still got the photos of that evening, including the ones of Sister Josephine. My friends bought me gifts, and the girls in the group all wrote letters to me, which were gathered in a small folder for me to take away and keep. They all wrote lovely words of good wishes and encouragement, and it made me feel very supported, but even more sad at leaving. On my final day, when lessons had ended on Friday lunch time, I walked up to the playroom to collect my things. As I was removing items from my locker, in walked Mrs. Errington, my P.E. teacher. She came over, hugged me, and said, "I'm really going to miss you." I wanted to say the same thing, but I just hugged her, knowing that if I spoke a word, I would burst into tears. Even as I write this I can feel a lump in my throat, just thinking about that last day. It's quite surprising all these years later. I must just be far too soppy and sentimental for my own good.

As I walked out of the front door for the last time as a St. Vincent's pupil, I felt a sense of loss. That feeling would continue for far longer than I wanted. All through the summer holidays I remember thinking, "I'm not a part of that school any more, but I don't feel like a Chorleywood girl either". I know that's rather a silly thing to say. How could I possibly feel like a Chorleywood student when I hardly knew anything about the place? On occasions when I was alone with time to think, I felt very uneasy. During the holidays, a member of pastoral care from Chorleywood came to our house to introduce herself and talk about the college. She spent the evening with the family, and ate a meal with us. I tried very hard to be enthusiastic but, unfortunately, I wasn't convinced. During our meal, she told me that at school we were allowed to be excused one food item, and if there was a particular food that I really didn't like, it would be written on a list and kept in the kitchen so that I would never be made to eat it. There are a number of things I don't like, but the worst, the very worst is, yes you've guessed it, liver, and without hesitation, I chose that. I was unaware at the time, but this was the first of countless rules which would govern my daily life at Chorleywood College.

Mum and Dad must have had to spend an utter fortune on clothes and the never ending list of things we needed sent out by the college. Amongst other items, we were required to have a trunk in which to bring everything. Mum and Dad searched high and low to purchase one, but they weren't readily available. Luckily, Mum saw one advertised in our local paper, and it turned out to be only a few doors away from us on the same street. Passers-by must have thought it rather strange, as Dad and I carried it down the road.

I tried to take my mind off the matter by busying myself with lots of activities. Dad asked us to clear out a shed that was at the bottom of our garden. He didn't make much use of it, and it still contained numerous items owned by the previous occupants of our house. Some of Kirsten's friends joined us in the task, and they became my friends too. We cleared everything from old pots of paint to rusting hamster cages. When finally it was empty and clean, we put a bench in there, and some cushions. Posters were stuck on the walls, and the window given a good clean. We spent many hours in there, and decided to call ourselves "The White Hand Gang". I haven't got a clue how this name originated, but we had a great time.

My sister had a friend called Melanie, who lived opposite our house. Melanie would make us laugh, because when we would walk to the shops together to buy sweets, she enjoyed surprising drivers in their cars by waiting for the traffic to stop, and then casually cartwheel across the road, get to the other side and wave to them before turning and making her way into the shop. It also became a summer holiday tradition for the three of us to go out and collect jumble and hold a sale to raise money for a local charity for the blind. One year, someone donated several dresses of the same style in various colours. The colours were so garish, and the collars were huge rounded flappy designs. Sometimes Kirsten and Melanie would try on some of the donated items, and pretend to have a wacky fashion show. Melanie suggested I should try one of the aforementioned dresses, but I refused, exclaiming, "I'd look a right wallie in that!" From then on, Kirsten and Melanie referred to them as "wallie dresses." During the jumble sale, whenever someone bought one of them, Melanie would sidle over to me and whisper in my ear, "Someone's just buying a wallie dress." I would then have to stifle a snigger, but Melanie would try to make me laugh.

Although we made a respectable amount of money during those sales, we almost got ourselves into huge trouble one year. As we were carrying items of clothing out of the house one morning, ready to begin the sale, we were unaware that Mum had thrown an expensive skirt down the stairs for Nanna to put in the washing machine. Somehow, it must have got mixed up in the jumble items. The first moment I became aware of anything, was when Kirsten said to me that a lady had just bought Mum's old brown velvet skirt. The following evening while we were eating dinner, Mum asked my Nan, "Mum, have you seen my brown velvet skirt I asked you to wash?" Nan replied, "I didn't realise you'd asked me to wash your skirt love, I haven't seen it!" At that moment, if Kirsten and I could have exchanged a look across the table, I'm sure we would have done so. When the meal was finished, we both retreated to our bedroom not really knowing whether to laugh or to panic. In actual fact, we did both. First we laughed, until it hurt, but then eventually, when Mum was searching the house to find it, we started to feel rather uncomfortable.

It was lucky in one sense, because Kirsten remembered the lady she had sold the skirt to, and also where she lived. However, we had a restless night, wondering what to do. Should we try to go to the house and buy the skirt back? Or should we just leave things the way they were? Would the lady concerned be in, and would she be willing to sell it back to us? What we hadn't previously known, was that this skirt had been very expensive, so the woman must have thought she had acquired quite a bargain. I remember thinking, "I wish the woman had just bought a wallie dress instead!" The next morning, without telling anyone else, we made a reluctant journey to the house. We both felt rather silly, as we told our story of the mistake we had made, and eventually persuaded the woman to sell the skirt back to us. We were both so relieved to get it back, and I don't remember if we ever told Mum the truth about what happened.

One of the most memorable moments of that summer was when my Dad called me to go upstairs. I found him sitting on the floor in my bedroom. I thought it rather strange, but went over and sat beside him. He gave me a large hammer of all things, and calmly said, "Jane, bang a big hole in that wall." I paused, feeling rather confused, and said, "What?" He repeated the request once more. Had he suddenly taken leave of his senses? Was this some kind of weird test? I asked him if he had gone mad, and he said "No, I dare you, knock a big hole in that wall." I just laughed and continued to sit where I was. He repeated once more, "I dare you, knock a hole in that wall." Well, in for a penny, in for a pound, I thought, and he did dare me twice! So I simply picked up the hammer, and whacked the wall as hard as I could, making a large hole in my bedroom wall. "Aaah!" he shouted, "What on earth is your Mum going to say?" I replied, "It's too late now, and you did dare me." Then I leaned forward and whacked the wall again.

I did eventually learn that, for a while, Dad had planned to extend our bedroom, and make it into two separate ones. Beyond the inner wall, was around three feet of space which wasn't being used. I spent most of the following week knocking that wall down. While Dad was out during the day, I got to work with that hammer, bashing the wall and breaking up the wooden slats behind the plaster. I must have looked a sight, dressed in my baseball cap, and a pair of swimming goggles to protect my eyes from all the dust, but I really enjoyed myself. It was great fun. Dad called me "Demolition Dennis", and he still has pictures of me at work but, luckily, this book doesn't have photos.

7. Chorleywood Days

All too quickly, the summer was over, and, at the end of September 1981, Mum, Dad and Kirsten accompanied me on the journey to Hertfordshire to start the new term at Chorleywood College. We arrived mid-morning and were shown straight up to my dormitory on the top floor. All the dormitories were named after well-known ships, and mine was called Argos. The dorm housed eight girls, and I was given the top bunk of the only set of bunk beds. Mum helped me unpack as other girls came in to do the same. Each class of girls had their own member of care staff, and ours was Miss Larsen. The building was a large mansion house which had been converted into a school. A sizeable extension had been added to the main building, and the grounds were huge. It had a long drive, which led to an almost circular lawn, known as The Penny Lawn directly in front of the main entrance.

The large heavy front door opened to reveal an entrance hall with an oak floor, and marble pillars. Over to one side was a huge open fireplace and entrances leading off either side to other rooms such as the library, and the dining room. Further ahead, was a wide oak staircase, which led up to the first floor, where some dormitories were situated, and also our classrooms. The stairs then continued up further to another corridor of dormitories.

After unpacking our things, we were taken downstairs for lunch. I was taken to a long wooden table which was in the entrance hall, just outside the main dining room. This would be our form's table for that first year. A few steps away was a large trolley, and we were asked to line up in front of it, take a plate and wait to be served. Our parents weren't invited to join us, so mine sat in the large empty hall until I had finished. Following lunch, I was allowed to go and say goodbye to my family. As I entered the hall, Mum and Kirsten were in floods of tears, and I ended up joining them. My first impressions were that this was quite a cold place, nowhere near as friendly as St. Vincent's. We hugged each other, before they had to go. It was awful. They didn't want to leave me, and I certainly didn't want them to go.

There were fourteen girls in my year, indeed, we were the largest class in the school. After lunch, we were taken to our classroom, and introduced to our form teacher, Mrs. Henry. We each chose a desk at which to sit, and were given a key for our lockers. After she had spent some time with us, we immediately began the last two lessons of the day. In English we read "The Wind in the Willows", and then had a history lesson. At four thirty, it was time for afternoon tea. We made our way down the huge oak staircase, and over to the long table where we had eaten lunch, where we were given orange juice or tea, with an iced bun.

The early part of the evening was spent with Miss Thorpe who was in charge of pastoral care. She talked with us about the college, and got to know us all a little better. I was deeply unimpressed to learn that we had to be in bed by eight forty-five, and so began a long list of many rules and regulations I would hate. So at eight forty-five, I found myself in bed, feeling thoroughly miserable, and wishing I wasn't there.

The typical day at the college ran to the following schedule. At seven o'clock a bell, known as the rising bell, would ring throughout our dorms and we would get up, wash and put on our uniform, which consisted of a brown skirt, gold blouse, and a brown jumper. At seven fifty-five, the bell would ring again; this time refered to as the warning bell and we would make the trip down the oak staircase and line up outside the dining room. A loud gong would sound at eight o'clock and that would be the cue to take our places at our table. Before each mealtime we would be required to sing grace. There were several short songs, and it took a few weeks to learn them all. The eight o'clock news on radio three was played on a large booming archaic radio, and we had to sit in silence, eating a bowl of cereal while listening to the news. When it was finished, we were allowed to talk, as we ate toast and drank milk, tea or water. When breakfast was over, we had to wait until each table was dismissed in turn. We had to return to our dorms and make our beds before going to our classroom, to wait for our form teacher.

Mrs. Henry would spend around ten minutes with us every morning, passing on relevant information, and handing out mail to us, before we went downstairs to the hall for assembly. The morning was divided up into three forty minute lessons, followed by a twenty minute break. At break time, we congregated in the dining room, and lined up in front of a serving trolley. We were offered coffee, tea, or hot chocolate. As we walked past the trolley, there were two biscuit tins, one filled with plain biscuits, and another with cream biscuits. We were told we could pick one of each, and then sit at a table. If we were caught taking either two plain, or two cream biscuits instead, then we would be banned from having biscuits for the rest of the week. Break was followed by two more lessons, and then it was lunch time. I have to admit, that in the main, the food was much better at Chorleywood, than at St. Vincent's. There were a number of exceptions though, such as macaroni cheese, which was absolutely disgusting. The worst, however, was what we used to call "dustbin delight." This dish was savoury flan, which seemed to be a mixture of left-over food cobbled together served with tinned tomatoes. Most of us really hated it, but, as I mentioned earlier, we had to eat it. Indeed, as promised, the list of excused foods did hang on the kitchen wall so that staff could check when you announced that you were excused a particular food item.

When lunch was over, we were all required to take part in what was known as walk. We made our way down to the cloakrooms, took off our indoor shoes, and put on our out-door shoes, and brown gabardine macs, which I used to call my sack, and lined up at one of the doors round the back of the school. Walk, was a type of mobility lesson. Older girls would be paired up with new or younger girls, to teach them their way around the grounds, and later their way to the local shop, or railway station etc. Each day we stood in pairs in a long line waiting to tell the teacher on duty our names and where we were going. In the grounds, we had an outdoor swimming pool with a pavilion, a tennis court, and a ha-ha field amongst other areas. It took virtually the first half term just to learn your way around the grounds. At one thirty, we were allowed to go back indoors and return to lessons. Just don't forget to change those outdoor shoes, or you could be in trouble!

We had three lessons in the afternoon until four thirty, when we had a half hour break. We were allowed to change into our own clothes and have afternoon tea. At five o'clock it was time for prep, or homework as it's also known. This would last for an hour for the first year students, and then we would have forty-five minutes of free time before supper. Supper was normally over by around a quarter past seven, and we had around half an hour before we had to get ready for bed. At a quarter to nine, a member of staff would come and check that we were all in bed. If anyone was late, her name would be put in to what was known as The Late Book. If you were late three times in a half term, then you had to go to bed an hour early the following evening. If you were in the morning late book for being late for breakfast three times, then you had to get up at six a.m. the next morning and ring the rising bell at seven. Once we were in bed, we were allowed to talk until nine thirty, after which the lights were turned out and we had to go to sleep. My first impression of my new school was that it was a boring old bag of rules and punishments. It was no fun at all, and I hated it. I remember feeling like I didn't live in the real world anymore. There was no time to watch TV or listen to the radio, it was just do what you were told, when you were told. I laugh about it now, but at the time I remember feeling really miffed, because my new routine was so regimented, I didn't even know what was number one in the pop charts. I started to think that boot camp would be a softer option.

I found my first year very hard. I was so terribly homesick, and cried frequently. I am a little ashamed about it now, looking back, but I missed my friends so much. I didn't realise at the time what a hole I was digging for myself. Because I was so upset, some girls started to tease me, and things only got worse. I became the girl who most people didn't want to be with. If I asked if anyone was coming down to breakfast, they'd say "no thanks" and I would be left to go alone. I did try to make friends, but life seemed very tough. After two weeks, our parents were allowed to visit us. My Mum and Dad were very supportive. I dread to think how much it must have cost them to drive all the way from Lancashire, and find somewhere to stay for the weekend. It was great to see them though, but heartbreaking to watch them leave. We didn't get a great deal of time to ring home. Each student had an allotted ten minute phone call once a week. We were given one hour on Saturday and Sunday afternoons to be shared out between the class. I found this unfair, because a class of fourteen pupils had to share an hour whereas a class of just seven were given the same amount of time. If we missed our call because the person before us went on too long, we were not given any extra time.

It seemed forever until the half term holiday. We finished lessons at lunch time, and then put on our brown sacks and outdoor shoes before collecting our luggage and lining up in the front hall. We all boarded coaches which took us to the station. We travelled by tube to Baker Street, where we would be met by a family member or an escort from our education department to accompany us for the rest of our journey. I remember that first trip home very clearly. My escort collected me and we travelled to Euston station, where we took a train to Preston. The duration of the journey from Euston to Preston was around two and a half hours. A group of men on the train were quite rowdy, singing songs and laughing. They began to talk with me, and offered me a glass of whiskey. I declined, but thanked them for their offer. I just wanted to get home. When I eventually did, around seven in the evening, it was dark and very cold. I didn't mind at all; I was home at last.

During that week, Miss Josie came to stay with us for a couple of days. I had really missed her, and it was wonderful to spend time with her and the rest of the family. I enjoyed myself so much that I forgot all about school, until the day before I was due to return. On the Sunday morning, I lay in bed, dreading going back. I clearly remember going in to Mum and Dad's bedroom, and begging them to let me go back to St. Vincent's. I sat on their bed in floods of tears pleading with them, but they wouldn't budge. I remember thinking at that time life seemed so unfair. I was so unhappy at Chorleywood. So, early the next day I was once again on a train back to school.

The same escort met me at Blackburn railway station, and accompanied me back to Baker Street. She wasn't an unpleasant lady, but obviously hadn't had a great deal of training when it came to guiding a blind person. As if the prospect of going back to the college wasn't bad enough, what I didn't know was that my day was going to get worse. Feeling completely miserable, I boarded the train to Preston, and sat in total silence. Not only was I going to miss seeing my parents for the next few weeks, but I also couldn't help but think about my friends who at the same time would be making their way to St. Vincent's. On arrival at Preston, we had to cross the bridge to get to the platform where we would catch the train to Euston station. I held on to my escort's arm while carrying my suitcase in the other hand, and we began walking up the steps of the wooden bridge. As we were about to make our descent, unfortunately she forgot to inform me when we reached the first step, and gravity took over, as it always does. I went flying down the stairs, and reached the bottom quicker than my suitcase. I slowly picked myself up as my escort repeatedly shouted "Be careful! Be careful!"

It sounds rather over-dramatic, but at that moment, I hated the world, I hated Chorleywood College and I hated being taken away from St. Vincent's. College rules stipulated that on travel days, all the girls had to wear a skirt, definitely not trousers. I hated that too. So as we slowly walked to a seat on the platform to wait for the train, I took a tissue from my pocket, and wiped away angry tears, and then the long trail of blood that ran from my right knee down to my ankle. Eventually the train arrived, and the arduous silent journey began, dragging me far away from the people I loved, and to a place that made me tremendously unhappy.

When we returned to college after a holiday, we had to go through a set procedure. The first port of call was the common room. As we opened the door we would shout "Reporting in!" The member of staff on duty would write down our name on a list and then ask us a series of questions. We had to choose three bath nights, which would be logged so they could check we were having them. We were not allowed to bath on any other night. Then we were asked if we wanted cooked breakfast. If we chose to have this, then we would have to eat it every breakfast time until the next holiday. If we chose not to, then we would simply have toast and cereal every day. In short, we couldn't have a cooked breakfast if we particularly fancied it on a given day; it was all or nothing. We then had to choose from tea, milk or water to drink with every meal. We were not allowed to swap and change, this was fixed for the half term and would be put at our place on the table ready for us. I had always dislike plain milk, and tea so, for the whole five years, I simply drank water. Looking back, it seems rather petty, but that's the way it was - no arguments. After taking our luggage to the dormitory, we would line up outside the surgery, where a nurse would call us in and take our pulse and temperature. When the details had been recorded, we were allowed to go and unpack.

The six weeks which followed were quite eventful. One Sunday morning, the school was thrown in to a state of emergency. I was making my way across the entrance hall from the common room to the stairs, when I heard a curious sound. I walked closer to find out what was happening. It was the sound of torrential rain, only the rain wasn't outside, it was in the library. I was immediately shouted at, and told with other girls to go straight up to our dorms as people ran around frantically. Apparently, two girls had been messing around in their dorm, and had managed to knock a sink off the wall. Consequently, torrents of water had begun to flood the library below. As staff rushed to remove books, the fire brigade was called. Everyone was confined to the dorms, while the matter was dealt with. I stood on the large landing at the top of the main staircase, listening to the chaos below. Suddenly, a fireman rushed over to me, and asked me if I had got some string or anything to tie back a fire door. The only thing I could think of was a strong piece of string I had on a novelty shaped comb on my dressing table, which someone had given to me as a present. I rushed up the stairs to collect the string and quickly tied the door back, as various fireman rushed through with different pieces of equipment. One of them asked me to stand at a given point on the landing and relay messages between firemen upstairs and downstairs, which I did. At one stage, the head mistress walked past me, and not realising the situation, shouted at me and practically bundled me back up the top staircase. I gave her enough time to disappear, and crept back to my duties. It was a considerable time before the situation was under control, and I guess there must have been an extensive amount of damage. I don't know what punishment the girls received, but some of us found the whole episode quite exciting.

At the end of that highly eventful day, we were unaware that further drama was to come our way. About two weeks later, Mrs. Henry had just finished teaching us our last lesson of the day, and dismissed us to go for tea. As one of the girls attempted to open the classroom door, she was surprised to find that it was stuck. She shouted over to Mrs. Henry, exclaiming that the door was locked. Mrs. Henry retorted incredulously that there was no way it could be locked, and strode over to open it. She tugged and pulled, but her efforts were fruitless, and she nervously concluded that the door was, indeed, well and truly stuck. As panic began to fill the room, I sat calmly in a state of deja vu. I found no reason to be distressed, why should I? I was a seasoned pro at this getting stuck in a classroom lark! It then took a considerable amount of shouting and banging to arouse a rescue party, and when several people had tried in vain to release us, it was decided that reinforcements must be called for. We had very few men in the college. There was a computer teacher, an elderly gentleman who came in to repair our specialist equipment such as Braillers and variable speed tape recorders, a history teacher, who couldn't be located, and a caretaker, who also couldn't be found. Our last hope was a cheery chap who happened to be the head chef. No problem! At least he could cook food and send it up to us through the window if necessary. Mr. Collins was a portly gentleman, and we thought we would soon be free as he proceeded to throw his weight, together with several other weighty objects at the door. Disappointingly, the door stayed put. It made a stubborn and staunch effort to keep us in our classroom.

The classroom was on the first floor. I say first floor, but, being a large mansion house, it was considerably higher than a standard first floor room. Our teacher tried to calm those of us who were genuinely frightened by the experience, but it was not difficult to discern that she was just as worried as they were. I would love to have been a fly on the wall in the staffroom, as discussions were taking place as to what was to be done. Suddenly, as people outside in the corridor grappled with the door, our PE teacher, Miss Sharpe put a ladder against the wall, climbed up to one of the windows, and delivered a large tray of currant buns. I found this rather curious but it was nice to think that concern had been shown for the fact that we had missed afternoon tea. Some of us tucked in gratefully, while others continued to fret. Miss Sharpe and Mrs. Henry engaged in a conversation, and eventually Miss Sharpe persuaded our teacher that we could climb out of the window one by one and, with her help, descend the ladder. "Cool!" I thought. This was one of the better Chorleywood moments.

So began the long process of each girl, in turn, climbing out of the window and slowly making her way down the ladder, with Miss Sharpe a couple of rungs below, keeping a close eye on her progress. Once the girl in question was safely on the ground, Miss Sharpe would immediately go back up to assist the next pupil. As time went on, a crowd of staff gathered and gave a warm round of applause each time someone made a safe descent. Like the captain of a sinking ship, Mrs. Henry stayed in the classroom until the last girl was safely down at ground level. As I remember, she still felt scared to go down the ladder, and waited until, eventually, the door was prized from its place. The following morning just before assembly, Mrs. Henry praised us for our courage, and handed out medals for bravery. These were large chocolate mints, wrapped in gold paper, which had been stuck to lengths of red felt. She pinned them to our sweaters, before she led us all down to assembly. We all felt very pleased with ourselves, as we marched down the oak staircase and across the entrance hall proudly displaying our medals. Unfortunately for most of us, the temptation to consume the chocolate overcame the need to display our awards, and we ended up walking around with scrunched up pieces of gold paper hanging from our sweaters, which didn't quite look so becoming.

Weekends were also very structured. We had school on Saturday mornings. After breakfast, we would collect our laundry bags from the chair beside our beds, and walk downstairs to the toilet block, which also had two rows of large sinks. Firstly, we would wash our hair, and then we would be shown how to hand wash all our clothes. Yes, at twelve years old, I stood scrubbing my jeans at the sink, and they didn't even provide us with hand cream afterwards. We later had to spin the clothes in an old fashioned top loading spin dryer, before hanging them on various rails in the drying room. After break time, we had further lessons such as drama or biology before lunch. Even on a

Saturday afternoon we had to go on walk, so the weekend didn't really begin until around two pm. However, that didn't mean the rest of the weekend was yours to relax and do exactly what you wanted. Each Thursday morning a list of activities would appear on the notice board. Each one lasted for an hour, and it was compulsory to do one activity on Saturday afternoon, one on Sunday morning, and one on Sunday afternoon. We had to make our choices, and line up to read them out to a member of staff so she could log them to make sure we attended. These included everything from knitting and sewing, through to making soft toys and collages. Some activities were ok, but many were incredibly boring.

I was still getting a hard time from some girls in my year, and it wasn't just the daily drip-drop of nasty words, but my possessions began to go missing. At first it was just a few sweets from my suitcase, but it gradually got worse. One weekend, some friends of my family who were visiting the area took me out for the day, and when I returned to school, they gave me a box of chocolates. I should have locked them in my locker straight away, but I put them in my drawer, and the following day they were gone. At the end of term shortly before Christmas, a friend came to visit me, and I asked them to wait until I got their Christmas present. I went to collect it, only to find that it was gone. I had bought a box of chocolates, and some bubble bath. I knew after searching for a few minutes what must have happened. Feeling dejected, and very embarrassed, I returned to apologise, saying I must have misplaced the gift and would give it to them next time. It was after this incident that staff finally got involved and eventually the culprit was caught. The stealing stopped, but the bullying didn't. It was a very lonely time for me. I was trying my best to settle in to my new school, but my heart was still in Liverpool. As I lay in bed each night, I always found myself thinking about my friends and wondering what they were doing.

From my perspective, I got the distinct impression from an early stage that a certain member of staff at college didn't like me much either. One evening just before supper, letters were handed out to us that had arrived late that day. When we were seated at our table, waiting to line up for our food, I read my letter and was sad to learn that one of my friends from St. Vincent's had died. I was visibly upset, but said nothing. When a friend commented to this particular member of staff who was on duty at the time that there was something wrong, she simply said, "Don't worry about her, she just doesn't want to eat her meal." She never took the time to enquire about what was wrong, and didn't seem to care. During another meal time, my class mates were discussing a subject that puzzled me, and I was curious to find out more. I kept hearing the phrase mother hen but didn't have a clue what they were talking about. I later learned that each student had been appointed a member of staff to be their personal tutor, or "mother hen". Each pupil would regularly meet up with their mother hen to chat about any problems they were experiencing, and to seek any advice they needed. It turned out that my tutor had not by then had the time to meet with me, and that was the reason I was, for want of a better phrase, left somewhat in the dark. Even though I had made it clear at the time that I didn't understand what a supposed mother hen was, the same member of staff never made any attempt to explain to me, anything about the procedure. I decided that I needed to devise a plan to somehow become part of the crowd and I needed that idea fast.

8. Crime and Punishment

Bedtime was staggered in fifteen minute intervals ranging from eight forty-five to ten o'clock, depending upon which year you were in. Once in bed, everyone was allowed to talk for thirty minutes before lights out. Care staff would have to take it in turns to be on night duty or "prowl" as we used to call it. They would make sure each dormitory was in bed, and then return later to turn out the lights and tell us to go to sleep. They would then wander the corridors, listening and making sure we obeyed. We soon learned that Monday evening was Miss Thorpe's night off, and that was our licence to make more mischief. Most evenings, we would be told off at least once for whispering after the allotted time. But as the weeks progressed, we became more adventurous about what we could attempt to do without getting caught.

Playing Dares became our favourite pastime. Some of these included the following:

knocking on Miss Thorpe's door which was on our corridor and running away; filling a tooth mug with water or talcum powder, and placing it on top of the door in the hope that the person on prowl would get covered or creeping down the corridor and removing an item from the staff fridge, bringing it back to the dorm to show everyone, before returning it without getting caught. I once had to run down the corridor, banging a large metal bin, and shouting, "any rubbish?" repeatedly. I was also dared to run a bath in the bathroom at the end of our corridor, and stand in it for ten seconds. As I was getting out, I heard someone coming up the stairs, and ran so quickly to the dorm that I went flying across the lino on the floor. Many of us ended up with badly stubbed toes as we did similar things. We rarely put our slippers on, and would often bang them on the metal legs of the bed frames.

The dorms all had lino floors, and the same furniture. We had an old hospital style metal bed with a very thin foam mattress. Next to our bed was a chair, and alongside the bed was a small mat. Parallel with the bed, was a single wardrobe, with a dressing table and chest of drawers. We would often end up inadvertently skidding across the floor on those mats. Each dormitory had two or three sinks, with the toilets and bathrooms further down the corridor. If we were caught talking, we would invariably be issued with punishments. The most common one was to be made to sit in silence at the top of a flight of stairs for around twenty minutes. I was once sitting at the top of one set of stairs, when another staff member walked past me with her dog.

She had just taken him for a walk, and was very wet. The dog walked past me, and stopped for some attention. She pitifully related that the dog had dragged her through a huge puddle. Was she looking for sympathy? My response was to smile, and give the dog an extra pat, all the time thinking "Well done doggy". I was once caught chatting, and made to go down to the sewing room, to do some ironing. Feeling particularly defiant on that night, each time I was asked if I was now ready to go back to bed, I replied "No I'm ok!" I spent the best part of two hours ironing half of the school's laundry, before being ordered to go to bed. Two of my friends were once sent down to the main corridor to stand there for around half an hour as a punishment. They ended up being told off again, because the school nurse walked past and enquired, "What are you doing there, waiting for the number ten bus?" They laughed so loudly, that the member of staff heard them and they got into more trouble.

About four of us were particularly mischievous one night and so were sent down to the toilet blocks to do some hand washing. As we stood at the sinks scrubbing, the door opened, and we were surprised to find that it was the head teacher. We rarely saw Miss Woods, except during assembly, and immediately fell silent, thinking that now, we were in deep trouble. She asked us what we were doing and who had sent us there. Miss Woods was a lady in her sixties. She often seemed rather stern, and not particularly approachable. However, on that night we were to be surprised. Minutes later, she returned, explaining that she had confirmed our story. She then paused, and said, "Girls, are you sure you are warm enough?" We assured her that we were, and she left us to our work. After that incident, even though I didn't see very much of her, my view of Miss Woods changed. My only criticism was that I wish she had spent more time with the pupils. I was to learn at a later date, that she was quite a warm person, with a surprisingly good sense of humour.

I'm pretty sure that Miss Woods knew nothing of one of the worst punishments that was inflicted upon us by some of the care staff. Again, after being caught talking after hours, we would find ourselves standing at a sink with our little cup of washing powder, only this time it wasn't our own washing, it was someone else's. To be frank, we were made to hand wash other girls stained underwear. Believe me, it certainly shut you up after lights out for a considerable number of nights. However, sometimes you get yourself into so much trouble, that you finally realised that there's only one way out, and that's to simply admit your crime, before they get to you first.

One winter evening, one of the partially sighted girls in our year, noticed some lights beyond the ha-ha field, near the woods, and was intrigued. I'm not sure how, but she managed to persuade three of us to accompany her in exploring where they were coming from. I say one evening but, actually, we decided that we would go during the night, around eleven pm. I wouldn't consider doing it now, let alone at the age of fourteen! I simply don't know how we had the guts, or probably lack of sanity, to go ahead with the plan, but we did. After creeping down the stairs, we exited by the door of what was known as the listening room, made our way to the ha-ha field, and through the woodland beyond. After wandering around for I don't know how long, we couldn't seem to find whatever it was we were looking for, and decided to go back. When we finally returned, we were vexed to find that none of us had had the presence of mind to leave the heavy door on the latch, and so were locked out. We wandered aimlessly around looking to see if a downstairs window had been left open, but to no avail. Finally, someone came up with the notion that in the winter garden, a large conservatory, was an old rickety iron fire escape. This was deemed to be unsafe to be used unless under extreme circumstances, but hey, we were in enough trouble already. What difference would it make unless, of course, the structure was to buckle under our weight and then… Well, we wouldn't think about that yet. So off we went climbing the spiral metal stairs, which led to a narrow landing, and wound around the perimeter of the building close to the ceiling, and through the fire door into one of the dormitories. Of course, we woke all the girls in there, but we were warm again, and safe.

I'm not sure who told Miss Larsen, but the following day, she told us that as soon as Miss Thorpe came back from her night off, she would tell her, and we would be in big trouble. As we all crowded on a bed in the dorm, we contemplated what would happen to us, and feared our punishment. In one of my bolder moments, I suggested that we simply knock on Miss Thorpe's door when she returned and admit to our travels before Miss Larsen got there first, thus killing two birds with one stone. Neither of them would foresee our intent, and maybe our punishment would be curbed by our blatant honesty. I clearly remember the feeling of trepidation, as we sat waiting to be called into Miss Thorpe's room. She, however, was much calmer than any of us expected, and even took our classmate to explain whence the lights were coming, adding that if she was curious about anything else in the future, it was better to enquire first. I cannot remember what punishment we received, so I suppose it wasn't actually that bad.

So, some you win, some you lose, but winning will always give you that warm feeling of satisfaction. One afternoon, a group of friends and I had arrived back early from walk, and were desperate to get indoors. It was very cold. As I leaned against a window frame, I was surprised to find that one of the cloakroom windows had been left open. Without hesitation, I climbed in, and called the others to follow. We quickly changed in to our indoor gear, and made our way along the stone corridor to ascend the stairs to our classroom. I was first in line, and, just as I got there, the door behind us opened and we heard Mrs. Henry's voice, loud and disgruntled. She saw my companions, but I was lucky enough to have just turned the corner on to the stairs. I pinned myself flat against the wall, hoping that she wouldn't see me, and I was pleased to learn that I was in the clear. The door closed, with Mrs. Henry still chastising my classmates, as I tiptoed up the stairs, and took refuge in the warmth of my form room, while the others were sent outside again, to brave the cold.

That wasn't the only occasion on which I experienced a sense of glee at simply getting away with something. One evening before April Fools' Day, I hatched a plan, and managed to persuade a member of my form to assist me in some mischief making. The day fell on a Sunday, which gave us a better opportunity to arrange more tricks. Our main target was breakfast time, and we really went to town, or dining room as the case was. Breakfast was at eight thirty, but we got up at seven, and made the most of the time. We began by taking a trip to our classroom. I had the idea that we would write the week's meal menu, which normally appeared on the noticeboard in the main corridor, on a Monday morning. Today it was to appear a day early, and be our own creation. We included some usual dishes, but slipped in a few surprises. I suppose it wasn't truly a menu, because you had no choice, it was simply a way to inform us what we would be having for each meal the following week. When we had compiled our version, we hurried down to the noticeboard, removed the old menu, and replaced it with ours.

Then began a flurry of activity. We rolled up the large carpet that lay in the front hall and hid it in the library. We hid the gong in there too. We made sure that the beater for the gong was hidden separately, so that if the gong was located, it still couldn't be struck. Next came the dining room part of the plan. We removed random seats from the wooden frames of the dining chairs and swopped linen napkins which, incidentally, had people's names on them on their napkin rings, from table to table. We selotaped cups to saucers, tipped the sugar out of the sugar bowls, stuck the spoon in the bottom of the bowl, and put the sugar back in on the top. The long line of metal toast racks which stood on a high shelf, were removed, tied together with string on the inside, and put back in to place, as well as a host of other dares of disruption. It felt like we had done a day's work as we tiptoed back to bed unseen and feeling very proud of our work

We certainly felt we reaped our reward at breakfast time, as we sat back and enjoyed the show. There were gasps of surprise when a member of staff went to bang the gong that had mysteriously disappeared. Peals of laughter and screams as certain people went to sit down and fell through the frames of their chairs. An almighty clatter filled the room, as one of the kitchen staff pulled down one of the toast racks, and the whole lot followed. Sugar sprayed the tables, as girls tried to remove the spoons from the bowls, and, eventually, someone finally noticed that the carpet from the hall had gone. No one found out who was responsible, and we were to enjoy further merriment later that afternoon. We were in the common room listening to the record player, when a member of the kitchen staff came to sit and chat with the member of care staff on duty. A couple of girls had already read the menu, and were surprised to find we were having lasagne for supper one evening. Up to that point, we had only had this dish at lunch time, never in the evening. They quizzed the relevant staff member, who protested, saying that we weren't having lasagne that week, and was quite indignant. As we lined up for supper that evening, we heard a disgruntled conversation going on with some of the fifth form girls. They were complaining that they had been making orange surprise in a cookery lesson that week, and now the kitchen staff were stealing their ideas, because it had never been on the menu before, and now suddenly it was. That was an unexpected bonus for us. That morning we had known nothing about the fifth form's cooking schedule, orange surprise was simply a coincidence, something we'd just pulled out of the bag, as an unexpected item. It surprised us too, but gave us plenty to laugh about. Our day had been not just a success, but a triumph, and something we reveled in for weeks.

There are times though, when things go very wrong. Each summer, we held a school swimming gala in our outdoor pool. Because our class was large, we had to be split into two separate teams. It so happened, that when we took our O-level options, history and geography were timetabled against each other. By chance, seven girls had opted for geography and seven for history and that dictated how we were split into the two teams. We were asked to think up names for our teams, and discussed the suggestions between us. At the time, we had been studying rivers, and one geographical term associated with this is interlocking spurs. I proposed that we should call our team "The Interlocking Spurs" so that we could cheer each other on by shouting "Come on you Spurs"! The idea was immediately adopted, and on the day we did so, and I'm pleased to report we were the better team. The gala, however, did involve the whole school, and took up most of the afternoon. At the end I was amongst a few who, instead of staying to revel in victory, chose to get changed quickly. As we stood in the pavilion, we suddenly heard a great deal of noise outside. As girls began to come in we became aware that something unpleasant had happened. Some of the girls had become rather over excited, and thrown one of the mobility teachers in to the pool, fully clothed. It turned out that she was very frightened of water, and couldn't swim. Miss Thorpe had to jump in and save her, and the girls were in a great deal of trouble. To add insult to injury, this teacher had been wearing a watch that was given to her by a close family member who had died. The watch was ruined, and she was devastated as it was of great sentimental value. I have to admit, I was so glad not to have been involved, and felt very sorry that the incident had happened.

Danger isn't something for which you have a great deal of respect, or consider much when you're young. Two girls from my year got into trouble during the first few days at college when they decided to give each other rides in the trunk lift. This contraption was only used at the beginning and end of each year to store or retrieve all the trunks. My friends decided that what was good enough for the trunks, was good enough for them and one tugged on the rope, while the other travelled up and down, not at all worried that at any moment it could have given way under their weight. A friend and I also sat casually on the wide window sill of our dormitory late on summer evenings, dangling our legs out of the window, over at least a thirty feet drop, just to feel the cool breeze, completely oblivious to the fact that, if we'd slipped, that would have been the end of us.

You would also have thought that a group of blind girls would have shown respect for a teacher having the same disability. Never, this was our chance for a laugh. Our English teacher was an elderly lady, who had no sight at all. She was gentle, but definitely what you would call old school. We'd often laugh when we asked the time, and she would feel her tactile watch and reply "It's five and twenty past ten!" We would pass notes to each other, often sharing answers, or just exchange silly messages. We thought it very funny to do stupid things like wear the covers from our Braillers on our heads during the lesson, just because she couldn't see us. Once, one of the partially sighted girls took pleasure in walking across the desks during a lesson. She was stepping across the teacher's desk, right in front of her, and just managed to move her foot, before the teacher's hand came into contact with her shoe. This bad behaviour wasn't restricted to one member of staff. During our first year, we had a new French teacher who found it difficult to keep adequate discipline in the classroom, and we gave her such a hard time that, eventually, she simply walked out of a lesson. The head of French was furious and, as a result, had to teach us instead.

You would expect that by supper time we would be allowed to chill out, and enjoy our meal, but no, rules were still rife. After supper, we were normally given a small fairy cake, and a piece of fruit. It always seemed unfair to me, because, if someone on your table didn't want their cake, and offered it to you, you were at liberty to take it. However, this wasn't the same with fruit. On several occasions, I witnessed others and indeed myself being banned from having fruit for the rest of the week if we were caught trying to have a second piece. I recall an occasion when I sat at the table for supper, to learn that half of the girls on our table were ill and would not be joining us. To my delight, instead of the usual fairy cakes, which we began to call duplicates, had been replaced by Penguin biscuits. As if this wasn't enough to be glad about, no one else on my table wanted one, and I asked if I could have theirs. They replied that I could have the lot if I wanted, and I dug in. When supper was ended, I rose from my chair. I was wearing a rather baggy hand knitted jumper at the time, and it must have looked like I was simply pulling it down as I left the room. However, clasped in both my hands, hidden under the sweater, were six chocolate biscuits. What a catch! I wasn't the cat that got the cream, but the kid who got the biscuits. It created the same sort of feeling you get when you bite into a Kit-Kat to find that it's solid chocolate. Yes, you've been there too!

9. Oops!

As you've probably gathered, food ranks quite highly in my world, but, sometimes you can just have too much of a good thing! Christmas dinner was a fairly big event, so much so that it had to be held on a different day from our Christmas party. We were always treated to a decent traditional meal, which was followed by vast amounts of tangerines and After Eight Mints. During my third year, I specifically remember eating so much that I felt quite sick afterwards. We were allowed to go to our dorms for an hour after to chill, following the meal, but I vividly recall feeling so bloated that I spent the majority of the time kneeling in front of a toilet, feeling extremely sick. I did however learn my lesson, and was far more conservative in my choices at future celebrations.

However, the person who decided to serve up turkey soup for supper one evening, would need to learn from their misjudgment too. It was indeed, the one and only time I remember ever having soup at school and I will explain the reason. At lunch time, dishes of food were placed on our tables, and the teachers served us. At supper time, we lined up in front of the serving trolley and carried our food back to our places. For someone without any sight, it can be difficult to make sure that they are carrying the plate absolutely straight. So, when there are plenty of people wandering around with full soup bowls, that's where the fun starts. As girls proceeded to make their way back to their tables, and others stood up to join the queue, the show was about to begin. People banged into each other and soup slopped on the floor. Then others slipped on the spilt liquid. The floor was soon awash with turkey soup and bodies. Soup spilt, and students slid. Kitchen staff ran around frantically trying to mop up, and help up, and try not to fall themselves. Needless to say, we didn't really drink much soup that evening - no marks to the turkey who planned that meal! Soups-a-daisy, it's not very pleasant when you get a bowl of it down the back of your neck, but I've literally cried laughing, as I've related the story several times since.

Once we'd finished indulging in all that food, there were plenty of opportunities for exercise. As I have already mentioned, we had a large outdoor swimming pool which was used during the spring and summer terms. In the summer it was great, but there were plenty of occasions when it was cold and pouring with rain. As we made our complaints, they would be met by the answer that we were going to get wet anyway, so why bother about the rain. One dry summer day, we were enjoying a swimming lesson, when we had a surprise. There was suddenly a huge splash, as a stray dog jumped straight in the pool. He played quite happily, unaware of the disruption he had caused, while we were ordered to get out until he could be retrieved and sent back to whence he came.

That wasn't the only time we had an unwelcome guest in the school. One February evening, we were woken suddenly around midnight by the fire alarm. We had already practised fire drills, and were not overly concerned. We put on dressing gowns and slippers, and made our way downstairs and outside to line up. It was freezing, but we all thought it was quite exciting, and stood patiently for around twenty minutes, as we waited for the fire brigade. They conducted a thorough check of the building and concluded that it had just been a false alarm. We were sent back to bed and thought nothing more of it until we were woken again around three in the morning, and followed the same procedure. As I made my way out of the dormitory, I heard someone walking in the wrong direction, and quickly followed to tell her. The girl was clearly very sleepy and disorientated, and I had to grasp her hand firmly, and pull her to follow me on the correct route. We waited once again, this time feeling very cold, and just wanting to go back to bed. The firemen took longer on that occasion, to check that everything was ok, and eventually after around half an hour, we were allowed to go back to bed. Some girls seemed to be enjoying the experience, whereas others were clearly not amused.

When the fire alarm rudely interrupted our sleep at five-thirty, our groans almost blotted it out. Who in their right mind would want to exchange their warm bed, for a pair of cold damp slippers, and trudge across the muddy grass again, to wait for another half hour? We stood in line, and shivered, and moaned, and yawned as the fire brigade returned again. I didn't believe it was possible to sleep standing up, but some of us got close that morning. Eventually, we were allowed to crowd into the common room until all the equipment was thoroughly checked again. We were told that a bluebottle had been responsible for triggering the alarm, but we were all too tired to reason or care. Around six-thirty, we were sent back to bed, with the promise that the first lesson would be cancelled so we could have a lie in.

Remember those little accidents I was rather prone to at St. Vincent's? Well, they didn't stop just because I'd changed schools. A girl had once taken one of my folders, and I was chasing her around the classroom to get it back when I tripped. I fell forward, and my face hit a desk, and then the corner of a chair before I fell to the floor. I immediately tasted blood, and instinctively put my hand to my mouth. I remember thinking that my teeth were all there, so it couldn't be that bad! The bleeding carried on, and when one of the care staff saw me, she was horrified. Apparently, I had cut my gums and it looked quite a serious injury. I was rushed to the nurse, who immediately called my parents to inform them that I was being taken to hospital. Miss Downing was surprised at how calm I was, but she didn't know my history. This was no major incident, but I wished at the time that Miss Josie had been with me. I wasn't particularly enamoured at the prospect of having stitches in my mouth, and was relieved to find that the Doctor thought I didn't need them. In a matter of fact voice, he said, "Mouths heal very quickly, just be careful about the things you eat over the next few days."

I always looked forward to Thursdays because on those evenings it was judo club. For the first few months, the college lent us judo suits, but one Christmas, I asked for my own suit. I was very pleased as I entered the gym in my bright white crisp new suit. My instructor commented as soon as he saw me, and I swaggered to my place on the edge of the mat. It wasn't a heavy scratchy material like my borrowed one, but a much lighter weight fabric, known as a competition suit. The novelty soon wore off though when I travelled to a club outside school and learned that a decent bloodstain down the front of the suit gave you much more street cred and was more intimidating for prospective opponents. I didn't suffer any blood loss in my own judo injury, but wow did it hurt! During a competition fight, I somehow managed to break one of my toes. The worst thing was that I didn't even notice until I got into bed later that evening. As I lay there, the pain grew worse. In the morning, I visited the nurse who reported that my toe was completely black and blue, and I would have to wear my slippers. Oh no! Not the hospital again!

There was one instance of my being very glad to have escaped another hospital visit. Snow had fallen very heavily; indeed, it was up to my knees. We all had tremendous fun, building snowmen, having snowball fights, and sledging. One afternoon, Miss Turner took four of us to go sledging on the common. We had a brilliant time. I had a girl on the front of my sledge who had a little sight and could see where she was going. I, on the other hand, didn't have a clue, but just enjoyed the ride: yee-hah! Towards the end of the afternoon, we decided to have one more trip before going back to school, and it definitely was the last one. As we gathered speed down the hill, I heard Miss Turner scream. What I didn't know was we had just managed to miss crashing into a tree, and had, thankfully, slid accurately between two of them. Our speed increased further as we carried on down the hill, but it was a little too fast. Instead of stopping at the bottom, we hit the bank, and my friend and I, suddenly parting company from the sledge, went flying into the air and over the bank, into the road. As I hit the ground, I heard two car horns in stereo on either side of me honking furiously. As I rolled over and began to pick myself up, I could hear Miss Turner's voice, full of anxiety as she called out our names. Luckily, neither of us was badly hurt, but my friend was very shaken up, and felt quite sick. We were all very grateful, that both drivers had managed to react so quickly, because it could have been an extremely serious accident. A very upset, but relieved Miss Turner took us back to school to get warm and dry, but it didn't deter me from sledging again at the earliest opportunity.

There are times in life, when a simple joke can go horribly wrong. Several of us were getting changed following a drama practice, when a member of my class decided to take great pleasure in approaching each of her companions in turn, tugging at her hair, and exclaiming, "Ooh, I like your wig!" Some girls found this amusing, while others were rather irritated. I'm sure she must have foreseen the mixed reactions, but she certainly wasn't ready for what was about to happen. She approached a new girl, who had just joined the sixth form and tugged on her hair, uttering the same phrase. Suddenly, the girl's hair came away in her hand, and I'm not sure which of them was the more embarrassed. The sixth former in question, had joined the school after experiencing sudden sight loss as a result of suffering a brain tumour. The treatment she had received caused the loss of her hair, and she was wearing a wig. It was one of those moments when you really wanted to laugh, but also felt sorry for the girl in question.

It's also hard when you know you shouldn't be laughing, but try as you might you just can't stop yourself. During my first year, I was sitting next to my friend in a music lesson. We had been handed Braille sheets of the words of a song we were about to learn. As Miss Coates proceeded to teach us, my fingers wandered across the paper, and I noticed the name of the person who had composed the music and lyrics of the song. I sniggered as I read the surname, Bellock. As the class began to sing, I nudged my friend, and whispered to her to look at the name and substitute one of the letters for another. There was a pause, and then the penny must have dropped, because my friend let out a huge burst of laughter. I joined in, until our teacher suddenly stopped playing the piano and angrily demanded to know what we were laughing at. Neither of us divulged the information, and so received a thorough dusting down. Although we tried very hard not to continue laughing, the damage had already been done, and we giggled through the rest of the lesson.

That may have been the first time I was severely reprimanded by a teacher, but it certainly wasn't the last. I remember the day when we learned that we were to have a new English teacher in the department. Her name was Mrs. Underhill, and she was to teach us for a couple of sessions a week. She seemed to be an eccentric character, with a rather austere voice. I remember feeling a little uncomfortable because from my perspective, it wasn't always clear when she was joking with us, and when she was being serious, that was until I made a huge mistake. At the end of one lesson, she told us that our homework for that evening was to write a poem on a subject we felt particularly strongly about. As we sought further instruction, she made it clear, that there were no boundaries, we could simply explore any subject we liked. I apologise in advance for my teenage naivety, as this topic may affect many readers. I waded in, and chose the subject of smoking. When she arrived at our classroom a couple of days later, the atmosphere was well I could say smoking but, actually, it was positively frosty!

As she walked in, and sat at her desk at the front of the room, she said nothing. Now, you don't have to be able to see, or to hear someone's voice, in those instances. You just instinctively know when something is wrong. The atmosphere was heavy with her simmering wrath! She handed out marked homework to individuals, providing feedback, but saved mine till the very last. As my paper was pushed back in front of my face, she unleashed her full venomous criticism of my work. I felt like a condemned victim, waiting to be thrown into the witch's cauldron, ready to be thoroughly boiled. From that point on, her manner with me was, shall we say, anything but cordial. In fact she constantly referred to me in an intimidating tone as "ratbag"! Naive I was, but not completely stupid! There were no warning signs of Mrs. Underhill's smoking habits. We never smelled it on her clothes and, if I had, then I certainly would have avoided the subject. I honestly cannot remember details, but after a few weeks, suddenly, just as quickly as she had arrived, she had left without explanation. I never tried to find out further details, I was just glad to put the whole sorry episode behind me.

At college we had two horses; a small white one, named Pixie, and a larger brown one, called Brandy. I began riding in the first year, and enjoyed the lessons. I grew in confidence as I learned to trot and then had a go at jumping over large logs arranged in the field by the paddock. During one lesson, my PE teacher took a friend and me into the woods to ride, and we felt a tremendous sense of freedom out there. I was caught napping one day, however, when Brandy grew bored of trotting, and broke into a canter. Because I wasn't concentrating, I dropped the reigns and had to grab on to the saddle. I lost my balance and went flying off the side of the horse and fell flat on my back. As I rubbed my bruises, and indicated that I was ok, my teacher took care of regaining control of the horse. I didn't get back on that day, but when I did, I made sure I kept my mind on the job.

Remember the member of staff I mentioned earlier? Well, we had a number of confrontations over the years. I suppose it's fair to say that in more ways than one, we didn't really see eye to eye! One morning during my first year, we were all having a moan about how strict she was, when she walked past our dorm. One of the partially sighted girls noticed her and told us to be quiet. Unfortunately for me, it was my comments that she heard, and not the others. I immediately got that sinking feeling, and knew I was in for it. If I'd been that much smarter, I would have chosen a different route to breakfast that day, because as I reached the bottom of the oak staircase, there she was waiting for me. Breakfast I certainly was: stirred, grilled, and fried!

On a different occasion, my uncle and his girlfriend, who lived about an hour away, had invited me to spend the weekend with them. It was great, and the time to return to college on Sunday evening came around far too quickly. I was amused to learn that when we got into the car to drive back, it wouldn't start. We were forced to make the journey by tube train, which took considerably longer. It was dark, and late in the evening as the three of us walked across the common and over to college. My uncle had called the school earlier to inform them, but as we entered the common room, there she was waiting for me. She immediately sent me upstairs as my uncle explained our predicament. She seemed perfectly civil with them, but the following morning, I was questioned again about what happened. I felt uncomfortable, and got the impression that she wasn't convinced about our story. There was no cover-up, however, the car really had broken down.

The rules clearly stipulated that, at school, we were to wear brown shoes, both indoor and outdoor. My mum had spent hours dragging me round the shops one half-term to find me a new pair of indoor shoes, but, because I have a very narrow foot, we couldn't find any that fitted correctly. The only suitable pair we found was black, and the choice was simple, I either wore the black shoes, or my slippers. I went back to school and kept a low profile, hoping that no-one would notice. I was ok for around a week, but eventually a member of staff saw them and I was taken aside and told to change my shoes. After explaining the situation, I was told that my mother must buy a new pair in two weeks' time when I was due home for a weekend break.

When I told my Mum on the phone, she was furious, and felt that the staff member should have been more understanding under the circumstances. In fact she was so unhappy, that she then rang the head teacher. After minutes of conversation, Miss Woods decided that the member of staff in question should be given the job of taking me to find suitable shoes in the required colour, and my Mum was not to be put to further inconvenience. Around ten minutes later, Miss Woods rang my parents following further consideration. She told them that she had changed her mind, and had simply left a message on the staffroom notice board saying, "No comments about black shoes!"

Similarly, in the fifth form, as we were nearing our O-Level exams, the same staff member approached our breakfast table one morning to make arrangements for refreshments during our exams. We were all given some extra time, because Braille reading of the test papers took longer. Therefore, during that time we would be allowed to have something to drink. She informed us that we could have milk, or tea with biscuits, and we were to choose the drink we wanted. As I have already stated, I dislike tea and milk, and during the five years at College I had only drunk water. When it came to my turn, I politely asked if I could have water. She sternly replied that I could not, it would have to be milk or tea. I told her I only drank water, but it made not one bit of difference.

I was so angry at her attitude, that I devised a plan. I bought a plastic cup which had a screw top lid, and one morning before the exams began, I tentatively knocked on Miss Woods office door. She gave me the call to enter, and with much trepidation, I did so. I explained my predicament, and asked for her permission to take my cup of water into the exam with me. Considering that most of the exams would last at least three hours, and that it was likely to be hot, I hoped that Miss Woods would be willing to give me permission. She was extremely thorough in her explanation. Miss Woods opened a large filing cabinet, and removed a weighty folder, containing exam regulations. She read them out to me, explaining that the rules clearly stipulated that I was not allowed to take anything in the room other than my Brailler, and some paper. She added, however, that she understood my request, and would speak with the particular member of staff. The following morning I was surprised and pleased to find that the same member of staff appeared again at our table after breakfast, informing us that we could have water during the exam, and did anyone wish to change their choice. I was astounded, but did feel rather smug as ninety per cent of my class opted to have water.

So finally I was taking control, not in a manner that was rude or malicious, but simply standing my ground. As I sat at the table for breakfast one morning, I was somewhat peeved to find that my cereal bowl did not just contain two Weetabix, but also what looked like enough crushed cereal to feed my entire table. As I mentioned earlier, it was compulsory to eat cereal. It was a fifth form privilege to be allowed only to eat toast. We could have toast only when we had eaten a small portion of cereal. A small portion of Weetabix, I'd learned over the years was half of one serving. So, I removed one of them from my bowl, placed it on my side plate and cut it in half. I ate the half portion dry--well I washed it down with a glass of guess what? Water. Once I had dutifully obeyed rule number 35627, I pushed the bowl aside, and helped myself to some toast.

It wasn't long before someone walked past me, and in a rather direct tone said, "Eat your cereal." I did my best to explain but she was having none of it, she simply repeated her order, and walked away. The seeming injustice of the situation made me want to bang my fist on the table. I had done nothing wrong, in fact I had been completely compliant. Why then should I just cave in. This was even worse than the time Miss Downing had confiscated my teaspoon, because she decided I was stirring my hot chocolate too much. I had to be bold, and fight my corner. As she made her way around the dining room, she once again saw the offending cereal bowl, and hissed her request for me to eat my breakfast. I gave her the benefit of the doubt, believing that maybe I had not adequately explained what had happened. However my words were in vain. She was adamant. I must obey orders. So when she approached me again for a third time, uttering those same words, this time in a voice that was determined to enforce her authority, I turned toward her and confidently exclaimed, "No!"

Despite my resolute behaviour, I was actually expecting to receive punishment of near nuclear proportions, and was, therefore, flabbergasted to find that she simply walked away without a single word. I don't know who was the most surprised, but my moment of victory was one to revel in, and to treasure. My only regret was "Why the heck didn't I do that years ago?"

I wasn't the only pupil to end up in conflict with a staff member. I recall an incident during our third year, when another girl from my year had a major bust up with our form teacher. We were to attend a musical at a theatre in Windsor one afternoon, and had been told by our teacher that we could wear our own clothes, as long as we wore a skirt. "Here we go again," I thought, "The skirt thing," but our teacher was insistent. I submissively dragged the only skirt I had from the back of my wardrobe, and got ready on the day. The other girl, however, decided that she was going to wear trousers. We all gathered in the large entrance hall, but when our teacher turned up and saw the trousers, the show began. A major argument took place, with raised voices, and angry confrontation. The student was told repeatedly to go and change or she wouldn't be going to the show. The problem was that the girl had enough sight to see that our teacher was wearing trousers. As I realised the situation, all I could think was, "Josie would never have told us to wear a skirt, and then turned up in trousers herself!"

10. Home and Away

In the first year after leaving St. Vincent's I was pleased to find that our term dates were different. Auntie Jenny therefore offered to drive me back over to Liverpool, during my holidays. I was so excited to be going back, and couldn't wait for the day to arrive. Nanna came with us, and we chatted enthusiastically. Auntie Jenny had a particular liking for wine gums, and I remember a large plastic box of them which she kept in the front of the car. We usually arrived just before morning break time, but didn't warn anyone. I liked to make it a surprise.

As I walked through the front door and into the hall, I smelled that distinctive smell of what I guessed was floor polish which told me I was back in the place I loved and had missed so much. A permanent smile covered my face, as I walked to the empty playroom, and decided to hide behind the bookcase. This was my home from home, where my real friends were. I remained still and silent, and Nanna and Auntie Jenny, sat quietly in the little dining room, adjoining the playroom. Soon I heard the girls coming down the corridor and into the room. I suddenly jumped up and shouted, "boo!" Then there were hugs and shouts and loads of laughter. It was wonderful to see Miss Josie, I missed her humour, her warm caring nature, and the laughter we all shared.

All too quickly, it was time for everyone to go back to lessons. I said "Goodbye", and everyone went to their classrooms. Often, Miss Josie would take me to walk around the school, visiting my teachers, to chat about what I was getting up to. I always ended up wishing I could stay longer, and not have to leave. As we walked outside, and over to the car, I was filled with a sense of melancholy. The journey always seemed twice as long on the way home. I kept my thoughts to myself, however. I was very grateful to Auntie Jenny for taking the time to drive us there. She repeated this trip every holiday for over a year. Thanks Auntie Jenny, I owe you a large box of wine gums!

While I was still at St. Vincent's but home for weekends, I had begun attending a club for visually impaired children. We met once a month on a Friday evening, and were collected from our homes by minibus and driven to the venue. The age range was from toddlers to teens, so there was always plenty going on. My sister always came with me, and also Nanna, who very soon became a valued volunteer at the club. We would chat together, play board games, and listen to music. It was good to meet friends in my home town, because I didn't really have any, they were all at my boarding school.

Each year we met together for our Christmas party, where there was always loads of food, party games, and a present from Santa. Around the same time we would be taken to the local pantomime, which we all loved. During the summer, a number of day trips were arranged. A group of us would dash to the back seat of the coach for our journey. One memorable occasion was when we visited Alton Towers on the day that Prince Charles married Lady Diana Spencer. There were very few people at the theme park, and we didn't have to wait long to get on the rides. Our particular favourites were the corkscrew, and the log floom. The summer outings usually included visiting the seaside, and time on a fun fair. Needless to say, that the journey home was always a great deal quieter than the outgoing one because we were pretty tired.

The person in charge of running the children's branch of the society was a woman in her early sixties. Mrs. Alexander was a good humoured lady, who was always keen for us to enjoy a range of activities and experiences. She had a good attitude toward disability, never wrapping us up in cotton wool, but encouraging us to reach beyond the constraints of visual impairment. Her favourite phrase concerning blindness was, "It's not a disability, it's just an inconvenience!" Each year, she would take us on a trip to Lake Windermere, where we would spend the day on sailing boats and speedboats. Another favourite activity involved two people sitting astride a long pole, facing each other, in the lake. We would then have a pillow fight, until one person fell in. She also took us horse riding, and dry skiing among other activities.

There was once however, a trip which didn't take our fancy. We were driven to one venue, I shan't say where. Most of us were seriously unimpressed to find that when we arrived, there was very little to do. There was a kids' playground, a cafe, and the opportunity to play table hockey, or hire a pair of roller skates. We hung around chatting, and wondering what to do, when one of the sighted guides, noticed something. Remember, each visually impaired person had with them a sighted guide who was either a sibling or a close friend. Kirsten always came with me. We noticed that each half hour, a small train was making trips across the bay to the nearest seaside town where we knew there was a funfair. We decided that the next time it came back we would be on it. As we waited, someone from our little group of friends casually suggested to Mrs. Alexander, that she deserved a cup of tea, adding that we would be fine for a while and that she should take a well-earned break. Gratefully, she accepted our offer and went into the cafe. As the little sand train returned we took our chance, and made our escape. Feeling rather smug, we spent the next two hours and all our money on the funfair, while the majority of the kids stayed at the cafe. We had indeed spent all our money, but on our return, we were to pay! We were late, and the coach had to wait for us. I've never seen Mrs. Alexander so angry! She was normally a very cheery easy-going person, but not any longer. It wasn't the fact that we were a few minutes late, but that we had disappeared without permission. The day had been hot, but the atmosphere in the coach on the way home was certainly cooler than outside.

One summer, when I was about thirteen years old, the family spent a considerable time at the BBC studios in Manchester. Mum had a friend who worked there, and managed to get tickets for a number of live kids shows on a Saturday morning. The show was called "Get Set For Summer", and we attended around five. They were broadcast live at nine o'clock in the morning, so we had to arrive early, at around seven thirty. The only part which was recorded, was the opening music. We all sat on tiered benches in the studio, and the cameramen recorded a part where they ran the opening music and someone shouted across the music, "Are you ready?" We had to jump in the air and shout, "Yes we're ready." This was then played at the beginning of the show. Every week, there was live music from at least one or two current bands or vocalists. We were lucky to meet acts from the eighties music scene such as Duran Duran, Shakin' Stevens, Hazel O'Connor, and The Beat, among others. We had a fantastic time, filling our autograph books, and chatting with our favourite band members. Everyone at school was very jealous, especially when I met Simon Le Bon, from Duran Duran.

Mum, Dad and Nanna usually sat in the canteen having breakfast and watching the show on a monitor, while Kirsten and I sat with the other kids in the studio. One morning however, they attempted to squeeze into a corner of the room, to see how things were run. Each person taking part had access to a huge weighty tome, which was the script for the show. My Dad had picked one up, and was perusing it as he stood and observed. Suddenly, Mum and Nanna were asked to leave, but it was presumed that because he had a script in his hand, Dad was taking part, and he was left to continue watching. He stayed until the thought of that BBC bacon butty got the better of him.

Music always played a big part in our family life. Mum had spent a long time as part of an amateur dramatics group, where she often sang. From being a teenager, Dad had built up a sizeable record collection which included, The Beatles, Buddy Holly, The Peddlers and Roy Orbison. Music was always played in the car, and during my teens, I became aware of a female singer by the name of Barbara Dickson. Dad had an album that he really liked, and he played it round and round. That became one of our family favourites, and Dad went to her concerts a number of times. Even today, all those years later, we are big fans. Whenever the family gets together, we can be found sitting around the table with a glass of red wine, chatting and singing along to our favourite Barbara Dickson songs. It's become quite a tradition now, and a must for all our iPods.

I loved school holidays, going shopping with Mum, and listening to football with Dad. We had some good friends who lived across the road, and we would have brilliant parties over Christmas and the New Year, and barbecues during the summer. Sometimes other neighbours would join us, and one Christmas, we all did the conga right down the length of our street. I remember one party at which a neighbour had joined us, and had a little too much to drink. Norman was a slight mild mannered gentleman in his seventies. On that night he had really let his hair down. During a dance, he had lost his balance, gone flying in the air, and, I'm told, managed to do a back flip before landing on the floor. Incredibly, he had travelled the length of a long glass coffee table, which was covered in glasses containing an assortment of drinks. Not a drop was spilled, and not a glass was broken. I'm convinced a trained stunt man couldn't have done a better job. Once we had established that Norman was ok, the place erupted into hysteria as we recalled the event in disbelief.

In school holidays, we would make intermittent visits to Leeds, to attend appointments with my ophthalmologist. He was a gentleman with a glowing reputation, but sometimes had a formidable manner. Indeed, my mother often felt quite intimidated in his presence. During a consultation, he prescribed some new eye drops for me. Mum made the comment in regard to the medication, "So Jane takes these three times a day?" He spun round from his desk and retorted, "Are you asking me or telling me?" Mum recoiled and remained silent. His expertise however, was without question. He was always very pleasant to me. One day shortly after my loss of vision, he turned to me at the end of my appointment and told me to enjoy a few more weeks off school. To a nine year old, that's definitely how to win friends and influence people.

When I was fourteen, he proposed that he should perform the same operation on my left eye that he had carried out on the right. The sight in my left eye had deteriorated further, and he was confident that it could be improved. The date was set, and I tried to prepare myself. I kept telling myself not to become too hopeful, but I was confident that the operation would make a marked improvement. As I remember, due to industrial action, the procedure had to be postponed, and I had to wait an extra few weeks. Finally, we were given another date and, in the summer holidays, I was taken to the hospital. I was taken to my bed and asked to get changed and into bed. The operation was scheduled for nine o'clock the following morning, and around four o'clock, the consultant came to make his final checks, and speak with us about the procedure. I was led down the corridor and into a darkened room where he examined my eye. I vividly remember him suddenly turning around with a heavy sigh. He spoke with my parents, and then the disappointing news hit me. My sight had deteriorated further in the extra few weeks that preceded the operation, so much so that he was unable to carry it out. A very tearful Mum walked me back to the ward where I got dressed, packed my things and went out to the car. It was a very long and silent drive home. I was immensely disappointed, but said little. No one could do anything about it, and I was fully aware how upset everyone was, why add to that? We did have a short conversation in the days that followed. I made the decision that I didn't want to pursue any more surgery. I'd had enough disappointment, and just wanted to get on with life.

Back at home, there were important things to do to take my mind off the disappointment, such as shopping. There weren't many opportunities to spend my pocket money at school, so I would save it in my post office account until the holidays. I remember the first time Kirsten and I were given permission to go in to the town centre by ourselves; we felt so cool. We boarded the bus, and once we arrived, hit the shops. We looked at clothes, and tried the latest perfume. Then it was time for lunch. One of our favourites was a bakery called Grandma Lee's. We bought a pasty, and ate as we walked around the shops. Then it was time to search all the music shops for our favourite albums. We made the most of the day and had loads of fun, usually returning with a couple of carrier bags each containing our purchases. I once needed to buy a camera. Yes, you read correctly! I needed it because I was about to go on holiday to Denmark with some friends from school, and wanted the staff who accompanied us to take some photos for me. We searched until we found a bargain. One shop had a camera which was reduced from thirty pounds to only six pounds. I bought it, and it did a great job. Following the trip, my family used it, and it went on working for years. In fact, it probably still would work if you could get the correct film. I felt very nostalgic only a short time ago, when I spent the week with my parents during the school holidays. I reached into a drawer whilst unpacking, and to my surprise, there was the camera. My Dad had kept it all this time, and thought he'd leave it there knowing I'd find it and smile. For many years, it became a joke that I owned the best camera in the family. How ironic is that?

During one trip into town, Kirsten and I decided we needed a change from the normal lunch time pasty. I had saved up some extra money and suggested we go to a pizza restaurant called The Queens. Mum and Dad occasionally went there, and we felt very grown up as we sat at our table. We ordered pizza, garlic bread, and a glass of cola each and laughed as we wondered what our parents would say when they found out what we had done. They were, indeed, very surprised when we told them, but found the episode quite amusing.

On the run up to Christmas one year, we deliberated about what to buy for Mum and Dad. Kirsten told me that the toaster had broken, and we should buy a new one. So off we went to choose. We ended up buying a matching iron, toaster and kettle. On the way home, feeling very proud of ourselves, we wondered where we could store the goods until the big day. In the end we asked a neighbour if we could hide them in their house until Christmas day. On the afternoon of Christmas Eve, we made an excuse, and went to wrap the present. We found a large cardboard box, and filled it with the items, then wrapped it carefully. That evening, we had a party with family and friends. During the evening we collected the box, and carried it excitedly back home. Everyone was surprised as we put the large box under the tree, and Mum and Dad wanted to know what it was. The next morning, they were amazed, as I don't think they had expected us to have saved enough money for such a present. We got just as much pleasure out of the experience, as they did in receiving it. Even so, I'd like to take this opportunity to strongly suggest to my husband that he mustn't under any circumstances follow this example.

Talking of Christmas and presents, it reminds me of the time when Nanna took Kirsten and I to a pantomime. We hadn't planned to go, but were out shopping one morning when we saw the advertisement outside the town hall. The show was due to begin within a few minutes, and we begged her to take us, and she obliged. During the performance, different children were picked from the audience to take part. Kirsten and I were called up to sing a carol with some of the cast. We were given a present each for our efforts as we left the stage. Toward the end of the panto, they announced that those who had come in fancy dress should go on the stage for the competition, which had been advertised in advance. Strangely, no one had bothered, so it was decided that they should have a talent contest. Several people stood in line to take part, and Nanna encouraged me to go up and sing. She laughed later, because she related that all the children were smartly dressed and I stood there in my jeans, as I'd not planned to be there. I sang my song, and then it was time for the judges to make their choice partly based upon the amount of applause we had received. I was very shocked, but elated when I found out that I had won. Kirsten had to come on the stage to help me carry all my prizes. I won a huge bundle of toys, and we all struggled to carry them home on the bus. For days later, Nanna kept saying, "And there you were, standing on the stage in your scruffy jeans". Maybe it wasn't my voice, but the state of my jeans; perhaps the judges thought they were the only toys I would get for Christmas!

Kirsten and I have always got on very well together. Yes, we've had our fair share of arguments, which is only natural, but there's been more fun than fury. Mum and Dad once took us to the seaside, and although it was a warm spring day, we were surprised to find that there was no one else on the beach. We spent some time paddling while they watched, and then left us for a few moments while they got some coffee. When they had gone, we became somewhat overzealous in our pursuits and got rather wet. You know those moments when you say, "Are you thinking what I'm thinking?" Well we had just one of those moments. In a split second we both jumped into the water fully clothed, and swam around having a brilliant time. We hadn't taken any other spare clothes with us, and didn't know what the reaction would be when our parents returned, but that was all part of the fun. Luckily, they all had a laugh about it, and Dad had a picnic blanket in the back of the car, so we dried off as we travelled home. It was ages though, before Dad managed to finally get rid of the sand from the car.

One school holiday I returned home to find that we had acquired two cats. I say acquired; in fact a relative had gone to live in South Africa, and couldn't find a home for them. One evening when my parents were visiting them, he explained the situation, and they offered to adopt them. They were British Blues, and I loved them. Kirsten renamed hers Lucky, and I called mine Scampi, although I haven't a clue why. We had them for years, in fact they both must have been quite an age when they died. Lucky died just before my parents moved house, but Scampi kept going strong. He once caused quite a stir in the village where they moved. They ran a shop on the main street, and Scampi used to take himself off for a regular daily walk. A customer once ran into the shop enquiring if we owned the cat she had just seen having been prompted by a knowing member of the public. Apparently, Scampi had perfected the art of wandering over to the zebra crossing and patiently sitting until someone came along and pressed the button. When the bleeps sounded and the traffic had stopped, Scampi would walk across the road and over to the public gardens opposite. The lady who had entered the shop was highly amused, and couldn't believe what the cat regularly got up to. Motorists in the area must have got used to seeing that quirky cat taking its daily stroll.

11. Cause for Celebration

The run up to Christmas has always been my favourite time of year, and was very busy at College. When we returned at the end of October, the first School tradition we would take part in, was preparation for tree presents. As we all left assembly on a given morning, we would be required to pick a name out of a basket, and keep it a secret. You then had to make a gift for the pupil or staff member you had picked. The names were always kept secret, and I'll explain later why. We would all get to work deciding and planning on what we were going to make as a present for our specific person. We made everything from soft toys, to wicker baskets and jewellery boxes. In the four or five weeks that followed, the building was awash with sewing needles, knitting needles, all manner of textiles, crochet hooks, and beads to name but a few. The place was a hive of activity, as we worked hard to finish our gifts in time to meet the deadline.

In October of our first year, we were all given a carol folder, or two as the case was. They contained a selection of traditional carols, and other less known seasonal songs. We had extra choir practices to learn the songs, and each year, new songs would be added to those folders. I loved all the choir practices, because we normally sang the carols in two, three or four part harmonies. Much preparation was needed because we always held several carol services each year. A vast number of people were invited, such as friends of the college, and volunteers. During a service to which people from outside the school were invited, one gentleman sang so loudly, and enthusiastically, that some of us started to giggle. We were soon met with reprimanding whispers from a teacher sitting nearby, and we struggled for the rest of the time not to laugh. When the concert was ended we all met together to enjoy mince pies and coffee. I used to like mince pies, but I ate so many of them during those few days, that now I don't care that much for them.

In between Christmas preparations, and before celebrations began, we enjoyed bonfire night. Around six o'clock in the evening, we would gather in the haha field where a huge bonfire had been made and lit. Staff joined us to watch a large firework display. I always felt sorry for my friends who couldn't see them at all, but staff would stand close by, describing the colours and patterns they made in the dark night sky. I was lucky enough to still be able to see the bright colours, although not really much definition. We ate baked potatoes, and hot dogs, which were closely followed by pumpkin pie, coconut ice, treacle toffee, and gingerbread. When the display was over, we stood and sang songs around the fire for a long while. It really was great fun. Eventually, the fire died down and the cold got the better of us and it was time to go back indoors. The night was always a huge success.

The Christmas party was the main event of the year. We had lessons as normal in the morning, but once we'd had lunch, it was party time! We all met in the gym, and were split into groups of around eight girls, with a member of staff. We spent the whole afternoon playing games such as name that tune, and many other quiz games. Afternoon tea was at four thirty, and then it was time for the staff panto. I always looked forward to this part. Mrs. Henry was usually responsible for writing the script and all the staff would have to take part, including domestic staff. Mrs. Henry had a great sense of humour, and was very clever in her script writing. One year, she went around the school speaking with all the girls, to collect all the phrases or funny sayings synonymous with different teachers. The panto always made us howl with laughter as we heard staff taking the mickey out of themselves. One year I was making my way down the main corridor when I heard a voice behind me in a loud whisper. It was Mrs. Henry who enquired, "Jane, have you got your football scarf; could I borrow it for the panto? I want Miss Woods to wear it." I ran to my dorm to retrieve it, curious as to what Miss Woods would be saying that year. It was indeed a great show, and I don't know how Mrs. Henry came up with such funny material every time.

After the panto, it was time to hand out tree presents. A couple of weeks previously, we had wrapped our presents, and taken them to a collection point, where staff would check them to make sure everyone had one, and store them safely. We never left our names on them, just the name of the person it was intended for. When you got your present, then it was time for everyone to walk around the hall, trying to find out who had made their gift. In my first year, I made a basket for a member of staff, and received a soft toy from a girl in my year. Strangely, the following year, I picked her name out and had to make her a present. My most difficult and ambitious present I made, in my final year there, was a large brass rubbing coloured in gold, and placed in a frame which I made myself. I had previously done some brass rubbing at the local art gallery at home, and decided that the staff member I had picked would like this idea. It took me several hours one Saturday afternoon during the half term holiday to complete the task. I used black paper onto which I put special gold crayon. I made the wooden frame and varnished it before fitting the picture inside. It was quite large, around three feet by two feet, and was very difficult to store without anyone seeing it. I bought a huge plastic Santa sack, and covered it, and placed it in a large walk-in wardrobe in my room until the day of collection. I was pleased with my work and, later at the party, I found that my satisfaction was justified. All the teachers were very impressed, and ran around trying to find out who had made it, because they wanted one the next year. The teacher in question was delighted, and many other staff members later stopped me to compliment me on my efforts.

After the tree presents, came my absolute favourite part of the day. The entire school, including every member of staff, congregated in the large entrance hall. Chairs had been placed around the edges, and staff took their places. We all sat on the floor with our carol folders on our laps. All of the lights were turned off, and the hall was illuminated by a huge roaring log fire, and the lights from a massive Christmas tree in one corner. The atmosphere was amazing, like nothing I'd ever felt before. Staff chose their favourite carols, and we sang them in harmony. One carol we sang every year was "Ding Dong Merrily On High". It was Miss Woods' favourite. I can't possibly find the words to describe the scene accurately. It still brings a smile to my face as I recall the scene: the bright orange glow of the fire, and the warmth that emanated from it; the distinctive smell of those burning logs; the smell of the Christmas tree; the sound of singing that filled the room. I so wish that someone had taken a video of us all, it would have been something to treasure. It was magical! One of those very special and precious times that money could never buy. As the fire burned brightly, we continued to sing, and to me, that's what Christmas is about. Even though I say it myself, the sound that everyone made was beautiful, and I was always disappointed when we had to pack away ready to go to the disco and the rest of the party.

Another seasonal tradition was entrusted to the sixth form girls. On the last day of term, they would get up around five-thirty in the morning, and walk around the school grounds visiting each dormitory or the accommodation of residential staff members. They would shout up to the windows around six in the morning, "Good morning! Merry Christmas! Which carol would you like?" The air was once again filled with singing, and we loved it. We were warm and snuggled up in bed: they were out in the cold, but they were obviously having a great time. We heard their merriment as they left and made their way to other dorms or staff rooms. One year my parents were staying in the home of the head chef at the school. They had become friends with his family, and sometimes visited at weekends. Kirsten and I got on well with their children, and we spent a good deal of time socialising with them. On this occasion, Mum and Dad were unaware of the tradition they were to be treated to. The girls knocked on the windows of the house, which was in the grounds, and asked what carol they would like to hear. Mum and Dad have said on many occasions since how moved they were, as the girls started singing outside their window. They tell how they lay in bed with tears in their eyes, as the beautiful sound of singing filled the room. There were so many things I really disliked about the college, but Christmas time was fantastic. Ever since leaving, it's never felt the same. I still really miss the wonderful atmosphere, and especially all the carol singing during the party.

A couple of years before I left the college, a few houses were built on some land just beyond the grounds. We didn't think much about it, until the Christmas after they had been occupied. At the end of the main carol service, which our parents were invited to attend, Miss Woods told the following story. She had been upset to find that an anonymous letter had been delivered to the college, and brought to her attention. It was from an occupant of one of the new houses. They were vehemently complaining that they had been awoken that morning by girls talking and singing and were clearly not at all appreciative. Miss Woods was so incensed that she had taken the decision to compose her own letter. Not being able to identify by whom the letter was sent, she had written letters to everyone on the new site and hand delivered them herself. Her letter explained her disappointment, at whoever was responsible for not entering into the Christmas spirit for only one day a year. Here, however, was where her command of the situation and sheer genius lay. She firmly stated that if the person in question was unhappy with their new neighbours in the place to which they had chosen to move, then we were more unhappy with them, as we rather preferred the trees to their company. As her story concluded, laughter, and a huge round of applause filled the room. Well done Miss Woods, you always did know how to fight your corner.

I say this because she once told my parents about a time when a film crew visited the college. They asked if they and some prospective actresses could spend some time observing the students as part of their research. They wanted to make a film, which included the part of a blind woman. Miss Woods firmly turned down their request, stating that they didn't need a sighted person to take on the role. If they were serious, then they needed someone who was blind, and she already had the perfect candidate in the sixth form. The film crew left, and that was the end of the matter. The sixth former in question however, did go on to have a successful acting career after leaving the college. Another win for Miss Woods!

During the October half term holiday of 1983, Kirsten and I were spending a Saturday morning watching T.V. The programme was Saturday Superstore hosted by the radio and T.V. celebrity Mike Read. If I remember the story correctly, Mike was an avid collector of juke boxes. Due to moving house, he had to downsize his collection, and was planning to give one away in a competition. Viewers were required to write him a letter giving an explanation of why they would be the most worthy recipient of the aforementioned prize. Kirsten and I thought it would be a brilliant item to have at the club we attended for visually impaired children. So when the programme had ended, we got to work compiling our letter.

I wrote the letter in Braille, and Kirsten wrote the transcription on the page, beneath each line. We described how we met together once a month and the fact that we didn't have any music to listen to. Our radio was currently broken, and we would love to have his juke box. It sounded quite a sob story, but it was actually true. When it was complete, Dad drove us over to the house of the lady who ran the group, Mrs. Alexander, so that she could read the letter, and give her approval. When we got home, I rolled up the Braille letter, and Kirsten addressed it. It was around four-thirty in the afternoon when we walked down to the post box to send it. On the way back, we chatted excitedly about how we would feel if we actually won the competition.

There then followed a period of weeks where we waited, wished, hoped and dreamed, and still waited. The results were to be announced during a show early in December. I didn't get the chance to watch the programme, because I had to attend Saturday morning school. Kirsten was on a weekend trip at Whalley Abbey with her school. When she explained the circumstances to her teachers, they allowed her to watch. The whole class joined her excitedly to see who would win. Kirsten told me later, how the programme had seemed to last for ever, as she waited for the announcement. Before the result was officially announced, she became extremely excited, because as Mike Read spoke to a guest in the studio, she could see that in his hand was my rolled up Braille letter. Had we won the competition? Or was he simply going to mention it?

Back in college, I found it hard to focus on my lessons. My mind kept drifting to the subject of the results. My parents had promised that if we won, they would ring and leave a message for me. The morning seemed to drag on endlessly, as I waited for news. Not long before lunch, one of the care staff came running over to me. She said, "Jane, your parents have rung to leave you a message. It just says you've won!" I was completely beside myself with joy and amazement. This was surely going to be an exciting time to look forward to. Several phone calls were then exchanged between my parents, and the BBC, in order to make arrangements for me to appear on the programme and collect the prize. As part of the show, Keith Chegwin normally did outside broadcasts around the country at different locations. Because the juke box needed to be transported over to where we lived, it was decided that they would do a broadcast from one of the parks in Blackburn. I was lucky that the date fell on one of our pre-arranged holiday weekends from school, known as long weekends. These were two weekends per term when we didn't have Saturday lessons, so we could travel home on Friday afternoon, and return on Sunday evening.

When the big day arrived, it was snowing heavily, not the best of conditions for a live T.V broadcast. My family went to the park, together with Mrs. Alexander, and children from the club. A well-known band, which had a song in the charts at the time, were performing a song in the snow, and were complaining about the cold. I can't say I blamed them. It really was freezing. When it was our turn to be interviewed, my sister and I walked on to the stage, and Keith Chegwin interviewed us, as I stood next to the juke box. I was nervous as it was a live broadcast, so no room for blunders! Everything went well, and at the end of the programme, a large van took the juke box to our house, until it could be transported to its new home.

That afternoon, Kirsten and I walked to the shop. We giggled, as a young boy walked toward us and exclaimed, "I saw you on the telly today. Can I have your autographs?" Feeling rather impressed with our new-found local celebrity status, instead of going straight home when we had been to the shop, we decided to walk around a while longer to see if anyone else noticed us. We arrived home to find that a reporter from the local newspaper was waiting for us. He interviewed us and took plenty of pictures. It certainly was a weekend to remember.

As I began my fifth year at college, I was aware of some changes which would affect our daily lives, but completely unaware of the big changes which would be put in place by the end of the academic year. Moving up to the fifth form meant that we no longer slept in dormitories in the main part of the building. Instead we were to have single or twin bedrooms, which were in a part of the school known as north wing. This was a large two-storey extension, which had been added to the building. It contained the gym, our separate common room, and a number of bedrooms both for pupils and residential staff. I shared a room with my best friend Summera, and we had a great laugh. We were allowed to stay up until ten o'clock, and once in our rooms, could talk for as long as we liked. The days of prowl were long gone, and it made for a much more relaxed atmosphere.

We had our own small kitchen equipped with a fridge, which was quite a luxury, and our own twin tub washing machine. It sounds pretty archaic now, but then it was a welcome piece of kit. Best of all, we had our own pay phone in a little phone kiosk. We were allowed to use it whenever we wanted, and I took the opportunity of regularly ringing home, and also Miss Josie. I'd always kept in touch by letter, but a telephone call was much better. I recall the first time I rang her on her birthday. I made a special trip to the local post office, to get two pounds in ten pence pieces, so I'd have enough to phone Mum, and then Miss Josie. All these little changes helped to make us feel that little bit more independent. That year was quite a crucial time for us all, as we were not only sitting our O-Level exams, but would need to choose our A-Level options.

I was still experiencing problems with certain members of my class, and spent most of my time, with Summera, and another girl who had joined our class the previous year. whose name was Kirsty. She spent loads of time in our room, and we all got on well together. As we mused over our A-level options, Summera decided that she wanted to attend a college closer to her home. She also lived in Lancashire, and over the course of the year, she tried very hard to persuade me to join her, so we could study together. It sounded a very good option; it would be great to live at home again, instead of staying on at college, but I wanted to explore other opportunities before deciding.

Summera had a fantastic sense of humour, and we laughed a lot. I returned to college after a holiday, and noticed that she had put a poster on the wall. I enquired what it was, and she told me it was a picture of Euripides. If you are familiar with the classics, then you will know that he wrote Greek tragedies. Her love of the classics never rubbed off on me, but then again, she was much more intelligent than me. When she announced "Euripides," I said in a clownish voice, "Oh yeah, I know all about him!" I then said, "Knock, knock," to which she immediately replied, "Whose there?" "Euripides" I said, and she enquired "Euripides who?" I kept a straight face as I said, "You rippa-dees trousers, you mend-a-dees trousers!" Summera fell on her bed in a heap of laughter, and obviously found it much more amusing than I did.

One evening, we awoke around midnight, to hear someone shouting outside our room. They banged on our window, and at first, as we woke, we were quite scared. It quickly became apparent that it was one of the residential care staff who had been out for the evening and forgotten her key. The door to our wing was locked, and she couldn't rouse anyone. She then shouted, "Why won't you let me in?" for some reason this tickled Summera. Maybe it was the irony of the fact that now we were in charge! We had the power to let her in or leave her literally out in the cold. I couldn't understand why no one else had gone to help, but was amused by the repeated question. Enjoying our little bit of power, I made my way very slowly down the corridor, to the back door. Summera was still laughing at the cries of "Why won't you let me in?" I'm not mentioning any names, but it was a very grateful member of staff that greeted me when I opened the door. As I returned to bed, Summera kept me awake with her laughter, and mocking chants of "Why won't you let me in?"

In the summer just before we began our fifth year, I had spent three weeks in Denmark. I really enjoyed my time there, and would love to visit again one day. I stayed with a host family who were wonderful. I had some fantastic experiences, such as visiting Lego Land, some underground caves, where concerts were held - only just watch out for the bats! I stood literally with one foot in the North Sea, and the other in the Baltic at the point where they met. You could feel one current coming from the left, and one from the right. I remember my first visit to a Danish cheese shop. The smell was so overpowering, and I held my breath till we left. Lucky it was only a short visit. I was introduced to the music of Kim Larsen, a singer who had many hits in the Danish charts. I liked his songs, even though I couldn't understand the words. Before I left, I was given one of his albums on cassette, and we still have it today.

Talking of music, someone who was on the holiday with me was a huge fan of Chris De Burgh. He played the songs round and round. I developed a liking for the music, and when I got back to this country, I looked out for a cassette. One Saturday when we returned to school, Summera and I walked across the common to the village, where there was a small record shop. I asked if they had any tapes by Chris De Burgh and was surprised to find that they had one album. It was "The Very Best of Chris De Burgh", and I immediately snapped it up. When we returned to college, I played it round and round on my huge ghetto blaster, that I had been given the previous Christmas. I was pleased and surprised to find that Summera fell in love with the music, and became a big fan too. We played that album so many times that we wore out the cassette. One of her favourites was a track called "Lonely Sky," while another was "In a Country Church Yard". That year we were reading the George Elliot novel "Silas Marner", and Summera thought that the lyrics of the song perfectly described a scene in the book.

One Sunday morning, Summera and I were rather rowdily singing along to the afore-mentioned album, when she suddenly stopped. We heard voices outside our room door, and they weren't ones we recognised. They were very well spoken adult voices, and we were intrigued to know more. Eventually we learned that a new member of staff was moving in to the room next door to ours. Her name was Jessica, and her parents had driven her to the college for the first time. I have to admit that my first reaction wasn't great. I thought "Oh no, she sounds very posh. I hope she's not going to be constantly telling us to shut up." I couldn't have been more wrong. Jessica was fantastic, even though my world and hers were far removed. She had just completed her studies at Oxford University, and was unsure about the type of career she wanted to pursue. She had decided to take some time out, and work as a community service volunteer at the college for a year. Jessica and I soon became firm friends. She introduced me to Brahms, and I introduced her to Chris De Burgh, and Phil Collins. She showed me how to make a rug, and I taught her how to knit. One thing that we did share which neither of us needed any tuition in, was our mutual love of chocolate and cake. Usually on a Sunday afternoon, Summera and I would go to her room and enjoy tea, or coffee and loads of cakes. We all had a similar sense of humour, and I think that's what drew us together. We were all from very different backgrounds, but got on so well, and learned a great deal from each other. I still keep in touch with Jessica, and talk on the phone frequently. I was gutted to hear around four years ago that Summera had died. She was an amazingly intelligent person, yet unassuming and very gentle. I always remember her with a smile, and feel very privileged to have been her friend.

12. All Change!

I was still unaware at that time that a radical change was in store. While chatting one day with Summera and Kirsty, Kirsty told me that she wanted to study A-Level physics, an option that wasn't available at Chorleywood. She had asked staff if there were any opportunities to attend a local college, but this option didn't seem to be viable. Kirsty had then come up with a novel but pretty ingenious idea. She posed the question as to whether she could transfer to the boys college for the blind in Worcester, where they did offer physics as an A-Level. I told her to go for it, and admired her out of the box approach. Amazingly, it seemed that the head mistress was open to exploring this option. As discussions took place between various members of staff from both colleges, Kirsty dared to mention to me that it would be great if I went with her to do my A-Levels. I was quietly quite excited about the idea, I'd never really enjoyed my time at Chorleywood, and relished the prospect of a viable escape route.

There were also other options to consider, apart from the obvious choice of simply staying on at the same college, but for me, that was the last option. Some of my class members were discussing the prospect of moving to another college for the blind in a different part of the country. I never discussed my thoughts with any teachers, so I was very surprised during my next phone call with my parents. Aparrently, the details of my most recent conversation had been overheard by a teacher, who had passed this on to more senior staff. My Mother had received a call from both Miss Woods, and the deputy head, strongly urging her to dissuade me from transferring to that particular place of study, and to stay on at the college to continue my education. I found the whole scenario quite amusing, as I had never considered that particular college to be my first choice, but was instead drawn to the idea of moving to Worcester.

Kirsty and I continued our deliberations over the subject, until one day I announced that I had decided that I did want to join her in Worcester. Following lengthy discussions with Miss Woods, and other staff including the Head Master of Worcester College, it was decided that Kirsty and I should visit the College for a day, to look around, and meet the teachers of our chosen A-Level subjects. By this time, some of our class members had learned of our intentions, which up to then we had kept to ourselves, and were not amused. They made known their opinions that they considered us to be disloyal, and the word "traitors" was one we heard on numerous occasions. We however were undeterred and looked forward with anticipation to our first visit. Anyway, if things didn't work out, it would be a welcome day away from School.

The prospect of amalgamating the boys' and girls' grammar schools was not a new concept. In fact, it was a matter which had been discussed for many years, but as pupils, we hadn't heard much about. A couple of years earlier, we were in a lesson, when the subject arose about combining the two colleges, although I have no recollection how we arrived upon the subject. After learning that it had been discussed as a possible option, but no action had ever been taken, we talked about the idea together in our class. After we came up with some suggestions and opinions on the matter, the teacher chairing the debate announced that we should share our views with Miss Woods, and immediately led us down to her office. Although we arrived unannounced, Miss Woods was extremely accommodating. She sat us all down and listened to our ideas. We then sat quietly as she removed a huge folder from a filing cabinet and asked one of our partially sighted peers to read out the title on the aforementioned folder. There was a pause, and then a nervous class member read out the word "merger". That colossal folder contained copious notes and information gathered during lengthy dialogue over the matter. We left feeling rather deflated, as Miss Woods related that the discussions would probably continue for years before any real activity would take place on the matter.

It's strange to think that less than three years after that day, Kirsty and I would be travelling to Worcester with the strong possibility that we would be the only girls in the School. I'm very thankful to Mum and Dad who were extremely supportive. They both took time off work and drove down from Lancashire to Chorleywood and stayed overnight, before driving us both to Worcester the following day. When we arrived, we were given lunch, and then Kirsty and I were shown around the College by two of the sixth form boys, while the Headmaster, Mr. Kingsley spoke with our parents.

We sat and chatted with the boys for around half an hour until it was time for afternoon lessons to begin. We were then taken separately to be introduced to our prospective teachers, and learn about the syllabus. I remember thinking that two of my teachers seemed quite eccentric, but I liked them and this made me more enthusiastic about the move. The atmosphere was friendly, and seemed much more relaxed than Chorleywood. We both left feeling buoyant and excited about the prospect of becoming honorary Worcester boys!

Following our return to College, life resumed its normal pattern. Our O-Level exams were imminent, and continued to be the focus of our attention. On a weekend during the spring, Mr. Kingsley made a trip to Chorleywood to speak with Kirsty and I. I vividly recall a quiet Saturday evening when I was instructed to meet Mr. Kingsley in the assembly hall. I opened the heavy door, to find him sitting at one end of a long table. He invited me to take a seat at the other end, and enthusiastically informed me that he had spoken with my parents. It had been agreed that I could make the move to Worcester College in the autumn, and he officially wished to congratulate me as the first girl to join Worcester College. I experienced a sudden rush of elation. It was real--I would be leaving Chorleywood and going to Worcester. He shook my hand, congratulated me again, adding that this was a momentous occasion, and that in the future, he would be presenting me with a certificate, officially welcoming me as the first girl to join Worcester College. As I smiled and thanked him, the only thought that bothered me, was that this had originally been Kirsty's idea, and she should have been the first girl to be welcomed. The incident had only occurred because my parents had been available to confirm the details over the telephone, while Kirsty's had not. Nevertheless, I left the room feeling totally elated. A new start in a new place was an exciting prospect.

In celebration of this momentous occasion, I decided to go and play my flute in one of the four practice rooms. For those of you who remember Chorleywood, I stood in practice room 1 and played my flute as I revelled in the prospect of leaving. That night, I went to bed happy, the only person who wasn't was Summera--she had been hoping that I would join her up in Lancashire.

Mr. Kingsley made several visits to Chorleywood in the weeks that followed. Other girls in our class had started to express their interest in also making the move to Worcester. I distinctly recall one meeting where other members of the class who had not committed to the move but wished to ask questions, were interested to enquire about facilities at their prospective new place of study. One girl asked if they could have a kitchen facility so they could cook their own meals. Mr. Kingsley announced in a loud bold voice, "You can have a kitchen each if that is what will make you happy chum!" I clearly recall one Sunday afternoon that closely followed when there was a knock on my room door, and several girls danced across the floor announcing, "We're coming to Worcester!"

By this time, everyone had decided what they would be doing following their O-Levels. The majority would be transferring to Worcester, while others chose different colleges. Only one student decided to stay on at Chorleywood to continue with her A-Levels. In fact, it was decided that all the girls due to begin their GCSE courses the following year would automatically transfer to Worcester, and the rest of the school would stay at Chorleywood for one more year before joining everyone else. What had Kirsty started? Once everything was decided, the only thing that then mattered was achieving our O-Level grades in order to proceed with our A-Level options.

Summera was a good influence on me, when it came to studying and revising, she was a serious grafter. In school holidays, if exams of any kind were imminent, she would set herself a schedule which would run from when she got up, till she went to bed. The arduous task consisted of two hours study, followed by a one hour break. I was so impressed with her dogged determination to achieve the highest possible grades, that I tried out this method (during one day), but family time at home was precious when you spent most of your time away at school, and anyway there were far too many tempting distractions, that I admit, I failed miserably in my efforts. I did discover later though, that her Father had made a promise to avail her with ten pounds for every A grade she achieved. Not bad--if I'd been made the same offer by my Dad I would have at least considered giving that grueling study-plan one more attempt.

Mr. Kingsley continued to make regular visits to Chorleywood in order to finalise arrangements, and It was decided that we should all make a visit to Worcester, as the rest of the girls had not yet been shown around the college. One Saturday morning in the spring of that year, we boarded a minibus and made the trip. On arrival, we were taken to the coffee bar. The room was well lit with a bar at one end and several alcove soft-seated areas with low coffee tables. It was far more up-to-date in terms of decor than we had been used too, and we were already suitably impressed. We were offered a drink, and then the staff left us to chat. The girls sat around the tables at one end of the room, and the boys from our year sat at the other. There then followed a long period of silence, as we all sat awkwardly wondering what to say. Eventually, we did all manage to introduce ourselves, before the staff returned to give their presentations. Once again as we were shown around, I noted that the atmosphere was indeed much more relaxed, and I have to admit, it did give me motivation in achieving those grades required to pursue my A-Levels.

Facilities at the College were very good. The first plus point was that we would be moving to a City. Woo-hoo! Thank goodness for that – stuff going on! Some pupils had enjoyed the grandeur of living in a converted Mansion house surrounded by large grounds, but it never really suited me, I found it rather isolating, not to mention boring. In our new school, we had an indoor swimming pool instead of outdoor, and as well as a gym, which we had been used to we also had a multi-gym. Cool! Unlike us at Chorleywood, the boys were allowed to make several journeys into the town centre per week and, the sixth form regularly visited the local pub. Enough said--I'm in!!! In noting another extremely important plus point, I firstly need to make a terrible confession--I LOVE MY BED! It's not just a place to sleep; it is a sanctuary, a place to ponder and dream and simply be downright unashamedly lazy. So when I discovered that we would be treated to the extravagance of modern pine beds with, you'll never believe it, a duvet, I thought it was a dream. I'm getting so excited now, I can hardly contain myself: to put the icing on the cake, we had fitted sheets. Bring on the 20th century. So-long to scratchy old blankets! Too-da-loo to tatty threadbare counterpanes. They say it's the little things that matter, and yes, they certainly did. Things were looking so good I started to wonder if there would be room-service? Hmm, maybe not.

After an eventful day we made the journey back to Hertfordshire, chatting about the people we had met and the facilities we had seen. The main focus now though was getting stuck into copious amounts of revision. We had a room known as The Quiet Room where Summera and I spent hours studying. This room was medium sized with a carpet and, for some reason, was always very warm. It had a large table in the centre, and along one side of the room was a long desk containing several tape recorders with headphones. We were only allowed to speak in there when necessary, and if so in a whisper. It was simply somewhere to relax and have a good read. Under the window there was a large old radiator, which had been adorned with a long soft cushion. Summera and I often carried heavy piles of Braille notes, and sat on the radiator to revise for our exams. I know you won't believe it, in fact I surprised myself, but I actually managed to get myself into a good routine. So much so, in fact, that I decided to stay at school for the long weekend immediately before my exams so that I could study. I explained my intentions to Mum and Dad on the phone and they seemed fine about it. However, it appeared later that Mum was not convinced. I distinctly recall having a bath one evening, when someone knocked on the bathroom door. I heard a voice instructing me that as soon as I'd finished, I was to go and see Miss Woods in her office. To be summoned to the head's office was always a big deal, but for it to happen reasonably late in the evening meant I was either in BIG trouble, or possibly some urgent bad news from home. I didn't want it to be either, so with much trepidation, I made my way downstairs. I arrived to learn that my Mum had called Miss Woods enquiring as to the real reason why I didn't want to go home at the weekend. I have to admit that I was completely exasperated. I thought that something terrible had happened. I explained very calmly to Miss Woods that I simply wanted to spend as much time as possible revising, and Summera was unable to travel home for the weekend so we would study together. The information was relayed back to my parents, and I left feeling very relieved.

At the end of one particularly long period of revision, we returned to our room to play some music and relax. This was brought to a sudden end when we had an unwelcome visitor. The day was warm and our room window was open. Unfortunately a bird flew in and Summera was hysterical. She screamed and ran across the room to the door as the bird flapped around. Although the window was large and open wide, the bird seemed to like our room more than the outdoors and didn't make any attempt to fly away despite the earsplitting screams of my room-mate. I tried to calm my friend down as I led her out of the room to find a member of staff brave enough to deal with the situation. The bird was eventually evicted and we returned finally, to relax. It was very hot in there for the rest of the day, as a certain person wouldn't let me open the window! Summera and I did get on very well. At weekends we used to take it in turns to make each other breakfast in bed which was usually Dairy Lee on toast. However, if she had the choice, Summera would have eaten salt and vinegar crisps and cola for every meal. I use to joke about buying her a box of 48 bags of crisps and 48 cans of cola for her birthday.

Before we knew it, we were standing outside the gym which had been converted into the exam hall for our first exam. I remember feeling very nervous. This was to be magnified several times over when I learned that my candidate number was 000006070013.

Thirteen at the end of my number? Oops! I decided to take the view that it would be lucky for me, and ploughed on regardless. So much for positive thinking guys, the next day I woke up with a stinking cold. For the next week, I made regular visits to the surgery to dose up on paracetamol, and my skirt pocket bulged with tissues. I didn't feel great, but this was no time to feel sorry for myself I simply had to get on with it. It's strange to think that we managed to do our exams and concentrate with all the noise going on around us. We were all bashing away on our Braillers. Imagine that you are taking an exam on an old typewriter, with fourteen other people doing the same. What a racket! I'm not sure if I could do it now but then it was something we had grown up with, got used to, and got on with.

Because it takes a blind person longer to read a Braille exam paper than a sighted person to read the printed version, exam boards allotted some extra time to compensate. This meant that my most gruelling day involved seven and a half hours of exam time. One of the tests on that particular day was geography. This was classed as an O-A Level, (apparently somewhere between the two.) I had done very badly in the mock exam only achieving a D grade and was particularly disappointed. When I had finished the paper, I checked through very carefully several times for any mistakes. If we finished early and were happy, then we were allowed to leave early. I however decided to stay to the bitter end. I was the very last one to leave, but I had promised myself that I would stay. If my mark was bad then I had done all I could, but if I was to leave early and do badly in the results, then I would not have been able to forgive myself. So I gritted my teeth and stayed painstakingly sifting through to see if there was anything meaningful I could add, and correcting as many mistakes as I could find. I am pleased to say that my diligence and probably stubbornness paid off as I managed to achieve a B grade.

The exam I was the most confident about was R.E., I always enjoyed the subject and received good grades. A few days following our mock exam, a teacher overheard me telling another student that I had finished the test forty-five minutes early. She gave me an immediate dusting down about working through methodically and not rushing. The member of staff I am talking about was not my specific R.E. teacher, but a different member of staff. Earlier that year, when covering for another member of staff, she had presented the whole class with an inopportune R.E. test. At one point, we were given a question to which I knew I should know the answer but, unfortunately for me, I simply had a mental block and sat there clueless while everyone else wrote furiously. Ever had those times where your mind goes blank and you feel such a plonker? Well my humiliation was to be completed, as she stopped proceedings to shout furiously at me, "Jane, if you don't know the answer to this question I don't know how you will ever pass your O-Level. My blood boiled, and my frustration surged. Although I was in a Religious Education lesson, I have to admit that my thoughts toward her at that moment were far from…Christian. I said nothing, and weathered the storm, all the time promising myself that I would get an A grade in my O-Level and send her a copy of my results.

After my second dusting down, I waited anxiously for my mock result. There were only four students who had chosen to take the R.E O-Level, and, as we entered the room, I walked to my desk and sat down in a state of apprehension as she greeted us. Miss Wells was a softly spoken lady from Yorkshire. She had a very calm and peaceful demeanour and was always very kind and encouraging. She proceeded to read out our results and when it was my turn I held my breath. Much to my surprise and relief, I was told that I had achieved 74 per cent. I allowed myself a brief smile as Miss Wells congratulated me, but warned me not to be complacent. To get an A grade in the exam I would need to get a slightly higher mark. This didn't bother me too much. I was looking forward to meeting a certain member of staff to give her the good news. When I did meet the person in question I sat quietly as she spoke with fellow students. As she approached me, I sat surrounded by an almost tangible aura of silent smugness. When she finally turned to me she said, "I hear you did well in your mock exam." It would have been nice to have been given the slightest sniff of an apology after humiliating me in front of my friends, but that I suppose was too much to ask for. It didn't matter anyway, I had got exactly what I wanted.

When I did actually sit the exam, there were a couple of questions I wasn't entirely happy with, and so left the exam feeling rather deflated. I was sure that I hadn't managed my target of achieving an A. We tackled the last couple of exams, and then fell in to a heap, never wanting to see all those notes again. There was nothing to do but wait for the results and hope for the best. It seemed strange to think that it was suddenly all over, the pressure was lifted and now we could relax. Sometimes it's hard to jump off that train of academia that you have travelled on for so long. Before and during the exams you spend all your time wishing they were over, but when suddenly they are, you just don't know what to do with yourself. Now I could start making plans for the summer. So for the last time, my trunk was hauled from the trunk lift and carried to my room to begin packing. From wellies to Walkman, and typewriter to toothbrush, everything had to be squeezed and squashed in there ready for the journey home to Lancashire and a very well deserved summer holiday. On a dull and wet Sunday morning at the beginning of July, I said my good-byes, and we loaded the car. As we drove slowly down the long driveway, I felt good. My Chorleywood days were over; some had been good and I had met some nice people, but on the whole it hadn't been the greatest of experiences. I was grateful for the high standard of education I had received, but it had come at a price. I waved my last "See yah" to the ponies across the field, and began the long journey home.

13. Chillin' Out in Summer

A few days after arriving home I made a phone call to St. Vincent's to see if I could get permission to spend some time there chilling out with my old friends. I was elated when Sister Josephine said I could stay for a couple of nights and began packing. Miss Josie was now in charge of the senior girls and it felt just like old times. I even attended some of the lessons. It was like being back where I belonged. In the evenings we hung out in the youth club, or watched TV but I loved it. It was strange, because in some ways it felt like I had never been away, everyone was so welcoming and friendly. During my first evening, I distinctly recall sitting outside the youth club, with the girl I had sat in the classroom with on my very first day there. We chatted and laughed, and I experienced a feeling of warmth and a sense of belonging I had not felt since leaving the place. On the second day, we went strawberry picking. I made the mistake of wearing a white Lacoste T-shirt. Half way through my endeavours someone shouted my name and I instinctively turned around only to find I was being pelted with fruit. Unfortunately I never managed to remove the stains from my shirt, but I didn't care - it was brilliant. In the evening the senior girls had a small group Mass. I was asked to take part with everyone else, either saying prayers, or singing a solo. The service was beautiful. I felt very moved that I had been welcomed so warmly and was almost moved to tears. Everyone was so sincere, I felt a warmth and acceptance I had never felt at Chorleywood and wished I'd never left Liverpool.

It was great to spend time with Josie again. We had always kept in close contact, but to actually meet together and chat was great. When you share the same sense of humour with someone it's easy to get on and just laugh the time away without really making any effort. She would tell me what everyone had been getting up to, and I would regale her with a wealth of stories about the embarrassing situations I had managed to get myself into. The worst part of that time was leaving again. My parents came to collect me, and I was glad to see them, but I did spend the whole car journey home wishing I could have stayed longer.

In late July, Kirsten and I joined a group of blind children and Mrs. Alexander for a week's holiday in Eastbourne. Some sighted kids came along to help as guides for those who had no sight at all. During the day we engaged in activities such as horse riding, sailing, and a wealth of other pursuits. In the evenings the younger ones enjoyed a disco while a few of us who were older went out with the young adults who had come as volunteer guides. We had a brilliant time. I experienced a rather embarrassing situation one night. My friend who was sitting next to me told me that a guy who was sitting across the room was trying to get my attention and simply couldn't understand why he couldn't catch my eye. I thought this was very amusing.

During one excursion, we visited a gift shop. As Kirsten browsed the items on display, she read out the caption on a fridge magnet. It read, "Love thy neighbour, but don't get caught!" At the time it tickled me so much that I let out a sudden roar of laughter that caused everyone in the shop to turn to see what was happening and Kirsten was so embarrassed that she nearly walked away and left me. However, to get her revenge, she noticed a bottle of smelling salts, and without telling me what it was, asked me to, "Smell this!" That was my first--and last experience of the aforementioned product. I know they are designed to revive, but they nearly killed me!! It's a wonder my head is still intact. Revenge wasn't sweet – it was incomprehensibly brutal, thanks Kirsten.

That holiday was closely followed by a two week excursion with Mum and Dad. We spent the first week in Bournemouth, staying with relatives. The weather was hot and we spent our time either on the beach, looking around the town, or sitting in the garden. We had a picnic in the New Forest, and went swimming. In contrast with this enjoyable week in the sun, the second week was spent in Devon. My parents must have been caught up in a temporary moment of madness, because they decided that we should go camping. Camping! Now there's a word that fills me with dread. I just don't get it...I really don't! Seemingly perfectly sane people make the choice to leave the comfort of their homes, and actually pay money to be allotted a piece of grass, sleep there in a tent and have the audacity to call it a HOLIDAY? Am I missing something here? You sleep on the ground and then wake up in the middle of the night, turn over, and find that water has seeped in because it has been raining solidly for the last five days. A holiday! When the sun finally does come out and you try and cook a meal you are plagued by pesky wasps. A holiday? You then feel so full of the joys of your experience that you cannot wait to fill your bucket with dirty plates, walk half a mile to queue for a place at a sink where you wash and dry your crockery. A holiday? Not to mention the excitement of waking in the night and fighting with your bladder for the next ten minutes before dragging yourself from your sleeping bag in a disgruntled stupor and trudging across a boggy field with your torch to go to the toilet. Oh what joy! As a good friend of mine once said, "If it doesn't have en suite, it isn't a holiday." Now there's a man of good sense and wisdom.

So if you are the sort of person who is irritated by people who are constantly happy, all you need to do is pay for them to go on a camping holiday, it's bound to make them miserable,. Seriously though, the one and only week I spent camping was certainly one to remember, even though it was for the wrong reasons. . It did indeed rain relentlessly for the whole week apart from one afternoon. I had been told that the tent was brilliant. It had a room where we all would sleep, and a separate area where we could put a small camping table and chairs. Best of all we could actually stand up in the tent! Wow! a palatial paradise in green pastures. I'm starting to like the sound of this…NOT!! I recall one late afternoon we all sat huddled around the camping table wondering what to do as the rain thudded on the tent. This was in the day before mobile communication, or games consoles. Mobile phones were larger, and much heavier than house bricks, and only for high flying executives. We didn't have a portable TV, so it was really down to the basics. The only outdoor activity on offer due to weather conditions was mud wrestling, but Mum wasn't really up for that. So someone suggested that we play cards, but when we finally located them it seemed that they had also succumbed to the rain. I heard the words "Oh no, they are wet." "Wet? Now how in the world did that happen? Ah poor Mum and Dad, when it was suggested that we just have an early night, with four of us in one room, it probably wasn't what they had in mind.

To make matters worse, Kirsten became ill during the evening of our last day. I did feel sorry for her, but struggled not to be sick myself as that awful stench filled the tent. Her symptoms got worse and she simply didn't know which way to turn (so to speak,). I buried myself at the bottom of my sleeping bag, and vowed I would never do this again. If we hadn't borrowed the tent, I would have burned it at the earliest opportunity. When I finally did get to sleep, I awoke to the sound of Kirsten throwing up all over the tent floor. The smell! Oh, the smell!

At that time, it was fashionable for teenagers to wear luminous socks, in bright pink, green and orange. The rules of fashion stipulated that one could never wear a matching pair, but must wear odd socks in different colours. The staff at School automatically assumed that it was our lack of sight which determined this factor, and so were often heard telling individuals that they were wearing odd socks and needed to change them. While we were packing to go home that day, Kirsten commented that she had lost one of her bright orange socks, Mum and I didn't have a clue where it was, but Dad did--He said that it was in a plastic bag because as bright as it was, it had been camouflaged within Kirsten's last offering on the tent floor. Kirsten blamed her illness on the clotted cream fudge she had consumed the previous evening. I however blamed Mr Tent--or at least the idiot who had invented this whole mad caper. I wanted to hang him on a guy rope, and cook him on the camp fire. Needless to say, when we did get home the tent needed to be put up in the garden and aired sufficiently before returning it to our friends. I don't think they would have been friends for much longer if we hadn't done that. The long car journey home was horrendous and my sister sat at one side of the back seat, and I at the other with a gulf in between us for the whole five hours. I was dreading her being sick in the car. Every time she moved, or opened her mouth, I cowered in my corner, dreading what would happen next. Car sick, car sick--I was completely sick of the whole darn business. As we drove up the driveway, all I could think about was a nice warm bed and the feel of carpet beneath my feet, with the bathroom across the landing, instead of across a muddy field. Ah, joy!

Summer holidays at home as a teenager always reminds me of the hours Dad and I used to spend riding on a tandem. It actually belonged to our local Society for the Blind, but we kept it in our garage, ready for anyone who wanted to use it. Kirsten often joined us on her bike, as we would ride around the streets of Blackburn. As we did so, we would often hear gasps of surprise from small children as we whizzed by. "Look at that funny bike!", and "that's a bike that they used to ride in the olden days!" My favourite part of these jaunts, was flying down St. James Road. For those who don't know, this is a very long steep stretch, and as you can guess, we never rode up it, just hurtled down. It was a great feeling of freedom and excitement. Conversely, I always remember the long drag, every time we ascended Preston New Road – now that did take some stamina!

We rode that tandem on many crazy pursuits. I don't know who came up with the idea, but one summer, we did a sponsored cycle from Blackburn to Blackpool. It was grey and wet on that Sunday morning, as we left our drive at eight o'clock in the morning. Dad and I cycled the first thirteen miles, and then another visually impaired lady and her sighted guide took over to complete the journey into Blackpool. I remember the rain lashing down, as we began the long drag up Preston New Road, but it was great fun, and raised a substantial amount of money for our local society for the blind. On a separate occasion, our family was invited to a garden party. The theme for the party was France, and Dad came up with an idea. On the previous day, he returned home and presented me with the largest box of onions I had ever seen, and a ball of string. He instructed me to tie the onions together and then tie them to the tandem. Ok!... On the day of the party, we dressed in themed attire, and rode the tandem complete with several pounds of onions and arrived to roars of laughter. My Dad still has the photographs, but there's no way they will appear in this book.

I do remember the party being very enjoyable, apart from one embarrassing moment. In the evening we had a raffle, and I was asked to fold all the purchased tickets, and place them in a large box. When it was time for the draw, I was asked to pick the first ticket. To my horror, I won first prize. Oh no! I tried to protest and draw another ticket but none would allow me to do so. The prize was a large bottle of whiskey, and the following week when I asked Dad if I could try a glass, he flatly refused. I was quite miffed. After all, it was my prize. He wouldn't budge though, and I never got to taste it. Dad doesn't like whiskey, so I'm not sure what happened to that large bottle.

I had spent some time pondering over what I might do as a career after leaving College. I came up with the notion that it might be a good idea to see if I could become a radio operator in the control room in a police station. I figured that the job may be quite interesting, as at the beginning of each day, there would be no way of telling what type of situations you may be dealing with. After sharing this with my parents, Mum took it upon herself to arrange a days work experience at our local police station. So one bright sunny day in August, we met up with a police sergeant, who gave us a guided tour of the station, and explained about the sort of tasks carried out by various different people. I spent the whole afternoon sitting in the control room. I was fascinated. There were different telephones with different ring tones which depicted specific departments, and it was quite noisy: certainly a hive of activity. I was shown how to operate the switchboard, and actually answered some calls and put the callers through to the correct extensions. Then it was time for me to sit with the radio operators. The only snag with that part of the job was the requirement to note down all the details of radio conversations on pre-printed forms. Today, this wouldn't pose a problem as everything would I guess be entered into a computer, but at the time I was disappointed that I was unable to carry out the task independently. One of the staff was very understanding, and assured me that if one day I still was interested in doing the job, then they were sure there would be a way to make things work.

At the end of the day, Mum and I went to have coffee with a senior officer, to see what I had made of my work experience. I thanked him for allowing me to stay for the day and informed him that it would be indeed a job I would like to explore. He informed me that they had enjoyed my company and I should keep the job in mind for when I left college, and that if during future school holidays I wanted to spend more time at the station, I would be very welcome. He then paused, obviously considering something. He then slowly asked with an air of caution in his voice. "There's only one thing that worries me Jane. If you're going to do this job it will mean you would have to work night shifts on a regular basis, and how would you get around at night when it is dark?" Dutifully, I stifled a giggle, smiled sweetly and replied, "I'm sure I'll be fine." What I really wanted to say was, "No problem Sir, I'll wear my night vision goggles…"

14. Worcester Sauce

Amidst all this activity, my mind momentarily mused over the day which drew near—results day! I clearly remember waking up on that important day, and waiting, and waiting, and waiting, for the post to arrive. When finally, I heard the distinctive sound of the letterbox, Kirsten gave me the letter and we ran to our bedroom. I opened the letter, and then held my breath as Kirsten started to read out my results. Amazingly, I had achieved one C grade, with the rest being all A or B grades. I was so happy, and couldn't take in the news. I had done so much better than I had expected. Everyone was very pleased and proud of me, and once again, I received cards and gifts for my efforts.

I was due to begin my studies at Worcester College in early September 1986. However, we received a couple of phone calls postponing the date as facilities for the girls weren't ready. These delays never bothered me in the least. As far as I was concerned, they could take as much time as they liked. However, each time my Mum became quite exasperated, and I recall one Sunday evening when we heard the phone ring around eight o'clock and learned that it was the headmaster informing us that term would not commence until the second week in the month.

Eventually the day arrived when we travelled down to Worcester early one Monday morning. Before arriving at college, we decided to take a trip around the city centre. Mum wanted to show me where the shops were and give me an idea of my surroundings. Finally, we arrived and went straight to the corridor where our study bedrooms were located. As I was the second person to arrive, I had a choice as to which room I wanted. I chose room number four. It wasn't the largest room available, but it was next door to a good friend of mine, and also had the added bonus of having a balcony. Now before you get all excited about there being a balcony, there was one small drawback. It had to be shared with the occupants of the double room next door and, also, whereas they had access via a patio door, I had to climb through my window to get out there. This didn't bother me though; I would just have to take care when trying to manoeuvre a chair out there during the summer months.

Along the same corridor, there were also a couple of bathrooms with toilets, and a tiny kitchen. This was not quite the salubrious kitchen we had been promised, but tiny and poky, equipped with a washing machine, fridge, toaster and kettle. Along one wall, someone had put up a shelf which contained loads of crockery. I will never forget one evening as I walked along the corridor and suddenly heard a huge crash. The shelf had given way, and all the plates, cups etc fell in a broken heap. The shelf obviously wasn't strong enough for all that weight, and we all had to spend the next half hour armed with large bin bags collecting the broken pieces.

Directly opposite my study was the College laundry. As we carried all my things into my room, a couple of the staff from the laundry began to chat with me. They were all really friendly, and I remember thinking that the Worcester accent was really comical. To me it sounded similar to the type of accent I expected to hear in Devon. I found it rather amusing to learn that if someone from Worcester was greeting several of us in a group, instead of using our individual names, they simply shouted, "Mornings!" Well, I suppose it's pretty logical, and it saves time--why not? Once I was settled and fully unpacked, Mum and Dad decided to leave me to it. This time it was a completely different story. Mum especially didn't seem too upset to be leaving me, and I was quite happy, even though I was in a completely different place, and didn't know my way around the building. No, this place seemed completely relaxed. I felt quite happy and was looking forward to my new life in Worcester. Not to mention meeting the boys. Oh it felt good to be in a mixed environment. I felt like this was going to be a new start: a place where I could breathe, a place where I could be allowed to just be myself without the fear of being shouted at, or shouted down, or pushed aside. I was ready for a new start, and new friends, and that's exactly what I was to get.

On that first day there were no lessons. We were left to get used to our new surroundings and settle in. When my parents had gone, I went to the room next door to see my friend Leah. Leah also came from the North-West of the country, and so often during School holidays, she would come and stay with me at my parents' house. During the hols, we would spend time playing Scrabble, reading loads of books, listening to music, or chilling out in the garden during the summer. We would often have a barbecue and Mum and Dad invited loads of friends, and they were always great times. One particular memorable occasion was when they took Leah and me to see the musical "Carousel". I'm not greatly familiar with that particular musical, but I do remember that Leah was particularly taken with a song which I think was simply called "June". It contained the lyric "June is busting out all over..." and Leah spent the rest of the evening singing that song

117

in a rather loud and jubilant voice. My parents found it hilarious at the time, and still talk about it now many years later.

So Leah and I spent most of that day together, in eager anticipation of what the new term would bring for us. I don't recall many details about that particular afternoon, but I do recall the evening. After our evening meal, we all gathered in one of the rooms to be given an introductory talk from the deputy head. As she was finishing her chat with us, there was a sudden loud knock on the door. A sixth form boy burst in, and asked rather confidently "Does anyone fancy coming down to the pub?" This was a very strange experience for all of us, as we had been used to living in a very closed environment, with very little opportunity to venture outside the college. Even if we had stayed at Chorleywood, the prospect of going to the pub would never have been considered. It would have been positively frowned upon. I had been told, although I cannot confirm that it was true, that for those sixth form girls over the age of eighteen, the following would happen. Each girl had to sign a form agreeing that they would not visit a pub within a three mile radius of the college. Indeed, in my five years at Chorleywood, I never heard of anyone going out for a drink. Needless to say, that this unsuspecting guy's invitation was met with a period of stunned silence. As the boys were allowed to go out, there was no legitimate reason to stop us, and so the meeting was abruptly adjourned, and we all walked down to the college local.

I was surprised to learn that the guy who had been bold enough to extend this invitation then asked if I was among the crowd, and when I rather sheepishly made myself known, he took my arm and introduced himself. Wayne had known me when we were both in the same class at St. Vincent's and had heard that I was to be attending the College. It felt great as we walked together down the road leading the way to the pub, getting to know each other once again. I felt a sense of freedom, and independence, I knew from that moment, I was going to enjoy my new life in Worcester. I also knew that it would take a while for some of the girls to let go of the life they had been used to at our previous school, and shake off all the constraints that they had become accustomed too.

A couple of other boys joined the group, and so I guess there was a crowd of around twelve of us. As we approached the bar, Wayne asked us all what we wanted to drink. All the girls in turn chose orange juice or lemonade. When Wayne asked me, I announced quite casually that I would have a half of lager. There were immediate gasps and tuts of disapproval from my class members. Most of them didn't like me much, and now I'd just given them something else to berate me about, but I simply didn't care. My Chorleywood days were gone, and I was determined to break free from all the grief they'd dished out to me over the years. It was time for me to be my own person. It was time for me to start enjoying myself, and I was determined to do so.

We all sat around two small tables and began making conversation for a matter of minutes until Wayne suddenly asked all of us. "Which one of you girls is in room four?" There was a silence and I started to feel slightly uncomfortable. I was in room four, but why did he want to know that? Anyway, I certainly wasn't going to tell him. To my annoyance, someone shouted, "Jane is in room four, why do you want to know?" Wayne then replied. "This afternoon, I asked the ladies in the laundry if there were any nice girls worth getting to know, and they had told me that there was a really nice one in room four!" There was then another pause while I sat there with an extremely red face, not knowing what to say. Eventually the conversation resumed, and that was the end of the subject, well, for me anyway. I got over my severe embarrassment, and enjoyed the rest of the evening. When it was time to leave, Wayne insisted on walking me back to College. Some of the girls had already left early. I think this was their protest after I had ordered my second half of lager. We strolled home, laughing about our evening, and about some of the things we had done at St. Vincent's. When we reached the front door, he suddenly turned to me, and before I knew it had kissed me goodnight. I was quite taken aback, but casually said "Thanks for this evening, see you tomorrow" before quickly scampering back to my room. The boys weren't allowed in our rooms after eleven o'clock, and it was nearly that time, I was glad; I just wanted some time to myself. As I got into bed that evening, I felt a combination of bemusement, excitement, and contentment. My first day had been quite a day to remember. What would the next day bring?

Mornings were a much more laid back affair than our previous routine. We could go down with the rest of the school in the large dining room for breakfast if we wished, or we could choose to make our own food in the kitchen along the corridor. I've never been much of a breakfast person, so usually took advantage of having a few more extra minutes in bed. I often took great pleasure in stretching over to my desk, switching on the kettle, and then enjoying a cup of coffee in bed before getting washed and changed ready for the day ahead. No

119

more gongs; no more late books – just coffee in bed and my own choice of music. Sixth form students were not required to wear uniform, but could choose their own clothes instead, something else which I thought was a welcome change. As I left my room that morning, Leah was just leaving too, and so we walked downstairs together, and over to library C, where we were to have our very first lesson which was to be English literature.

We took our seats along with the other students, and waited for the teacher to arrive. Instead of sitting at individual desks as we had been used to, here we all just sat casually around one large table. The room was filled with banter as we all got to know each other. It was strange to have boys in the class. Suddenly I heard the sound of rapid footsteps as they distinctively tapped down the corridor. The door burst open and a woman dashed in as if just coming to the end of a race. As she quickly motored across the room, she said "Good morning," in a rather preoccupied manner, she proceeded to regale us with the details of the fact that she was already having a bad day, and it was only just nine o'clock. I assumed that this was a humorous attempt on her part to help us relax and get to know her, but I couldn't have been further from the truth. As I sat there listening to her, with an amused smile on my face, suddenly she saw me and immediately stood in front of me, almost nose to nose, and exclaimed in a most disgruntled voice, "Don't you mock the afflicted Miss Readfern!" Ah, not a good start. For the rest of the lesson I sat stony faced, scared that I would inadvertently offend her again. I was going to have to be careful in Mrs. Chester's presence. I did, however, manage to get through the rest of the time without any further problems.

Those of us taking English Literature A-level would be taught by three different teachers. My first impressions of Mrs. Patterson, was that she was going to be very strict. I can't quite remember what gave me that impression at the time, but once again I was wrong. She was a very warm approachable lady. She even admitted to us that on occasions she had been given rather crumpled assignments from certain students, but instead of refusing them and demanding a well-presented copy, she had taken them home and carefully ironed them under a tea towel, before marking them and returning them to the students. How gracious of her. During one lesson, she referred to a particular character from one of Shakespeare's plays as a "quivering mass of alcoholism", which made us all laugh. The other teacher was a gentleman whom I found to be quite eccentric. A few years previously, he was involved in a horrific accident. He had been riding his motor bike, and somehow managed to collide with, and end up under a steam roller. Consequently, he had lost both an arm and a leg. Mr. Mills would spend a good deal of time during lessons talking about his accident, and I am almost ashamed to relate that on one occasion, I laughed uncontrollably when a fellow student one day exclaimed in his best Mr. Mills voice, "That accident cost me an arm and a leg!" I admired the man, though, for his dogged determination, and confidence. His recovery and rehabilitation was lengthy, but he returned to being involved in sporting activities in which he had participated in before his accident. During one lesson, he asked me for my opinion on "Emma" by Jane Austen. I boldly retorted that it was my view that the entire works of the aforementioned author was a scandalous waste of trees. As you can imagine, he was not particularly impressed.

I have no recollection of the second lesson of that first day, but I do distinctly remember break time. A rowdy queue formed along one length of the dining room, and out along the main corridor. I inched my way to the front of the queue, and when I reached the serving table, I was offered a choice of a hot or cold drink. After making my choice, I turned to make my way to a table, when a member of the kitchen staff tapped me on the shoulder and asked if I would like anything to eat. Expecting to be offered a biscuit, I indicated that I would like something. I was surprised to learn that I could have toast, toast and marmalade, or even a sausage sandwich. Wow! I wasn't used to this. When I reached out to collect my toast and marmalade, I was given TWO pieces! I again turned to find a table, but was tapped on the shoulder again and asked if I would like a biscuit to go with that. WHAT? Three biscuits were thrust in to my hand and I was then allowed to make my way to a table. I was so shocked at this unexpected outpouring of generosity, that I almost lost my appetite. Those poor girls back at Chorleywood, dutifully taking one plain biscuit from the plain tin, and one cream biscuit from the other tin, and the Lord help you if you tried anything else! Similarly, I was intrigued to learn that each evening dinner was served at six o'clock, closely followed by supper, at seven forty-five. Supper! That wasn't ever on the agenda at Chorleywood. This snack consisted of a choice of hot or cold drink, with sandwiches filled with everything from honey, chocolate spread, jam, fish paste, marmite, or peanut butter, to mention just a few. We were allowed to choose any combination of fillings we liked. It felt more like a hotel than a school. As I sat there, I thought to myself, "This is the life. I really think I'm going to enjoy it here." The only drawback was that I would have to eat rather less than I had done on that first day, and involve myself in plenty of physical activity if I wasn't going to end up the size of a house.

I was glad to learn that there were indeed plenty of opportunities to get fit. There was the indoor swimming pool, which I had visited as a St. Vincent's pupil several years previously, when I'd had to make that quick change during the swimming gala. The pool was usually open for at least an hour every evening for anyone who wanted to take part. I was also glad to learn that next door to the gym, was a smaller room, namely the multi gym. We could use this facility any time we liked, once we had been shown how to use all the equipment. We had PE lessons almost every day, which included, running, swimming, the occasional football lesson, even for the girls, and I recall one particular morning when we were introduced to cricket. I don't know much about cricket. I am aware that someone throws a ball, and someone else has to whack it with a bat as hard as they can and run, until the ball is retrieved, thus scoring something wildly complicated called a…run, or a series of runs! This process is then repeated over and over again until they achieve something called an "over?" Oh, and then there's the "googly" or a "google" which is when the ball is thrown but missed by the person wielding the bat, and hits another unsuspecting guy in a very painful area. Ouch! No wonder I could never get the hang of it. On that particular morning, I had to bat. Everyone laughed at me, because once I'd whacked that ball as hard as I could, I threw the bat down and ran like stink. Apparently, I was supposed to take the bat with me. Why? Who needs excess baggage when you've got to run as fast as you can? Anyway it all sounds rather vicious to me. Cricket boxes and and the requirement to wear a helmet, the prospect of balls flying around at one hundred miles per hour. I think grand prix racing sounds far more sedate.

Over the days and weeks that followed, we adjusted to our new environment and routine. It wasn't however just us who had to get used to a new lifestyle. In fact, I began to enjoy myself so much, that it came as a shock to me one day during a phone call with Mum. She was rather upset. Although I had been ringing them to keep them updated, it seemed that I wasn't calling my parents as often as I had done the previous year, and on many occasions when they did call me, I was often unavailable. I was either in town, or in a different part of the building and couldn't be located. This did cause some tension at the time, as I didn't always receive messages from fellow students who had answered the phone. My world had suddenly opened up, and my parents were having to get used to that fact. Life was busy, but a lot more chilled. We had lessons from nine until four in the afternoon, with a short period of time to relax after lunch. No more "Walk!" I would usually spend my time in the coffee bar before returning to lessons. During the evenings, it was a regular occurrence to find me in my room which was packed with people on my bed and sitting on the floor with cups of tea and coffee. Somewhere in between endless hours of socialising, we found time to squeeze in some study.

It was inevitable, that within a couple of weeks some relationships started to become established. One girl in my year had been friends with a guy when they had been together at primary school, and so they quickly rekindled their friendship. I had been spending some time with Wayne, but also with a guy from my year called James. He would frequently knock on my door, and invite himself for a cup of tea. This was no problem until I learned that he had a girlfriend who lived in Worcester. Although I liked him, I wasn't interested in pursuing a relationship with him, and so was quite upset when I learned that many of my classmates were talking about me, accusing me of trying to split up James and his girlfriend. On the evening when I learned of this news, I made my way to my room, locked the door and lay on my bed feeling very down. This was a huge blow to me. I'd been having such a great time, and thought that the days of being disliked were far behind me. I stayed there for ages, listening to the noise going on outside my room, and wondering what I was going to do. The accusations couldn't have been further from the truth, and now it wasn't just the girls on my back all over again, it was the boys too. The following day, a guy from my year approached me and asked to speak with me. He proceeded to tell me that I had not done anything wrong, the other students had got the wrong end of the stick, and I wasn't to worry everything would quickly blow over. He had explained to the rest of the year that I was not at fault, and they now understood. I was very pleased to find that he was right. I was really thankful to Paul for his support at that time, and thought he was a decent guy.

With things now back on track, I continued with my studies, and my room was again daily filled with people and cups of coffee. Leah and I began having horse riding lessons on a Tuesday evening after school had ended, and we also prepared ourselves to take part in the

Hyde Park fun run in London, which would take place the following month. I was filling my diary to its capacity, but having a great time. Amidst this busy schedule, I enjoyed my few minutes extra lie-in every morning, so imagine my annoyance at being woken up suddenly one morning by a knock on my study door at around seven o'clock. I put on my dressing gown, and cautiously opened the door to find Wayne standing in front of me. He greeted me with a "Good morning, I've brought you a cup of tea!" Feeling rather surprised, I thanked him, and said "See you later" as I closed the door. As you already know, I hate tea, but considered it to be a thoughtful gesture. I walked across the room to the sink, poured the tea away, put the mug on the desk, and got back in to bed. Around five minutes later, there was another knock on my door. Again I put on my dressing gown, and opened the door. To my surprise, this time it was James, who said, "Hi there, I've brought you a cup of tea." I thanked him and told him I would see him later, before closing the door. Now I didn't know what to think. I walked to the sink, poured the tea away and placed the mug on my desk before getting back in to bed. Part of me felt quite flattered to have the attention of two blokes, but I hated being woken up early, and for tea! Come on guys, if you're going to wake me, get it right and make it coffee! I was just on the edge of sleep, when there was another knock on the door. This time it wasn't funny. I ignored it. I didn't want any more tea, just sleep. I ignored the sound until it turned to a loud pounding accompanied by furious shouts of "Open this door immediately." It was Miss Lane, the member of pastoral staff in charge of the sixth form girls. She had a room at the end of the corridor, and must have seen something and become suspicious. Feeling just as angry as she sounded, I opened the door without saying anything. She burst in and proceeded to open my wardrobe, the cupboard, and search in and under my bed, even checking on the balcony of all places. When she found nothing, or should I say no one--she left all the while issuing instructions as to what would happen if she did ever find anyone. I said nothing and let it all wash over me as I closed the door, and got into bed again. My leisurely lie-in had been ruined, and now there wasn't even time for me to make my own cup of coffee. Grrr! Take me back to the boring simplicity of Chorleywood – NEVER!

15. Love Is In the Air

Not long after the "Tea Incident", I learned that on a few occasions, Wayne and James had disagreed about who should be spending time with me. It was a shame because I thought they were both good guys, but I didn't want to be the third person in that potential triangle, that sounded like far too much hassle for me. I am glad to say that I did remain friends with both of them, but that was the way it was going to stay. One evening during our first week at the College, Leah and I were sitting in her room. We were both fed-up of not really knowing our way around the building, and so decided that we would just take a walk and learn as we went along. During this venture, we found ourselves at the coffee bar. As we walked over to buy a drink, there were two guys standing at the bar drinking coffee and deep in conversation. Wishing to get to know more of the guys, we introduced ourselves, but were disappointed when they merely introduced themselves and then carried on with their conversation, making no attempt to include us. Both the guys were called Gaz, and that is as far as we got. So after finishing our drinks, we went on our way.

A few days later, Leah and I were playing the piano in one of the practice rooms when someone came in. The person in question was Gaz, one of the people we had met in the coffee bar. I'm pleased that this time he was a lot more chatty than on our previous acquaintance. After a while, he invited us back to his study for coffee and we followed him back to the sixth form boys' corridor. As I followed behind him, I remember thinking how tall he was. When we arrived, Gaz went off to borrow a power lead for his kettle, but came back empty handed, so guess what? Yes, it was back to my room for coffee. What started off as coffee for three soon turned into coffee for around ten. I didn't mind, I had become well used to that situation. On another evening Gaz and I also chatted briefly when Leah kindly offered to invite everyone for drinks in her room. We all seemed to get on well, although, I've never spent so much money on tea and coffee before or since.

Friday evenings were always feel good times. During one of those evenings, James and I had been having great fun playing catch with a full carton of milk along the length of the boys' sixth form corridor. Fortunately, we got bored of that game before any serious damage was done to the carton, and decided to take a walk along the front drive. At the top end of the drive we came across a stray traffic cone. I haven't a clue why it was there, and I also don't remember what gave us the idea to have a kick around with the cone. At first we booted it to see which one of us could make it travel the furthest distance, and then just decided to kick it from one to the other. When we tired of that, we made our way up to the sixth form common room, to see if there was anyone else around. A few people were gathered in there, including a certain person named Gaz. At some point during the evening, I heard someone suddenly shout "Oh, yuck!" It turned out that Gaz had been looking around the room, and found a stray jar of coffee. I went over to investigate, and he handed the jar to me. I sniffed it. It smelled ok, but then again, a little strange. I put my hand in to find that the contents were all stuck together and crusty. I said, "Ooh, that's really manky." For some reason, this expression made Gaz really laugh and we began a conversation which had us both in fits of laughter. The conversation ended with me saying, "Well if you're going to bring me coffee, you'll have to do a lot better than that." At the time, I never expected that he would take me up on the offer. When eleven o'clock arrived, we had to return to our respective wings, so we all said "Goodnight", and headed off for bed.

At nine o'clock the following morning, there was a knock on my door. I was already up and dressed, and opened the door expecting it to be Leah. To my surprise, it was Gaz, armed with a cup of coffee. I invited him to join me while I drank my coffee, which was actually quite a good cuppa. We talked, listened to music, and just as on the previous evening spent a good deal of time laughing. Gaz had a great sense of humour, and before we knew it, two hours had disappeared. He then had to leave because he had arranged to go into town with a friend, but before he left, he asked me if I would like to go to the pub with him. I accepted, and we arranged to meet at seven that evening. Gaz was in the upper sixth form, a year above me. However, I already knew most of the boys in his year including Wayne. Leah had become friends with another boy from the same year as Gaz, who was also called James. I thought it would be a good idea if the four of us went out together that evening and so it was arranged. That afternoon I spent time with James from my year. He had arrived at my study not long after Gaz had left and asked if I wanted to hang out. We spent some time playing the piano in one of the practice rooms, and then he tried to teach me how to play snooker, but I have to say the game didn't really appeal to me. My thoughts kept returning to my evening ahead, I was really looking forward to meeting with Gaz again. The afternoon seemed to drag on, but eventually, I told James it was time for me to go.

When we were both ready, Leah and I walked downstairs to meet Gaz and the other James and went to the pub. It was late September, and the weather was still quite warm so we chose to sit at a wooden table outside. James and Gaz went to get the first round of drinks and Leah and I laughed about how great it felt to be sitting outside a pub with two guys. It was so wildly different to the lifestyle we had been used too. However, neither of us was complaining. When the guys returned, we spent the whole evening chatting and we all got on really well. There weren't any awkward silences, or moments when we wondered what we should talk about next. The whole evening flowed as if we'd all been friends for ages. Gaz and I, however, as I remember, spent more time laughing than talking. When the men went to get another round, I gave Gaz a twenty pound note to pay for the drinks. When they returned, he gave me my change, and told me that I would have to find the remaining tenner myself. Feeling a little bemused, I picked up my drink to take a sip, and found that the note was floating in my drink. Everyone laughed, and so the evening continued. Around ten thirty, we all walked back to college, said "Goodnight" and went to our rooms. I had really enjoyed my evening, but it was more than that. I felt so relaxed in Gaz's company, and I loved the way we made each other laugh so much. I found myself wanting to meet up with him at the earliest possible opportunity the next day, and hoped he felt the same.

We met the following afternoon, and just enjoyed spending time together. It very quickly became apparent to me, that all I could think about was Gaz. When I couldn't be with him, I spent the time just thinking about him, even during lessons. I was seriously smitten. No, actually, I was well and truly hooked. Gaz was so easy to be with, all I had to be was just me, and that was enough. I'd never had a friend like that before. It was kind of strange, but completely wonderful. The only thing better than that, was the fact that he seemed to feel the same. Gaz played the bass guitar, and I can honestly say, that although I had a lifelong love of music, I hadn't really noticed much about bass lines before. Now however, I was introduced to this new world, but I didn't mind, as far as I was concerned, bass guitars were lovely; bass lines were lovely; the whole world was just a continuous haze of complete loveliness! It was truly, madly, deeply, fetch me a bucket stuff! Wherever Gaz went, Jane went and vice versa. Within a couple of days

127

news had spread through the college. We were definitely an item. If you couldn't find Gaz, then look for Jane and you would find him. If you couldn't find Jane then look for Gaz and there she would be. Everything was just naturally right, as if it was just meant to be. Some thought it was silly, and others thought it was incredibly sweet, but we didn't care one bit. In fact, I think we were completely oblivious.

I mentioned earlier, that Leah and I had started going to horse riding lessons on a Tuesday after school. The chap who took the lessons was fantastic. We had been used to riding the ponies at Chorleywood, but now we had the luxury of riding much larger horses in an indoor arena. The horse I usually rode was named Major B and he had a wonderful temperament. You may not be able to see exactly where you are going, but riding always gives a great sense of freedom. I really enjoyed those lessons, but was shocked one evening when I came back to college and met up with Gaz. He told me that he described Tuesday evenings as his "Depressed evening" because it seemed ages till I returned. Aaah! No one had ever missed me that much before. Similarly, I think he felt the same on the Sunday in October, when Leah and I together with a couple of other students, boarded a minibus to go to Hyde Park in London for the annual fun run. Some girls who were still at Chorleywood also attended, and it was good to meet up with them. We all sat together on the grass and had a drink and talked until it was our turn to take part. I don't have enough sight to run independently. In those situations, a sighted guide, or as in my case, a partially sighted fellow student wears a band which is tied to their wrist, and the same tied to the blind person's wrist with a short length in between so they can both run freely but one can lead the other. It was a great atmosphere, as we stood in a large crowd waiting to begin. As we ran, crowds of people on either side cheered us on, shouting and clapping us all the way. Luckily, the day was mainly dry, apart from the odd bit of drizzle, and the fact that it wasn't too warm was advantageous when you've got to keep on running. Debbie and I both had moments when we had to encourage each other and keep each other going, but on the whole it was brilliant. As we turned the last corner and were approaching the finish line, the shouts and cheers got louder, and louder. Feeling tired but pleased at our efforts, we ran over the finish line. We had done it, and those weeks of training had been well worth it. A few days later, I was surprised and very pleased to learn that Debbie and I had had our picture taken as we ran across the finish line, and our photograph was on the front page of the Sunday Times. Wow! That was one to keep for my family. It had been a thoroughly enjoyable day, but Gaz was definitely happier when we arrived home.

The only other thing that could prize us apart, was the outrageous interruption of A-Levels. Lessons still had to continue, so, while Gaz grappled with Maths and Computer Science, I tackled the likes of English Literature, and R.E. but as soon as lessons had ended, we could usually be found drinking coffee in the coffee bar, or listening to music in either his or my room. If we had been out to the pub for the evening, then we would often return, and study together in one of the libraries downstairs. It's true for most students, that some of our best work was produced after a good night out at the pub. On several occasions, this would also be accompanied by pie and chips. There was a very well frequented chip shop on the outskirts of the town centre which was a particular favourite of the sixth form at the college. Groups of students could often be seen lining their stomachs on a Friday or Saturday night before a pretty hefty session, or simply soaking up the alcohol on the way back. They became so popular, that they offered us a delivery service to the College. During the evenings, large orders from the College would be collected, and read out over the phone. Then a crowd would gather at the front door half an hour later, to collect the huge bags of food. In fact, during my first term there, just before Christmas, the owners invited the whole sixth form for a free Christmas fish and chips. They had a large dining area, and we filled it one evening. It was great fun and, when you're a student, free food always tastes good. So one evening, Gaz and I returned from the pub, took our books and Braillers to library C, and worked as we ate pie and chips. One of my assignments that evening, was to construct an essay written in the same language and style as guess who? Jane Austen. No wonder I needed a night out first! Gaz tussled with the Maths, while I reluctantly faced Jane Austen jeopardy. As I brushed away the pie crumbs from my Braille paper forty-five minutes later, I asked Gaz how he was doing, and he asked the same of me. It was clear that I was completely unable to understand anything about his Maths. So I decided to read some of my work to him. When he heard my efforts, Gaz fell about laughing. He shared my opinion of the aforementioned author, but actually thought I'd managed to produce a good piece of work. I have to say that when I got my result, to my surprise, I'd achieved an A minus grade. Not bad: from a member of staff who never gave A's for anything. There, it just goes to prove, that when you're a student, a pie and a pint can save the day. Come to think of it, maybe that's just what Jane Austen needed!

There were so many evenings when I would sit alone in my study writing assignments late in to the night, or should I say in to the next morning. There was simply too much fun to be enjoyed earlier in the day. As I was making my way down to the coffee bar one evening, I met Gaz and James who were coming in the opposite direction. I don't know why, but they proceeded to cross over their wrists, and join hands and told me to sit down, while they then carried me along the corridor and into the coffee bar. I felt rather stupid, and was glad when it was all over. That however, wasn't as bad as the event on my eighteenth birthday. My birthday is a couple of weeks before Christmas, and so everyone was in party mood. Gaz had promised to take me out for a meal to celebrate, and I was just about to start getting ready when someone knocked on my door. I answered it, and before I could do anything, four of the boys, including Gaz, had lifted me up on their shoulders, and proceeded to carry me down the main stairs and through the building. My shouts of protest rang around the corridors as they threatened to take me outside and dump me in the horse trough. They relinquished at the last minute, and, just as I thought I'd got away with it, they threw me in to a ready prepared bath of freezing cold water. I learned later that this was a Worcester College tradition for students on their eighteenth birthday.

This wasn't the only time I was to get wet. One evening, a few of us were out on my balcony, when Gaz decided to furiously shake a can of lemonade before opening it over my head. To add insult to injury, he then picked me up and dangled me over the edge of the balcony. It must be true when people refer to others as being MADLY in love. Students can sometimes be the most crazy people around. Gaz and I often played tricks on each other. At the beginning of that academic year, I had also taken up guitar lessons. My teacher was a pretty laid back guy, who let me learn the type of music I liked to play. For some reason, just before one of my lessons, I decided to take out my guitar from its case and quickly practise the piece I had been learning. As I attempted to remove the instrument, I found to my surprise, that an item of clothing had been put in the case on top of my guitar. I knew instantly, it was Gaz's doing. Right, I was going to get him back. It must have been the favour of God that I decided to play that guitar before my lesson. Phew! That saved a rather red face on my part. Just before your mind starts turning somersaults, Gaz hadn't been raiding my underwear drawer. It was a blouse he had put in there, not anything else. There would have been serious trouble otherwise. I was in love, not insane.

I made my plans to return the prank, and came up with the following idea. Someone had given me a small metal badge in the shape of a guitar, and so one afternoon, I crept into his study while he was in a computing lesson, removed his beloved bass guitar from its case, and replaced it with the badge. I carefully carried his bass back to my room and hid it under my bed. It wasn't long until Gaz appeared in a panic about where his precious guitar had gone. The worst trick he ever played on me though was months later. I had gone to London, to the National Theatre, to see Anthony Hopkins play the leading role in "King Lear". That is my favourite Shakespeare play, and it was wonderful. Everything had gone very well that day, until late in the evening when we had all left the venue and gone to take our seats on the minibus ready for the journey back to Worcester. It was already late in the evening, in fact it was not far away from midnight. Unfortunately, one of the exits out of the multi-storey carpark had been closed. This was an exit with a high roof suitable for larger vehicles. The only other exit was a much lower one, and a member of staff who had travelled with us went to find an attendant to see what could be done. At one point, we thought we were there for the night. Eventually, we left an hour later, and didn't arrive back at College until after three in the morning. I was shattered and more than ready for falling into bed. This potentially relaxing, welcome experience was brought to an abrupt end when I pulled back my duvet and was horrified to find that my bed was completely covered in scratchy dry breadcrumbs. It turned out, as I learned the following morning, that Gaz had crumbled an entire French stick all over my sheet, and left it there ready for when I returned. Much to my shame, when I did find the pesky crumbs, I was so tired and disgruntled, that I picked up my matress, emptied the crumbs on the floor, replaced the mattress, complete with now clean fitted sheet, got into bed, and fell asleep. Luckily for Gaz, I was fast asleep long before I could begin plotting my revenge. It was just as well, I would have to take my time over this one, and think long and hard. Watch out Gaz!

16. The fun goes on

Music surely must be the food of love, because Gaz and I loved music. At first, Gaz was slightly deterred because lots of my music consisted of popular stuff from the current charts. However, there was some middle ground. I had a limited edition album by the band Level 42, which Gaz had not heard before, and Gaz played his bass along with it. We also both enjoyed listening to Nick Kershaw. I hadn't noticed before, but there were some great bass lines on his albums too. Gaz bought a coffee machine, which, of course, he left in my room, and we would spend hours drinking coffee and listening to music. A couple of Christmases previously, I had been given a rather large ghetto blaster. At the time, I thought it was one of the best presents I had ever had. It was big and loud and also had detachable speakers which were definitely the in thing to have at that time. When I returned to Chorleywood after the Christmas holiday, I carefully took it apart, and wrapped each speaker and the main unit in separate bubble wrapped parcels, and placed them in the original box ready for the journey. Similarly, when it was time to leave college for a holiday I would perform the same ritual, always packing and unpacking my precious equipment with care. Now, however, the must-have item was something called a CD player! Only about two sixth-formers had hi-fi's which had CD players in their rooms. They were extremely expensive; not to mention the price of the CDs themselves. This was top of the range cutting edge technology during the mid-nineteen eighties, and I wanted one. I really wanted one. I'm not sure why, but on the day we all left college to go home for the Christmas holidays, I told Gaz that I was going to get one.

The following day was a Saturday, and Mum, Dad and I spent the afternoon going round the shops indulging in a little Christmas shopping. Now was definitely the time to broach the subject of a CD player for Christmas. I had saved some money from my eighteenth birthday, and wanted to put it towards the equipment. I don't think my parents were very sure at first, but then we stumbled upon a very good deal, which included a voucher for three free CDs of your choice when you bought one particular hi-fi system. So that afternoon, the hi-fi was duly purchased, and I proudly unpacked it and set it up in my room when we got home. Mum and Dad didn't see any reason to make me wait until Christmas day. It sounded brilliant. Gaz had introduced me to Lionel Richie's debut album, and I liked it. Not only that, but there was a song on the album, which we adopted as our song. So my CD collection started with "Lionel Richie", by Lionel Richie, "Human Racing" by Nick Kershaw, and a CD from the "Now That's What I Call Music" collection. I couldn't wait to ring Gaz and tell him the good news. When I did, he was amazed and, I think, a little jealous.

I loved spending time with my parents, but being without Gaz always meant that the holidays seemed to go on forever. We would spend hours on the phone, and always write letters to each other, which were so long, I'm surprised that "Royal Mail" decided to take them. I kept the letters that Gaz sent me for years, but unfortunately, I don't know what happened to them. The worst time, was having to spend Christmas without him. That year we all stayed at Auntie Jenny's house and had a really good time, it's just that it would have been even better if Gaz could have been there. It wasn't long though before the day came when it was time to return to school, and I was so happy to be with him again. When I went to his study, I found that he had also treated himself to a new hi-fi system. In fact he'd bought the same one as me. Gaz had bought a different album by Nick Kershaw, and also one by Level 42. During that term, our little CD collection started to grow. Saturday mornings would usually find us both taking the bus into town to visit various different music stores to buy our favourite CDs, followed by a trip to Macdonald's for lunch. We added albums from Whitney Houston, to Rush, but I was unaware at that time, that soon, very soon, the real music was about to begin.

One Saturday morning, Gaz bought a CD by an artist I'd never heard of before. His name is Al Jarreau, and from the moment I heard the first track, I loved it. At the next opportunity, I bought the same album, and then I bought another, and another, and another. Now, over twenty years later, I have over twenty-five albums by Al Jarreau, and I've been to at least seven of his live concerts. I would go to one every week if I had the time, and more importantly the money. He is simply my favourite artist, and my all-time favourite song is "Mornin'". It's a really feel good song, that always makes me smile. I have it as my ring tone on my phone, and also as my alarm in the morning, or should I say mornin'.

During my first term at college, I had made the decision to become a committed Christian. Gaz had already made that choice several years previously. He took the quiet calm approach, never forcing the issue, and when he tentatively invited me to join him one Saturday to attend a Christian conference, I was quite sceptical. My experiences at St. Vincent's had convinced me that God did exist, so I was quite open, but spending a whole day in Bible study was a little daunting. A gentleman named Reverend David Pawson, was teaching that day, and by the evening, I was so impressed with what he said, and so moved by the love of God, that I made my commitment that evening. Gaz was given a lift to church on Sundays by a couple who lived in a small village just outside Worcester. Eddie and Lin had been taking Gaz and his friends to church for a number of years, and now it was my turn to meet them. When I first was introduced to them, I found them to be a very warm and friendly couple. However, I didn't know then, just how much I would grow to love them both. In fact, they were to become another set of parents to Gaz and me.

Every Sunday morning, Gaz would hoist his huge bass amp into the boot of Eddie's car, and then the two of us would sit on the back seat with his guitar across our laps. When we arrived at church, Lin and I would find our seats, while Gaz and Eddie carried the equipment over to the front of the hall so that Gaz could join the music group. Invariably we would be a few minutes late, and Eddie and Gaz would be seen hurriedly dashing down the side of the hall. Gaz would unpack his bass guitar, while Eddie would be on his knees unraveling a very long reel of extension cable, and searching for a socket, before plugging in the amp. When the service was ended, everything would have to be packed away and carried to the car before beginning our journey back to college. I remember one day during the summer when Eddie stopped to buy some fuel, and came back with a Mars Bar ice cream for all of us. He said that he'd never tried them before, but after that, he would stop every week to buy ice cream. When Lin was away visiting friends for the weekend, Eddie would take us for lunch after church. Lin was, and still is a fantastic cook, but sometimes, one just needs a burger. In the City centre, there used to be a small burger bar called Viking Burgers, and that's the place where we would go. We used to tease Eddie about having a sneaky burger when Lin was away, but we loved it. Huge half pound burgers topped with fresh salad, would be accompanied by Cola or coffee, closely followed by a cherry pie or two. Just don't tell Lin…

The first Valentine's Day after the girls had joined the college was a memorable one. It was a Saturday, and Gaz arrived at my room with the largest box of Thornton's chocolates I'd ever seen and a beautiful card. I had bought a card and a gift for him, and after he'd opened it, we both went to join some friends who had received cards. By that time, some students had begun relationships, but not all. Lots of anonymous cards were received containing the most hilarious made up verses. I particularly remember one that began, "Nicola, oh Nicola, I'd love to tickle ya...", but that's enough of that. We nearly wet ourselves laughing, as various people read out their cards, and then made plans for the Valentine's party we were due to attend that evening. I remember thinking on that day how happy I was. I felt so blessed to have Gaz. I hadn't just found a boyfriend, I'd found my best friend, my soulmate. We continued to laugh continuously, and I couldn't imagine my life without him. Occasionally, I would consider what it would be like the following academic year, when Gaz would have moved on to university, and I would still be at the college, but I always pushed the thought aside. Now was time for enjoying myself.

Not long after Valentine's Day, I was walking along the corridor where our rooms were, when one of the girls in my year suddenly stopped me and said, "Jane, it's really good to see, you've come out of your shell since you've been here!" I was surprised, and didn't quite know what to say, but I made some short comment and we laughed before parting company. She was right though, I was really happy, the whole change in atmosphere, lifestyle, and Gaz had changed my life. A few days later, the sixth form was asked by the headmaster to attend an event at his house in the college grounds, specifically for a group of people known as "The Friends of the College". These were individuals who voluntarily gave up some of their time to raise money for the school, or helped with taking students out for the day. Eddie was part of this group, and so, that evening, Gaz and I walked across the grounds to meet him. I recall standing with Gaz and Eddie, as trays of sherry and orange juice were carried around for all of us, and we all chatted together. Also in attendance were a few members of staff from Chorleywood, who had come to visit. As the evening drew to a close, many people had left, but a few remained. For some reason, I found myself sitting on a sofa next to a member of staff from Chorleywood. As we chatted, I remember feeling a little self-conscious when she suddenly remarked, "Jane, you seem so much more relaxed and very happy here!"

So work continued day by day. I grappled with everything from the poetry of Thomas Hardy, and John Donne, through to Gnostic Dualism, interspersed with hours in the coffee bar, and evenings in the pub. Gaz and I would often study together because that gave us more incentive and we supported each other. Some may suspect this would have been more of a distraction, but it did work. Anyway, if I'd have

135

left Gaz to his own devices, I'm sure he would have quite easily found something different to do. The college by now, was considered to be the top educational establishment in the country, and each year, when the sixth form students had completed their A-Levels, over 90 per cent of them would go on to University. We were all considered to be high achievers. With this in mind, it reminds me of a story which was related by the college secretary. One afternoon she had answered a routine call only to find that the caller immediately launched straight into their particular request which went thus:

"Good afternoon, I have some wicker furniture which needs repairing, when could I bring it in?" The secretary was incensed by both the persons presumption, and the stereo-typing. Yes, basket weaving and furniture making was associated with visually impaired people many years ago, but by now this was ludicrous! In fact she was so angry, that she replied disdainfully, "No, I'm sorry, our students are far too busy studying for their astro physics A-Level to have any time to bother with wicker furniture." The story quickly circulated around the College, and we were all greatly impressed. Good on that lady!

The staff were fully aware of our relationship, and I was embarrassed one day when Gaz's computer science teacher approached me in the dining room. As he walked towards me he announced, "Here's the only one who has some influence with Gary, maybe you could persuade him to do some work." Work? What on earth was that? No wonder staff were commenting. On occasions, I would be walking down a corridor, when Gaz would walk past, hear my voice, rush toward me, and suddenly pick me up and carry me for the next few yards, much to my embarrassment. I sometimes thought he was completely crazy, but he always made me laugh so much.

Looking back, I can't believe how naive I was at times. One morning, I decided to take an early morning cup of coffee to Gaz in his study. I had nothing else in mind, just to leave the coffee and go back to my room. As I walked along the corridor leading to the sixth-form boys' rooms, carrying the coffee, I was stopped in my tracks by one of the boy's pastoral care staff Mr Hodgson. He was a friendly gentleman with a distinctive Scottish accent. We had got on well in the time I had been there, and often exchanged comments and quips about the town of Darwen in Lancashire, where I lived when I was first born. This particular member of staff had visited the place and wasn't particularly impressed and would often tease me about it. He suddenly stopped me as I walked and announced, "Where do you think you're going with that cup of coffee, mate?" Without thinking, I simply turned to him, grinned and said, "Aaaaaa!", before going on my way. He must have been so shocked, that he said nothing. I knocked on Gaz's door, left the coffee on his desk, and went back to my room. I'm sure however, that I was being closely watched on my return journey, but it makes me laugh to think how naive I was, and wonder how I got away with it.

Although Gaz is wonderfully talented, he has his limits. One day, we had found a large casserole dish, and decided we could use it to make some Angel Delight. We managed to make it without any problems, and when we had eaten it hours later, I washed the dish in the sink in my room, dried it and placed it on my desk ready to return it to the kitchen. I was a little irritated when Gaz picked it up and asked, "Do you think this would break if I threw it in your sink?" "Durrr!" I said disdainfully. "Yes, it WILL break, and it will probably break the sink at the same time!" All I could think was, "What a completely stupid question." He proceeded to disagree with me, adding that the sink was not far away from my bed and the dish would survive fully intact. I was completely adamant that it wouldn't and strongly advised him to put the dish down. Unfortunately, Gaz decided to take his chance, and the next thing I heard was the loud sound of shattering glass, followed by shrieks of laughter. I however was not amused. It was the first time I remember feeling really cross with him. I cleared up the glass, threw it in the kitchen bin, and didn't make further comment, although I have to admit I was thinking, "Stupid boy!"

As I've already mentioned, Gaz and I drank loads of coffee at that time. One day however, he decided that we should try some Cup-a-Soup. Gaz offered to make it, so I sat down and let him get on with it. There were two mugs ready on the tray, and Gaz began pouring a sachet of powder in each mug. He poured on the boiling water, gave the first mug a stir, and presented it to me. My first impression was that the soup didn't smell very strong, but went on to take a sip. Hmmm! plain boiled water--that wasn't really what I was expecting. It turned out that Gaz had accidentally poured both sachets into the same mug, and now he was stirring a very thick gloopy substance. Undeterred, he decided that all was not lost, he would simply pour half of his mixture into my now empty mug, top it up with water and everything would be fine. When both mugs contained soup, we sat down to taste them. Unfortunately, Gaz put his mug on the floor by my bed, went to sit down, kicked the mug, and soup went all over the carpet. After that, we decided to stick to coffee.

My resolve didn't last long. In a mad moment, I decided to buy a Sodastream for Gaz on his birthday. I also bought three varieties of syrup to make different drinks. Gaz really liked it, and it seemed that everything was going very well, until Gaz had an idea. He became gripped by what I thought was a ludicrous notion. Instead of filling a bottle with plain water, and allowing the Sodastream to do its job, Gaz wanted to fill the bottle with milk. I tried my best to offer a few words of sanity and wisdom, but to no avail. I stepped back as close to the door of his study as I could and cringed, as Gaz boldly loaded the machine and pressed the button. He learned that day that Sodastreams are made for water, not anything else. A few seconds later, there was the usual fizzing sound, only this time it was followed by a torrent of milk which covered him and the walls. Oh Gaz you silly soda!

As we eased our way into the summer, it was time once again for Gaz and me to be prized apart for the half term holiday. On that particular week, my family had arranged to travel down to Bournemouth to stay with relatives. They would spend Friday afternoon travelling down from Blackburn, and collect me in Worcester, before travelling through the night and making our way to our destination. As they weren't due to arrive until around seven in the evening, I was probably the last student to be left hanging around the building. I spent the majority of my time in my study, reading or listening to music. I had received a call to say that my parents were delayed, and didn't know what time they would arrive. I wasn't particularly bothered, I was quite happy in my room. Around seven thirty, I heard footsteps moving along the corridor, and then someone proceeded to knock on each door, open it, drop the catch on the inside to lock it, and then shut the door. I presumed that this must be Mr Smith, the head of pastoral care for the boys. He was a friendly chap, but shall I say, in my opinion, not particularly commanding. As I heard him move closer to my room a grin appeared on my face. By now he was getting in to the swing of things, and seemed to be enjoying his little procedure. When he knocked on my door, I called out in a low and austere voice, "Come in." He wasn't expecting that, because a rather girly scream emanated from the other side of the door, and he then exclaimed in a rather shaky voice, "Oh my God, there's someone in there!" I fell into uncontrollable laughter. This gave him the courage to open the door, and his terror quickly turned to anger. He ordered me to wait downstairs at the front door instead of being able to wait in my room, so I grabbed my bag, and very slowly and defiantly walked along the corridor, down the main stairs and through to the front porch. This small area was filled with laundry bags. I threw down my bag, sat on the laundry bags and waited. I was rather miffed with Mr Smith for not allowing me to stay in my room, but what had just happened kept me laughing for weeks.

The weather was great that week in Bournemouth, and we all had a brilliant time. I was glad though when it was time for me to go back and meet up with Gaz again. The family dropped me off at college on the Sunday afternoon. Some of the boys had arranged to travel back early in order to get some study time in on the run up to their A-Level exams, and Gaz was already there. I decided to play a trick on him and Kirsten came with me before my parents left. I went to the pay phone just by my room, and called Gaz. He answered the boys' pay phone in his corridor which was in a small cubical known as "the birdcage". I hadn't told him that I was returning early, and talked with him as if I was ringing him from Bournemouth relating how I would be returning early the next morning. I then asked him to wait a moment as Mum was asking me something. I left the phone and crept down the corridor, pulled open the door of the "birdcage", and tapped him on the shoulder, and shouted, "Hiya!" A rather surprised but pleased Gaz turned and gave me a hug. I then said goodbye to my family, and got myself unpacked, ready for the final few weeks of my first year at the college.

Those last six weeks seemed to fly by. More and more I found myself pondering about what life would be like the following year when I would be at college, and Gaz would be elsewhere in the country at university. I had enjoyed an amazing year, one of the best of my life thus far, and knew that the next year would be vastly different. Not only that, but it had been very easy for our relationship to flourish at the school, but next year there would be a wealth of obstacles that we would have to negotiate our way through for it to survive. Would we manage or would things change? I didn't really want to think about the possibility of us splitting up, and so I concentrated on the fun we would have during the long summer holiday.

17. New Challenges

During those last couple of weeks before the summer holidays, students started to let their hair down, and this became a headache for some staff members. I remember one break time when someone started a food fight in the dining room. The place was a real mess, as food was flying everywhere, accompanied by a cacophony of screams and shouts. One afternoon, some of us ended up in a rather exuberant water fight along the sixth form girls' corridor. What began with just flicking water, quickly escalated to cups of water, and culminated in someone launching a large pan of water down the corridor. Again the atmosphere was rather rowdy, as people ran in all directions, trying to avoid getting soaked, and slipping on an already wet floor. Lake Windermere had momentarily transitioned to Worcester. This rumpus was heard by one of the college nurses and she rushed down to investigate. I had never seen her so angry. She bawled at us at the top of her voice, and I thought at the time that if she didn't calm down, then she would be the one in need of urgent medical attention. The outburst ended with her running down the corridor in the opposite direction, promising to go and get the deputy head to see what we had done. I somehow got the impression that she was looking forward to watching the deputy head tear strips off us, so I suddenly announced in a loud voice, "Ok, guys, the fun is over. Let's get to work. By the time she returns she won't see anything she can punish us for. Luckily everyone responded. Towels were retrieved from every room, and we began the mopping up process. Minutes later, when the nurse did indeed return with the deputy head, we were all on our hands and knees, and most of the mess was gone. Someone really had the wind taken from her sails and we received the mildest of reprimands as there wasn't much evidence of anything to punish us for.

On the final weekend of the summer term, Mum and Dad came down to pick me up with all of my luggage. One of Gaz's best friends who had left the College a year previously had travelled down to spend some time with us. We were all invited to spend an evening at Eddie and Lin's house. They already knew Gaz's friend Chris, as he had gone to church with them on a regular basis. We spent time out in the garden until it grew chilly, and then spent the evening crowded around the piano singing and playing. It was one of those very special unplanned times, and will stay in my memory for a long time. There was a special sense of friendship, and pleasure in spending time with each other. Unfortunately, I would be the one responsible for spoiling such a great weekend. The next day was Chris's birthday, and although I was due to travel home with Mum and Dad, they begged me to stay and go for a meal with them to celebrate. Gaz said I should travel back to his house with him the day after, and meet his family and go home a few days later. I was hesitant at first, but soon they managed to persuade me that my parents wouldn't mind if I explained the situation. When I plucked up the courage to tell them, they were understandably hopping mad. As we stood on the front drive next to the car full of my stuff, my Mum was clearly upset, and my Dad was nothing short of livid. As he got in the front seat of the car and started the engine, I told him I would go home with them, but Dad was having none of it. As I stood there with tears rolling down my face, he growled some words in my direction, which I have no intention of repeating, and sped off. Looking back, that really wasn't one of my best decisions. I can fully understand now why they were so cross, but I was in that phase of life, where fun was the main deal, and that came before other important matters. Now I have a son who is in his late teens, and I see the self-same things in him from time to time. That's parenthood!

That afternoon I was thoroughly miserable. It had never been my intention to cause such a stir. I felt very guilty, and wished I'd never mentioned the subject. I knew that eventually I would have to get myself together, and put on my happy face, or I would end up spoiling the evening for Gaz and Chris. So that evening, off we went for a boiling hot curry to numb the senses. We did have an enjoyable evening, but my mind did wander at times to the sort of reception I would get at home in a few days.

The following morning I woke early and got up. I got my things together, although I didn't by now have a great deal. I had a couple of outfits and some overnight stuff. As it was the end of the year, Gaz's local education authority had sent a car to pick him and all of his belongings up to take him home. I joined him, feeling quite nervous in case the driver questioned why there were two passengers, but he never mentioned anything. On the journey I was a little apprehensive, going to a place I'd never visited before, and meeting family members for the first time. I had met Gaz's mum on a couple of occasions at college, but had not spent much time getting to know her. I had usually made polite small talk for a few moments before leaving them both to spend time together. My first impression of her was that she was a very quiet and gentle woman. Gaz had told me after our first meeting that she liked me, so I wasn't too nervous about meeting her again.

After a couple of hours journey, we arrived in bustling London. It was very different to anything I was used to. I had visited London on many occasions before, but not for more than a couple of days at a time. Gaz lived in the south-east of the city, and when we arrived, we were sorry to find that no-one was home. Luckily, Gaz had a key, so we let ourselves in, and hauled his luggage into the house. So, with the house being so quiet, we decided that the only thing to do was go across the road to the pub.

The pub wasn't exactly the most salubrious place I'd ever visited. It consisted of two large rooms, with a bar in between. One room had a bare tiled floor with a few chairs and tables, and a snooker table in the middle. The second room, I supposed, was the lounge part, because it was carpeted and a little quieter. Reggae music was playing on the juke box, and we sat down with a rum and black and talked about what I would say when I met Gaz's brother and sister. Both were older than him and fully sighted, and had always lived in that area of London. During our conversation, Gaz suddenly turned when he heard someone calling out to him. It was his brother Dalton, and he introduced himself to me. Dalton was a fun-loving easy-going character with whom I got on from the beginning. Gaz bought us all another round of drinks and we became acquainted.

Eventually, we decided to go back across the road to see if Gaz's mum had returned home. She had, and we hugged and said our "Hello's" before Gaz showed me into the sitting room, and went to the kitchen to speak with his mum. Despite the warm welcome I had received, I did feel slightly uncomfortable. I was in a strange house, in an unfamiliar city, with mainly people I had never met, and a completely unknown culture. Lancashire meets Jamaica: now that was a comical combination. It brought a smile to my face, as I imagined our two families meeting together. As I sat quietly musing, I was somewhat unnerved to realise that a disagreement was taking place in the kitchen. I heard raised voices, but couldn't make out what was being said as Gaz's Mum was, naturally, speaking with a Jamaican accent, and articulating at a rate of knots. I suddenly panicked wondering whether Gaz had forgotten to tell her that I was coming home with him. Maybe she didn't want me there? I hadn't caused more trouble had I? Not long after, Gaz's Mum, Irene, appeared with a huge plate of fresh mango, and said to me in a friendly voice, "You try some mango Jane?" I thanked her and took a piece. I'd never tried mango before, but thought it was absolutely delicious. Gaz came in to join me, or at least eat the mango, and Irene went back to the kitchen. When I asked Gaz if I had caused a problem by being there, he laughed and said that there was no problem. It turned out that Irene was vexed with Dalton for some reason, but thankfully, it was nothing to do with me. I was very relieved, and began to relax again.

Those three days were a crash course in Jamaican culture. It was different, but thoroughly enjoyable. Everyone I met was so welcoming and friendly, even though at times I struggled to fathom what they were saying, and they giggled at my Lancashire accent. On the first evening, Irene made jerk chicken with rice and peas, and homemade carrot juice. This was a drink I'd never tried before, but once again I was glad to say it was excellent. It turned out that Irene hadn't made carrot juice for a while, and when Dalton returned, and found it in the middle of the dining table, he quickly helped himself to a glass before turning to me and saying, "Carrot juice? Jane you can visit again!"

One evening, I was informed that we would be having soup for dinner. Well, there was no problem there. I sat at the table to find that in front of me was a huge Pyrex dish of soup. We chatted for a few moments, until Irene said "It's ok, you can start eating." I looked down at my dish, feeling rather puzzled, and asked, "Do you have a ladle, and I will serve the soup?" There was a burst of laughter, and I was told that the soup was just for me. Everyone had their own dish. What! I could never eat all that soup! Ah, but this was Soup with a capital S... This was a complete meal. In fact it contained all kinds of vegetables and huge chunks of meat. I was introduced to yam, sweet potato and dumplings all in the same bowl. This was more like casserole than soup, but once again, very tasty. So despite the obvious cultural differences, I seemed to be getting on with the family very well, in fact, better than I had expected. I had always been worried about their reaction to Gaz going out with "a white girl." They certainly had a far more relaxed approach than my parents, who had taken a long while to get used to the idea of their daughter's boyfriend being black.

When I'd started going out with Gaz, the fact that he was black didn't make the slightest difference to me. I had grown up with children from different parts of the world in the various schools I had attended. Looking back, I suppose I was a little naive, but at the time I really couldn't understand what all the fuss was about, when it seemed to be such a huge problem to my parents. I had never heard them air any racist views. In the town where we lived there was a large Asian community, and we had never experienced any problems, but when the issue affects one's daughter--I suppose the matter is different. I'm glad to say that we negotiated our way through questions about cultural differences, and when the two families met many months later, they became good friends.

Gaz also took me to his sister's flat to introduce me to her. Dionne had a daughter who was five years old. Nicole was incredibly sweet, and took great pleasure in drawing me several pictures, while Dionne introduced us to Nicole's new baby sister. Vanessa was only three months old, and as Gaz and I sat together on the sofa, Dionne handed her tiny baby over to Gaz to hold. When it came to my turn, I was quite nervous. I hadn't held a baby for ages. As I sat cradling her, I heard a sudden clicking sound and saw a flash of light. Dionne had taken a photograph of Gaz, me and the baby. She then announced with a mischievous giggle, that she was going to blackmail us, by sending the picture into the college, and tell them that the child was ours. Dionne's partner was white British, and so this scenario could have been true. We both laughed, wondering what type of reaction there would be if Dionne had gone through with it.

Irene loved sewing, and had her own sewing room filled with various machines and other equipment. The day before I was due to return home, she called me down, and proceeded to take out a tape measure and measure me. I didn't ask why, but that evening, she again called for me and presented me with a skirt she had made for me. Now, I hear you cry, "a skirt!" Yes, you would be right, but on this one occasion, and I firmly reiterate on this one occasion, I was so impressed at her talent, and kindness, that I did actually wear it.

The following day, Gaz escorted me to Euston station, where I boarded a train to Preston, to be met by Mum and Dad. The journey seemed very long, as I worried about the type of reception I would receive upon my return. The weather was warm, but would I feel the frost in the air, or would love cover a multitude of student sins? I'm pleased to say that the latter was true. Mum had imagined a London suburb with pedestrians armed with knives and shot guns on every corner, and police cars proliferating in the rush-hour traffic. Indeed on my return, she was so glad to see me arrive safely, that the upset of the previous weekend seemed to be forgotten.

The summer holidays were now in full swing, only this time things were to be slightly different. Mum and Dad had booked two weeks holiday just for the two of them, and Kirsten went on holiday with school friends at the same time. Coincidently, Auntie Jenny and Uncle Brian also had two weeks holiday, and so there was just Nanna and I left. Auntie Jenny asked us if we would stay at their house to look after the place, and so off we went. I had stayed at their home many times, so had no problem getting around while staying there. A couple of days after we arrived, Gaz joined us, accompanied by Chris. Nanna didn't mind at all; in fact she was brilliant. She enjoyed our company. She would cook our meals, and in return, we would take her out in the evening. Nanna was always very out-going and very young for her age, and so being with her was no hardship. Often we would walk down the road to the pub, and keep her in sherry for the evening, although she didn't need a drink to have a laugh. Nanna had a great sense of humour, and we laughed our way throughout those few days.

The weather that summer was fantastic, and we spent most of our time in the garden. Dad had transported Nanna and I in the car to Auntie Jenny's house and so I had taken my stereo with me. We found a long extension lead, and put the stereo out in the garden. Of course there was a substantial amount of Al Jarreau albums to see us through the holidays, and the one album which always reminds me of that summer is "Breaking Away". Gaz and I also found our competitive streaks when we began playing each other at the board game Othello. We became quite addicted to this pastime, and sometimes games would last for over three hours, and then we would often experience a feeling of anti-climax, when the game would end in a draw. It turned out that we were quite a good match for each other when flexing our Othello brains. It's very rare, to find me quite impressed with myself but, at that time, I was aware that Gaz had been the College chess champion on many occasions, and I was fully expecting him to thrash me every time.

When everyone returned from their respective holidays, Gaz and I went to stay at my parents' house for another week, and this was then followed by another few days down in London at Gaz's house. We spent the whole holiday together, and had a wonderful time, but then suddenly, summer was over. Before I knew it, I was packing my things ready to go back to Worcester for my last year of school. My term began in early September, whereas Gaz wasn't due to attend university until early October. Going back to the college without Gaz was so strange. I remember unpacking my case in my room and feeling very gloomy. It felt like all the excitement and fun had disappeared. I still had plenty of friends, but not my best friend.

It was all change at the College again that term, as the rest of the girls from Chorleywood had transferred to Worcester. Some new mobile classrooms had suddenly appeared on the front drive, and building work was due to begin on accommodation blocks.

Mr. Smith, the head of pastoral care for the boys had left the previous term and that meant that the accommodation where he had lived with his family, which was directly above our study bedrooms had been left vacant. This area had been converted into five bedrooms, a kitchen, and a large living room. Some of the girls from my year moved up to these new rooms, and Leah's room was directly above mine. Together, we worked out our own little system of communication. If either of us wanted to call the other for a coffee or just a chat, then we would have no problem in letting each other know. Leah would simply stamp on her floor, which was my ceiling, or I would take my white cane, and bang it on my ceiling. More often than not, it usually meant that a hot beverage was ready and waiting. A TV was put upstairs in the living room, and it was great to have the extra space to chill out. The first lesson on a Monday morning would always find Leah and me drinking coffee in the kitchen. Neither of us had a lesson at that time, and it was a good way to ease ourselves in to the new week. We would chat about what we had done over the previous weekend, as the weekends would always find me travelling to see Gaz.

Gaz had chosen to study computer science in Wolverhampton, and this had worked out quite well for us as it meant that he wasn't too far away from Worcester. It did however feel miles and miles away to me on most days. We used to spend hours and hours chatting on the pay phone each evening, it's a wonder we got any study done at all. It is true to say that I probably got much more work done than during the previous year. However, the time did seem to drag all through the week. I continued with my usual routine consisting of study time, socialising in the coffee bar, and trips to town or to the pub with friends, but it really was never the same without Gaz.

Each Friday afternoon at four o'clock when lessons ended, I would collect my already packed bag from my room, and wait for my taxi to take me to the railway station. I took a train to Birmingham, and then from Birmingham New Street, I would take another train to Wolverhampton. It took around an hour to get from Worcester to Birmingham, and a further twenty minutes on the train to Wolverhampton. I often engaged in interesting conversations during those Friday afternoon journeys. People would often ask inquisitive questions about how a blind person managed to get around independently. I once met a man who was an actor, who would often make the same journey as me. He would tell me many stories about his career, and the interesting people he had met. A member of staff from the college lived a few miles outside Worcester, and commuted into the city every day. He would often chat to me on my journey, and as he didn't teach me for any of my lessons, I felt a little less awkward. He was also visually impaired, and once related a funny story of how he had been riding a bike around a holiday site, and managed to ride it straight into a crowded swimming pool!

Gaz would always be waiting for me when I arrived at the student accommodation block where he stayed. I usually rang my parents to let them know I'd arrived safely, and then after I'd dumped my bag down, we'd go out for something to eat and then for a drink at the local pub. During my first visit, Gaz gave me a tour of the town centre. At the top end of Dudley Street, was Pizza Land, and this became a place where we could often be found. As we made our way through the busy shopping centre on a Saturday morning, I suddenly heard a lady shouting in a distinctive Black Country accent, "Come on ladies, get your Danish pastries!" Gaz loved Danish pastries; so naturally, we had to stop to purchase one. I say one, because they turned out to be huge horseshoe shaped offerings covered in icing, and one was more than enough for both of us. We also discovered a little coffee shop that served gorgeous scones topped with jam and fresh cream, which we would wash down with mugs of hot chocolate. This also became a place we would often frequent.

I got to know many of Gaz's new friends, and would often go out with them on Saturday evenings to have a curry, or hear some live music. The lifestyle was again very different from being back at Worcester, but I just wanted to enjoy being with Gaz, and didn't mind all the changes.

In stark contrast with the train journey on a Friday, when I would be excited to be with Gaz, came the misery of the Monday morning journey back to Worcester. I would get up around six, in order to arrive back at college before lessons began. I still have vivid memories of shivering on Wolverhampton station, waiting for my train to arrive. Nearly every week, a female member of staff at the station who must have been in her early sixties would approach me and exclaim, "Come on young wench, take hold of my arm," and then lead me to the train. When she first greeted me with this expression, I wasn't greatly impressed, until I learned that apparently, it is a term of endearment among Black Country folk. The journey always seemed to be twice as long as the outward one, but eventually, I would arrive in Worcester, and find my way to a taxi which would drive me back to college. As I related earlier, the first important appointment of the day was to join Leah upstairs in the kitchen for coffee. She would want to know what I had been doing over the weekend, and I would catch up on all the gossip that I'd missed. Leah was always a really good friend to me, and managed to cheer me up. She got on well with Gaz too, and seemed to understand how difficult it was for us being apart for most of the time. During those first few weeks, I was surprised at how many members of staff actually approached me and posed the question as to whether I was worried about Gaz meeting other girls, and the possibility of him starting a new relationship. Rather arrogantly I suppose, each time my answer was the same. I wasn't at all worried, I felt sure that we would be ok.

That first term eased along towards Christmas, and I got into my routine of college life during the week, and gate-crashing the university life at the weekend. Everything was going quite well until one particular bad weekend. This wasn't just a bad hair day. it was a weekend I was lucky to get through alive! After purchasing my ticket at the railway station one Friday afternoon, I tapped my way across the platform with my white cane. It was only a short distance from the ticket office to the bench where I sat waiting for my train, and the station was usually fairly quiet. On this particular day, there were more people around than normal, which meant I had to snake my way around them. As my cane hit an obstacle in front of me, I had to decide whether to move around it to the left or to the right. Unfortunately for me, I made the decision to go right. Because I had to avoid waiting passengers on my route, I must have lost track of my sense of direction, and suddenly I went flying through the air and landed on the track. Realising immediately what I'd done, I rather shakily stood up and hauled myself back up on to the platform as worried spectators hurried to help me. I was extremely lucky that no trains had been due, and made my way to a seat as people fussed around me. I felt like the biggest plonker in the world. I had done no serious damage, but people kept on fussing, and I just wanted to disappear. I did acquire a very sore bruised back for my poor decision making, but didn't tell the concerned crowd. It didn't matter how much that hurt, it was my pride that had taken the biggest thumping. And, in answer to your enquiring minds, I did wait for assistance before venturing further than the ticket office on future journeys.

My misfortune continued the following evening when a group of us went out to a concert, travelling together in a minibus. On arrival, there must have been a misunderstanding between the driver and the students sitting closest to him. The bus had long bench seats which were side facing, and we were required to use the two back doors to get out. When the bus stopped, Terry, one of our sighted friends, and I began to alight. Unfortunately for us, even though we had been told to get out, as I made my way down the first step the bus kept reversing. I nearly went flying through the air once more. Everyone shouted for the driver to stop, which he did, but as we stepped on to the street, the bus started moving towards us again. I have never run backwards as quickly as I did that night. As Terry grabbed on to my arm, we dashed across to the pavement. Again, thankfully, I was unhurt, but if ever I had a reason to become rather paranoid, it was then. By the time I was travelling back to college on the Monday, I was glad the weekend was over. Thinking that was the end of my rather eventful weekend, I sat back and waited for my arrival in Worcester. How wrong one can be? Minutes later, the train stopped and we experienced a lengthy delay. As we all sat and waited, and waited, we were to learn that there had been a fire on the train. Luckily, it had been a relatively minor incident, and when the matter had been dealt with, we continued our journey, but I was very pleased to get into my taxi and leave the memories of the weekend far behind me. I did, however, have some explaining to do when I returned to college over an hour late. I was rather worried about telling the member of staff on duty, but was very relieved when they were sympathetic, and were more concerned about my well-being. I certainly didn't want to experience another weekend like that one. Maybe it was Gaz's turn to come and visit me instead.

As Christmas drew closer, we started making plans for our sixth form Christmas party. This would take place upstairs in the girls' accommodation, and it turned out to be a party to remember. I was surprised to find that on this one occasion only, we were allowed to have alcohol. This was normally strictly forbidden in the college, but as it would be our last party, we were allowed to choose what drinks we liked, and the college was to pay the bill. Not only that, but they also provided some very nice food. Gaz came over to stay that weekend, as did some of the other boys who had left at the end of the previous year. As we both ascended the stairs, I remember hearing the music playing, and as we entered, one girl grabbed Gaz, and a guy grabbed me, and we all ended up exchanging a kiss under the mistletoe. No members of staff were present at the party, although we knew they weren't far away. We all had a really great time. We drank a lot, ate a lot, and most of us probably regretted it a lot the following morning. It really was worth it though, and although I did have a few drinks, I do remember clearly everything that happened. Towards the end of the party, we all danced to a slow song. As I danced with Gaz, it was one of those times when you just get caught up in the moment and everything else just drifts away. As the music stopped, I suddenly became aware that Gaz and I were in the middle of the room with a large circle of people joining hands around us. Needless to say, I was just a tad embarrassed! As the party came to a close, it was time for the boring stuff - clearing up. It wasn't just the cans, bottles, plates and left-over food we had to clear, but also the odd person who had rather overindulged. We found one guy lying on the floor, hugging an empty bottle of Bacardi, and that's as much as I'm prepared to divulge. I'm pleased to say that there were no lasting casualties, and I suspect that there are many other students who still have happy memories of that particular evening.

I knew that Christmas was going to be special that year because Gaz was going to join me and the rest of the family over at Auntie Jenny's. We all packed in to the house and had really good fun, even though it meant that some of us had to sleep on either the living room or dining room floor. Kirsten and I slept in the living room, and we awoke at a reasonable time on Christmas morning. The days of us waking Mum and Dad up at five o'clock, begging to see if Santa had been were long gone as we were much more concerned about getting a good lie in till at least eight o'clock. We couldn't stay in bed for too long because our bedding needed to be cleared away so everyone could use the living room. When Kirsten went to get a shower, Gaz came to wish me merry Christmas, and to give me my present. He handed me a small box, and when I opened it, I found an engagement ring. I had been right about it being a great Christmas day. We certainly had a lot to celebrate that day, and celebrate we did. We stayed for a few days and spent many an hour sitting around the dining table eating good food and laughing together. During the day, we would often take a long walk in an attempt to burn off all those extra calories. In the evening we would all crowd around the TV and watch a family Christmas film. Of course we couldn't watch without the obligatory large tin of Quality Street".

From that year onward, Gaz and I adopted a new routine in regard to Christmas and New Year. As we had spent Christmas week with my family, we decided to spend New Year with Gaz's family. The following year we would reverse that and spend Christmas with Gaz's family and New Year with mine. This would be a process that would run for many years to come. Although we had a great time with Auntie Jenny and the rest of the family, I'm sure it must have been quite strange for Gaz to be away from home over Christmas. It was the same for me over the New Year, but it was also a good deal of fun. Whether it was Christmas or New Year, at Gaz's house we would always be treated to a special Caribbean Christmas dinner. The day before, the house would be full of the most wonderful aromas. Turkey and beef infused with all kinds of herbs and spices, and oh, the smell of the cake Irene would make – mmm…!

It was always a struggle to squeeze the whole family around the kitchen table. The meal was always a choice of beef, turkey, baked potatoes, roast potatoes, rice and peas, various different vegetables, and fresh salad.

Once we'd made our way through that particular mountain of food, we tackled pudding. This was Irene's speciality sponge cake, covered in custard, and drizzled with Caribbean white rum. By the time we had finished, we were so stuffed that we each required a winch to lift us from our seats.

I returned to college a few days later wearing my engagement ring, but didn't make a big deal of it. Of course, I couldn't have been happier, but I was aware that there would be a mixed reaction from both students and staff. Some thought it was wonderful and rushed to congratulate me, while others were distinctly underwhelmed. During one particular R.E. lesson, our teacher was busy dictating notes to us and we were furiously bashing them out on our Braillers when he suddenly stopped. He had notice my ring, and in a rather surprised tone exclaimed, "Jane, are you sporting sparklers?" I had never heard that expression before, and it took me a moment to realise what he was referring to. When I quietly replied, "Ah, yes sir," I was pleased to find that he cordially offered his congratulations. A couple of days later, he passed me as I walked along the main corridor, and asked of me, "Jane, when Gary proposed to you, did he get down on one knee?" I was curious as to why he needed to know that information, and replied

151

by saying, "Why do you ask sir?" He answered me immediately, "Because if he did, then when he did it, you and he would have then been around the same height!" I suppose he wasn't far from the truth, as I am five feet four, and Gaz is six foot four. I turned to him and with a wry smile said, "Thank you for that sir." As I carried on my way, I heard his giggles echoing down the corridor. I didn't mind; better a little well-meaning light hearted humour, than a sharp disdainful remark. Some people thought that we were too young or rather silly. They were entitled to their opinions but for us it was different. Yes, we still had to get through university, and it would be a considerable time before we could afford to get married, but it was about making a commitment to each other, and all these years later, neither of us have any regrets about it.

18. On My Travels

As well as the rather unwelcoming distraction of looming A-Level exams, we also were required to travel the country attending interviews for our chosen universities. Unfortunately for me, the more I considered this prospect, the less I wanted to go. There wasn't really any other choice though. It was what was expected of us, but to me it felt like running on a never ending educational treadmill. Occasionally, I would find myself lying on my bed pondering over my years of education. From that awful day when I sat staring down at the work I couldn't complete, to the stage I was at then, I could honestly say that I'd worked hard at each school I'd attended and given it my best shot. Ok, maybe last year I'd done more socialising than normal, but I'd partied hard, and worked hard. My grades were perfectly acceptable, and I hadn't done a bad job so far. This year however, it was a different story. Yes, I had more time to get my head down and study, but sentimental idiot that I am, the fact that I missed Gaz so much was causing me to be rather less motivated, and my grades were slipping. Staff began to make comments, and I knew that I needed to knuckle down. Despite this dip, I knew that I could rectify the situation if I tried, but, all the same, I felt academically burnt out. I knew my parents were keen for me to attend university, so it was time to soldier on. Anyway, if I didn't go, then what else would I do? I didn't have a clue, and so without really saying anything to anyone, I simply kept plodding on that treadmill.

I was happy that none of my university visits impinged upon my weekends in Wolverhampton. Gaz had joined a band, playing his bass guitar, and weekends often meant live gigs. I recall one evening when I went to hear him play at a venue in Dudley. It didn't finish until late in the evening, and then we travelled back to Wolverhampton on a coach with a load of other students. Someone suggested that we should all go for a curry. I was sure that everywhere would be closed as it was around two in the morning, but to my surprise I was wrong. I thought it was quite comical as we all sat eating curry until three A.M. During a different weekend, we decided to book some time at a recording studio used by many of the students. I wonder if anyone reading this book remembers "The Sam Sharpe Project". We spent four hours recording a song in which Gaz played bass and keyboard, I played flute, and we both sang. I had never been in a recording studio before and found the whole process fascinating. The only slot left was on a

Friday evening at ten o'clock, and so it was after two in the morning when we walked back with our treasured recording.

As we eased into February 1987, Valentine's Day fell on a Sunday which was great for us. It was also the beginning of the half term holiday, and so I spent the weekend with Gaz before travelling to be with my parents. On that Valentine's Day, Gaz knocked on the door of the room where I was staying, and presented me with a bunch of red roses. I was delighted. I had never been given roses before. The following day, we both walked to the station together. It is quite funny looking back, because as I sat waiting for the train with my suitcase, guitar, and my bunch of roses, another girl about the same age as me sat with her boyfriend also clutching a bunch of roses. I was sad to be leaving Gaz, and as the other girl and I got on the train, we both leaned out of the window shouting our goodbyes and we both clung on to our flowers. She was quite tearful at having to leave her man, and she nearly started me off. The journey was uncomfortable, as there were no seats available, and I had to stand for the best part of two hours until we arrived in Preston. Lucky for me, I did manage to find a seat on the connecting train between Preston and Blackburn and, boy, did I need a seat by then. Mum and Dad were impressed at Gaz's romantic streak, and I enjoyed a few days with them before returning on the following Friday evening to once again spend the weekend with Gaz.

The time passed without any problems, and as it was the end of the half term holiday, Monday was a travel day, which meant I didn't have to return to college until the evening. This turned out to be the night when I would rather stupidly confront a lamppost and lose. I don't remember why, but I do recall that we were running late that evening when we went to catch the train back to Worcester. When I say running late, I mean it literally. Unfortunately for me, as I made my best efforts to break the four minute mile in order to be there on time, my face suddenly felt the full force of a rather resolute lamppost. I was very lucky that all my teeth remained intact, but I have to admit that the air turned a distinct shade of blue as I growled some expletives to help numb the pain, as my head rocked back. Nevertheless, in the words of Shakespeare, I was "Bloody, bold and resolute," and though battle worn, continued to make my way to the platform to catch that train. Ironically, when we did arrive, the train was late, and so there was plenty of time for me to mop the blood from my face. I must have looked a real mess. My nose and one side of my face was covered in a large graze, and there was blood everywhere. When my train pulled in,

Gaz was very reluctant to leave me. I was ok; more angry than upset. This time it wasn't a case of some bruising which could be easily covered, this time it was my face and I couldn't hide that away. It was on full display for everyone to see. It was one of those moments when I thought, "Why the hell do I have to be blind?" During my journey, many people saw me, but nobody made any comment. I must have looked like I'd been involved in a serious altercation. It makes me laugh now thinking about it, wondering what people thought, but it would be a further two weeks until my dad would see my injury, and he commented all that time later that just seeing what I had done to myself made him feel sick. Ah well, some you win.

I'm glad to say that my face healed nicely before I had to attend university interviews. The most memorable one was my trip to a teacher training college in Liverpool. Several days before I was due to attend, I made a tentative phone call to Sister Josephine at St. Vincent's to see if I could incorporate a night's stay at the school, as the journey was too long for me to return on the same day. I was excited when she gave me permission, and I packed an overnight bag in eager anticipation. I should have been looking forward to my interview, but instead, what I really cared about was a trip to my old stomping ground. I wore a broad smile as I found a seat on the train that was to take me back to Liverpool. I travelled on the day before my interview, which was scheduled for ten a.m. the following day.

I took a taxi from the station, and it wasn't long before we made our way along the drive and arrived outside the front door of St. Vincent's. I walked in to the front hall, and that distinctive smell filled the air. I breathed deeply. I was back. This was a home from home. During that visit, I would be staying in one of the senior girls' groups. I arrived not long before tea time, and after I had finished, Josie, (we had long since discarded the Miss bit), came to see me and we spent that evening together. We walked round the school, meeting up with old friends, and visiting those areas I particularly wanted to see. I was still feeling quite nervous about my interview the following day, but tried to push those thoughts aside. I took the recording Gaz and I had made a few weeks previous to play to Josie and she was very impressed. I remember her standing and listening , and then she said, "Gosh, it sounds very professional." I was pleased that she liked it, and thought nothing more of it. When it was time to get bedded down for the evening, I returned to the girls group, to get washed and changed.

When I had been a pupil at the school, I had shared a bedroom with three other girls. Me, Gemma, Dawn and Annie spent most of our time together: we were the four amigos for sure! In this group, small single rooms lined either side of a long corridor. Instead of doors, each room simply had a curtain, so even though we were all in bed, we were able to chat to each other. As we got into bed, we were allowed to chat for around half an hour before lights out, and even though it had been quite some time, I felt right at home. I knew some of the girls in the group, but there were a few I hadn't met before. During the conversation, one of the girls was talking when she suddenly lowered her voice. One of my long standing friends asked why she was whispering, and she replied that she didn't want me to hear, as I was not really part of the group. I lay there in my room, feeling just a little awkward, but then I was to hear something that stopped me in my tracks. My friend suddenly said, "Whatever you've got to say, just say it. Jane is one of us, she always has been, and she always will be!" It was one of the nicest things anyone had ever said about me. I was quite overwhelmed, and as the other girl proceeded to share what was on her mind, I wiped away the tears. I was glad to be in my own room, and glad that no-one saw me, but I was so moved that I have never forgotten that moment.

I enjoyed a very good night's sleep, before having breakfast the following morning and getting ready for the impending interview. To my surprise, it wasn't long after breakfast, when I learned that Josie had been telling the staff about the song I had recorded with Gaz. The next thing I knew, I was sitting in the chapel with the pupils from the senior school, and staff who wanted to listen to the cassette. Afterwards, many of the students whom I hadn't met before, came to say how much they had enjoyed the song. I was pleasantly surprised. Furthermore, I was not allowed to leave the building until several copies of the song had been made by various staff members. Minutes later, I was once again very reluctantly leaving St. Vincent's, having thoroughly enjoyed my time there, and wishing I could stay longer. Now it was time to visit another educational establishment: would it have the same positive impression on me, and more importantly, would I impress them?

As soon as I entered the building, I perceived a friendly welcoming atmosphere. I was taken on a tour around the college by one of the students, and then had my first interview. The course I had chosen involved studying English literature, R.E., and psychology. I survived the first interview without any problems, before joining a group of students for lunch. The afternoon however, was to be a little more eventful. My final interview of the day was in the English department. The gentleman conducting proceedings at first seemed rather frosty. I thought I was doing quite well, until he enquired of me, "What are you currently reading for pleasure?" There was a momentary pause. The truth was, I wasn't reading anything except for what was compulsory for my English Literature A-Level. When studying was over, I had other things to do rather than just reading. So I confess, I blurted out, "Emma, by Jane Austen." This was true in part. I was reading that novel, although as you already know, it would never be for pleasure. My interrogator, I mean interviewer, seemed suitably impressed. However, he then proceeded to ask me questions about the characters in the novel, and my opinions about the storyline toward the end of the novel. Luckily, I had read all of it, and was able to offer what I hoped he would consider to be constructive answers. I was sailing close to the wind though, and was glad when the interview came to a close.

I began the long journey back to Worcester, having enjoyed my mini break, and there was plenty of time to relax on the train before arriving back at college. I put on my headphones, and listened to the cassette that so many people had enjoyed, and felt a warm fuzzy feeling as I thought about my faithful friends back in Liverpool. Around three weeks later, I received a letter from the teacher training college. I was surprised to learn that I must have done something right, because they offered me a place provided I could achieve two grade D's at A-Level. I could hardly believe it. The college had a very good reputation, and this was almost too good to be true. Result!

All that travelling meant that I spent a good deal of my time on the train and I remember one particularly freezing Friday afternoon in February. I booked myself out at the staff room, and left to make my way to the station. There was snow on the ground, and I was expecting my train to be subject to some delay because of the weather conditions. Instead of shivering on the platform, I took a seat in the waiting room, where I chatted with the teacher from College whom I mentioned earlier. Unfortunately, the delay was longer than I expected, and we waited for over an hour till the train finally arrived. Again, this was long before mobile phones were the norm, but I felt sure that Gaz would realise that my late arrival would be due to the weather.

On arrival at Birmingham New Street, I was frustrated to learn that once again, my train was delayed. When I finally arrived in

Wolverhampton, I heaved a sigh of relief. That had been a marathon journey, and I was over two hours late. As I stepped out of the taxi, Gaz was there waiting for me. He gave me a huge hug, and we went to his study. He was almost in tears, and I was puzzled. What had happened? It became apparent, that he was simply extremely worried about what had happened to me despite the weather, and was so glad to see me safe and sound. It had been a long journey, and he had been really stressed out, so we decided to go for something to eat and leave the tensions of the last few hours behind us. We spent a thoroughly enjoyable evening having a meal. We didn't return back to the hall until after eleven, and went to his study to chat. All of a sudden, there was a thunderous bang on Gaz's door. When he answered it, there in front of him stood two large policemen. We were both shocked and rather embarrassed, as we listened to what they had to say.

Earlier that day, I had been reported missing by one of the staff at college, and West Mercia police force had been frantically searching for me, while I spent the entire evening at the pub oblivious to the chaos and panic. I made my apologies to the officers, explaining the story from my perspective, and they left. The next thing that crossed my mind was my parents. The college would probably have informed them what had happened, and they would certainly be frantic. Although by now it was past midnight, I ran downstairs, to call them on the pay phone. To my astonishment, they had not been told, and I apologised for waking them, and said that we would talk the following day, after we had all had a good night's sleep.

During the days that followed, I was able to piece the whole sorry story together. It had been a complete catalogue of misunderstanding, and miscommunication. This seems to be the way events unfolded. I left College as usual just after four in the afternoon, and went to the station. I met and chatted with one of the teachers from the college, in the station waiting room for over an hour until finally, our train arrived. Further delays at Birmingham, meant that I was over two hours late arriving in Wolverhampton, and Gaz was worried. He rang the college to see if I had left, and staff then began their own investigations in order to answer Gaz's question. There was a record in the staff room, of me having booked myself out for the weekend, so they were sure I was no longer in the building, and friends had confirmed this.

A member of staff had called the railway station, in the days when they could be contacted directly, and asked if I had been seen or assisted in getting aboard my train. Although I had been sitting waiting for over an hour, the person on the other end of the phone had reported that noone had seen a blind female on the station that afternoon. This set the panic wheels in motion and, not long after, the police had been informed of my disappearance. Because of my disability, I was regarded as a vulnerable individual. A full description was given to the police, and the search for my whereabouts began. News soon spread through the college, and pupils and staff gathered in one of the offices, waiting for news of further developments. Students were quizzed as to whether I had given them any indication as to where I was going for the weekend. Had they noticed anything different about me? Were they sure I was definitely going to see Gaz as normal?

When I had arrived in Wolverhampton, blissfully unaware of what was happening, Gaz was so relieved to see me arrive safely, that he completely forgot to ring college and inform them. So off we went to enjoy our evening. Meanwhile back at college, the office was now packed with curious students. Members of staff were busy making phone calls to hospitals, to see if I had been admitted, and to anywhere else they could possibly think of which might have useful information. At ten pm, everyone was sent to their rooms, and told that they would be informed if they received any news. It wasn't until the following morning that everyone heard that I was safe. What a mess! Now, thanks to mobile phones, that type of episode would probably be avoided.

Before I knew it, the Easter holidays had been and gone and I was dreading my exams. I had been given my exam timetable, and had a date firmly imprinted upon my mind. The 21st of June was the day of my last exam, and I would be free: Free from study, free from lessons, and free to leave the college and enjoy a lovely long summer. There was however, much to tackle before that date. A couple of weeks before the exams began, I stayed at college over the weekends to study instead of visiting Gaz. This was a huge sacrifice on my part, and I hoped that it would pay off when the results came in. The events of those last few weeks are quite hazy. I have vivid memories of standing outside the examination rooms, waiting to take my place at my desk, pondering over how difficult the exam papers would be.

When the day I had been waiting for did arrive, and I walked out of my last examination, I punched the air and went off to start packing my things. Over the next few days, there was much to do. A shelf full of cassette tapes containing notes, plenty of books, and various files and folders needed to be returned to the correct teachers. My sports kit was taken back to the P.E. teacher, and my room needed to be completely cleared of my clothes and other possessions. For the very last time, I began putting stuff into my trunk. I didn't intend using it again and we could now get rid of that old thing. So, on a quiet Sunday morning, we loaded the car, and I booked myself out of the college for the last time. I had been upstairs to say goodbye to my friends, and Gaz had travelled down from Wolverhampton the night before to travel home with Dad and me. As we drove out of the college grounds, I considered that on the whole, I had really enjoyed my time there and I'd met the best friend I'd ever had, who was now my fiancé. Now it was a case of waiting for those all important A-Level results.

19. When Lancashire Met Jamaica

There must have been Jamaican influences on my Dad's side of the family long before Gaz came on the scene. My Mum's side of the family always regarded being on time for something as being at least an hour early. However, my Dad's Mum had a timing completely of her own, which I suppose is best articulated as late. I noticed very quickly, that Jamaicans don't do early, they do "soon come!" which can be rephrased as "When I arrive, you'll see me!" The best example I can give you of this is of the night before our wedding. Gaz and I got married in Worcester, and so each of our families had to travel a considerable distance. My family arrived three days before the event, while Gaz's family said they would hire a minibus, and arrive for dinner, the evening before the wedding. We waited patiently for them, but nobody appeared. Several concerned phone calls were made during the course of the evening, with each one ending with us being told that they were just about to leave London, but this continued long after we'd finished our meal. , They finally turned up at six the following morning, and had a quick kip before breakfast was served. More about that later!

A similar situation occurred when Gaz's sister, Dionne, got married. We had spent the whole morning getting ready, and we thought the fact that we were all ready by the time the taxis arrived was a huge accomplishment. If we had all marched out straight away it would have been a miracle of grand proportions, but that would have been too good to be true. Just as we were stepping outside, Gaz's Mum Irene turned and shouted, "Oh! me forget to put on me bra!" and dashed back upstairs. We finally arrived at the church in a bustling fluster around twenty minutes later, to find we were the only group to get there later than the bride.

It was the language, or should I say the curious phrases we each had to get used to which caused the greatest moments of perplexity, and mirth. Let's start with expressions of surprise:

In these moments a Jamaican may say, "Kiss mi neck!", "Me fart!", and the most unfathomable, "Blouse and skirt!" Don't ask me to explain; it's not for me to question. Gaz was equally flummoxed when he heard a Lancastrian say in the same situation, "By the left!" No, I don't understand it either, and I'm the one from Lancashire.

It's funny the things you say without even thinking about it, until someone else finds it to be completely baffling. It is no longer the case with my generation, but with my parents and previous generations, it is a term of endearment to refer to a loved one as "cock" or "cockie". You can understand why our discerning generation quietly decided to ditch the phrase, but my parents and many others still use it. "Morning cock," or "Are you ok cockie?" was something I heard on a daily basis when I was growing up.

We have specific instructions pertaining to the illumination of one's home in Lancashire. This is specifically the case when making the distinction between lamps and other lighting. When using the main light especially in a lounge, we always refer to that light as "the big light". People all over the county could be heard saying, "Put big light on." While we're on the subject of the lounge, the main place where all the family sit together to watch TV, a curious code has been constructed. A request to turn up the volume would be, "Bring it in." Whereas if the T.V. was too loud, someone would shout, "Knock it down."

Gaz nearly choked on his beer one night as we were having a meal with my family. Mum was describing an unfortunate event that had taken place that day. She was telling how she had nearly fallen flat on her face, but the words she used were, "I nearly went full length!" He was distinctly unimpressed by our attempts to replace the word until with while. "Gaz, 'ave some of these crisps, they'll put you on while lunch." I found it all as funny as he did, because for me, it was second nature, and I really hadn't noticed what we were saying. After dinner, or tea as we called it, (for me it was always breakfast, dinner and tea,) Nanna would get up and announce, "I'll just side pots." that refers to the process of clearing the plates, and washing-up.

One of the terms which required explaining to me, was one used in moments of sudden amazement. The expression is "e-e!" pronounced as in "bed" or "fed". It wasn't long however until I started to use the phrase without thinking, and Irene and the family found this thoroughly amusing, especially as I appeared to know the correct context in which to use it. That reminds me of a time when we all nearly wet ourselves laughing. Jamaicans like to kiss their teeth, making a distinctive sound, at times of vexation or frustration. One of Dionne's children was running around her home, still wearing a nappy, and barely able to speak more than a few words when the incident happened. Dionne had given her daughter a few sharp words after she had done something naughty, but instead of the small child showing any remorse, she turned and kissed her teeth. I couldn't believe it, and ran out of the room to laugh uncontrollably. The timing was perfect, but how did she know how to do that at such a tender age?

There were some puzzling moments when it came to food. A much loved dish in Lancashire is meat and potato pie, or just potato pie is it is usually called. When Gaz was first offered one, he wasn't too enthusiastic about trying it. As far as he was concerned what was the big deal about filling pastry with just potato? He soon changed his mind when he heard about the meat part, and regularly eats them now. He also thought it strange at my family's use of the word "toffee". He soon learned that this didn't just refer to toffee but all other varieties of confectionery too. "Do you want some toffees?" could in fact cover everything from boiled sweets to chocolate. It's one thing talking about food, but a completely different challenge when having to eat a dish you've never tried before, and to be frank, would rather not bother with. On special occasions, Jamaicans eat curried goat. Irene had made some during a visit to her house, and proudly placed the plate in front of me. I have to confess that I was so glad when she left Gaz and me to eat together, as she had some sewing to get on with. Just the smell turned my stomach. I can't possibly begin to describe the smell or the taste, but in my opinion it was nothing short of truly vile. People often refer to the neighbour from hell, but this was definitely the dish from hell, no question. I've been in situations occasionally when I have been given food which hasn't been to my liking, but what Gaz calls my Chorleywood training, has caused me to clear my plate triumphantly. This time, I was happy to admit defeat.

There were, however, plenty of dishes I did enjoy. Some of my favourites were jerk chicken, beef with rice and peas, and patties. Oh patties! Irene made the most wonderful patties I have ever tasted. Filled with meat, fish or vegetables, and herbs and spices, they are similar to a pasty, but much, much better. Bun is also another which gets the thumbs up! This is a kind of mixture between sponge cake and fruit loaf, and is usually sliced up, buttered, and eaten with slices of cheese. There was never a shortage of wonderful food at Irene's house, and if we went out for the day, Gaz would have to drag a huge bag around full of picnic treats.

One summer day, Irene came home and announced that she had purchased four tickets for us all to go on a coach trip to the seaside with several other Jamaican people. We left the house a couple of days later, very early one Sunday morning, and walked to the place where we were to be picked up. We stood waiting in the warm sunshine, and

Gaz heaved a sigh as he dropped his bag containing our food for the day. I was most amused when, instead of a coach, a London bus drew up, and we found our seats. Irene's little granddaughter also travelled with us, and was very excited. The bus was full, and very noisy, as we made our way out of London, and travelled toward Southsea for the day. I'm pretty sure that it was around eight o'clock in the morning when we left, and the journey took around four hours.

We sat near the front of the bus, and opposite us sat a lady who had spread several bags on the seat next to her. At the time, we didn't think anything of it, presuming that like Irene, she had brought a wealth of food to share with her friends. When eleven o'clock came, I was to learn that this was not entirely true. I heard her place her bags on the floor, and then the clanking of glass bottles as she proceeded to lay several bottles of alcoholic drinks on the seat beside her. There, right in front of me, was the bus minibar. Moments later, the lady leaned forward and said, "You want some rum?" and thrust a disposable cup into my hand which contained a very large measure. Wait though! This wasn't just any rum. This was overproof Jamaican rum! Mind blowing, foot fumbling, tongue twisting, rocket fuel, and it was only eleven in the morning! Not wishing to seem rude, I mustered a nervous smile, and said, "That's very kind, thank you." Needless to say, as far as I remember, we had a very enjoyable day - I think!

Irene was a woman who was very talented in many areas. She was an excellent seamstress, and a brilliant cook, but I have to say, not so when it came to naming her pets. We once visited her to find that she had acquired a cat. When I enquired as to its name, she smiled and said, "Me just call it di cat!" Well, I suppose anything is better than Boo.

I guess that the phrase Gaz struggled most to interpret, was uttered one day by my Dad. I can't really remember what type of task Gaz was attempting, but he was certainly making hard work of it because my Dad shouted, "Eeh Gaz, that's like trying ta empty cut wit kit lid!" Gaz immediately stopped and laughed, before asking, "What on earth does that mean?" A cut means a canal, and a kit lid, refers to the lid of a folding cup, kept in a soldier's kit bag. In effect what he was saying was that it was like trying to empty all the water out of the canal with a tiny little lid. In other words, "You're really making hard work of that." Ah, the words of the gradely Lancashire folk. While we are on the subject, I need to make you aware of a little known fact outside of Lancashire. The county and its people are very special and this is endorsed by God himself. Let me tell you why. It is common for loved ones to refer to each other as "our Gaz", or "Our Kirsten". When Jesus taught us how to pray in the bible, He clearly stated that "This is how to pray," "OUR Father, who art in heaven."

20. Out in the real world

A good deal of my summer holiday was spent organising myself ready for my first semester at Wolverhampton. Although I really liked Liverpool, what mattered to me at the time was simply being with Gaz, and so all I wanted was a place there. There were so many things to do, like applying for my grant, for special equipment from the Royal National Institute of the Blind, and making arrangements for accommodation. When I finally did get my results, and secured my place at my chosen establishment, we made plans for a marathon day of driving. Dad took Gaz, Nanna and me firstly down to London, to collect some paperwork and my grant for my equipment. Then we drove to Wolverhampton, to pay my deposit for my room in the same accommodation block as Gaz. Dad must have driven for miles that day, I remember we were all very tired at the end of it. Then began the headache of buying my equipment; I needed a laptop computer, with a screenreader. For those of you who are unfamiliar with this, I will explain. Some special software is required to be downloaded on to the computer in order to produce synthetic speech. Whatever is typed into the machine, can then be read back, so that a blind person can use a computer successfully. I would need the computer in order to type my assignments, and make notes during lectures. I tried out so many different devices before finally deciding on the correct one for my needs, and I became quite weary of the task. Once I had made my choice, things were coming together, and there wasn't much time left before I was making my way on the train, armed with a large suitcase, a backpack, and my laptop bag.

My journey from Blackburn to Wolverhampton was, I'm glad to say, distinctly uneventful, and around three in the afternoon, I stood at the taxi rank, waiting for a cab to take me to the hall of residence on the campus, just outside the town centre. The day was sunny, and I stood there waiting, musing over a wealth of mixed emotions. I was elated at the thought of being able to see Gaz every day, but distinctly underwhelmed at the prospect of beginning another long three years of study. For the best part of the last nine years, I had lived in an environment where everything was geared toward my needs. I had been surrounded by a wealth of specialist equipment, and teachers with specialist knowledge and skills in the area of visual impairment. Now however, things would be vastly different. I was out in the real world, and it would be up to me, to negotiate my way through that sighted world, and the prospect was more than just a little daunting.

Eventually, my taxi arrived, and we drove through the busy streets, over to my hall of residence. As I ascended the stone stairs, and opened the front door, I told myself to remain positive; I needed to give this my best shot. I gave my name to the caretaker on duty, who presented me with a key, and the number of my room. He was an elderly gentleman with a broad Black Country accent, and a deep gravelly voice. He was however, a really nice chap, very helpful, and always cheery. He led me up the stairs and proceeded to show me where my room was located at the end of a long corridor on the first floor. There were six floors in the building, and as the lift was more than often out of order, I'm glad that I didn't have to trudge up and down all those stairs every day. With a friendly smile, he left me to unpack, and get used to my new surroundings. So here I was, at the beginning of a new chapter, my head full of questions about how the next few days would unfold.

My room was quite small, around seven feet wide, and 10 feet long. I had a small locker, a desk, a wardrobe and a sink in addition to my bed. At the end of the corridor was a toilet block with a bath and next door to that was a large kitchen. I can't say I made much use of the kitchen. It was always full of dirty crockery and utensils, in the typical student manner. On the occasions when I did attempt to use the fridge, I would return to find my stuff had been used. So began a diet of soup, pot noodles, and anything else I could make in my room with the use of a kettle. Luckily, there was a chippy and a pub just down the road, so it wasn't all bad. I quickly got to know the girls along the corridor, and some of Gaz's friends, some of whom I already knew from the previous year when I had visited at the weekends.

On that first night, Gaz took me over to the student union building, and we spent some time in the bar. I remember standing in a huge noisy crowd of people. The sound was so deafening, I could hardly hear what Gaz was saying. People stood shoulder to shoulder, jostling for some space, and infrequently, I would hear the sound of beer spilling on the floor as people pushed through the crowd. Some of Gaz's friends told me about different groups and societies I could join during that first week, which opened up a whole new social life for me. However, I was blissfully unaware of the obstacles I would face the following day.

My accommodation was around ten minutes' walk away from the main site, where I would need to attend lectures. The course I had chosen was a new one, and allowed me to combine three different subjects. On the first day, armed with my white cane and laptop bag, I tentatively made my way to the lecture theatre. Each new student, was appointed a personal tutor. This was a member of staff to whom they could specifically go, if they needed any extra help, or were experiencing any problems. I managed to find myself a seat in the crowded and noisy room, and waited. Various members of staff were sitting around the room, and at intervals, would call out a student's name. There then followed a dialogue between student and staff member, in order to introduce themselves, and get to know each other. I have to admit, that I felt very lonely as I sat there in that crowded room. It's not always easy as a blind person, to make the first point of contact with someone. You can't just glance around a room to seek out a friendly face, or break boldly into someone else's conversation. I thought to myself, "Give things time, it's only the first day." I didn't know anything about my tutor. Would the person be male or female? How would they react to my disability? It wasn't to be long before I would find out.

I stood up quickly when I heard my name called from a gentleman's voice far over to my left. I struggled to negotiate my way around students, chairs, and tables, but finally made it. At no point did he make any effort to assist me, and when I finally made my approach, he thumped his hand down heavily on the seat a couple of feet away from him without saying a word. I awkwardly located my chair and sat down feeling very embarrassed. The atmosphere was more than frosty. We sat a couple of feet apart, like two large magnets that were strongly repelling each other. I have never experienced such hostility from a person before or since, and an awkward silence fell before he introduced himself. This must have been the shortest dialogue of the day, as after a couple of questions, he told me I could go. As I arose from my seat, I was quite shell shocked. He gave me the impression that he found my very presence to be completely repulsive. As I walked slowly back to my room, I was very angry. How dare he speak to me in such a manner without getting to know me. I really hoped that not everyone had the same attitude. Later, when I told Gaz about what had happened, he tried to reassure me. He related how one of the staff in the department where he studied, had once said to him, "We're not used to dealing with freaks like you!" Gaz however, had a personal tutor who was brilliant. A really friendly approachable gentleman, who was always happy to help. Indeed, Gaz often said that he could not have managed the course without him.

I'm glad to say, that the rest of the staff I came into contact with were perfectly amiable. They offered to provide me with photocopies of hand-outs so I could scan them and transfer the notes on to my computer, and made provision for me to sit at the front of the lecture theatre, so that I could make a clear audio recording to take away with me. Another difficulty I grappled with at that time was mobility. I needed some time to learn my way around the main campus in Wolverhampton, but I was surprised to learn that I would have to travel to Dudley by bus to attend other lectures. What a headache! It really was. Now I needed to learn my way around Dudley, and the other buildings. On several occasions I experienced the following difficulties. I arrived at my lecture, to learn that the venue had been changed and we were required to travel to Dudley. A group of us then boarded a bus, and located the correct room, only to find a note explaining that the lecture was on a different site in Wolverhampton. We took the bus back and found the room, by which time, the lecture had almost finished. I found the whole process immensely frustrating, not to mention exhausting. On one occasion, I found myself running across the campus after undergoing the process I have just outlined, when the person I was following, forgot to tell me about a flight of stairs going down. Although I was behind her, I reached the bottom long before she did. As I rubbed my then sprained ankle, I thought to myself, "Stuff this malarky for a game of soldiers!" The site's first aid staff member, checked me out; bandaged me up, and drove me back to my hall, where I limped up the stairs, and went to my room.

At the weekend Gaz and I always found some time to relax. Saturday morning would usually find us in our favourite coffee shop having a hot chocolate. We would then buy a pasty and a Danish pastry to take back for lunch. Only a few hundred yards away from our hall, was the Wolverhampton Wanderers football ground. Whether you liked football or not, when there was a home game, you could clearly hear the singing and shouting of the fans. It didn't bother me. I actually quite enjoyed hearing them. Occasionally on a Saturday evening, we would go out for a curry. Once we were celebrating my birthday, and had treated ourselves to a three course meal, with several drinks. When Gaz went to pay, much to our surprise, he was told that a couple who had been dining in the restaurant, but had already left had paid our bill. We couldn't believe it! Anyway, if you ever end up reading this book, "Thanks!"

When I was at Worcester College, I had learned that it was a bit of a tradition among the sixth form boys to listen to "The Archers" on Radio 4. I had never given the programme a second thought until then, but once I got into listening, it was better than I had expected. In fact, I still listen now. So on a Sunday morning at the student accommodation in Wolverhampton, Gaz and I would drink coffee and listen to the omnibus of "The Archers". By this time, we had joined a church, and were both involved in the music group. Gaz played keyboards, and I the flute. The service was at three in the afternoon, and someone would always come to give us a lift over to the church. The service went on until around five o'clock. I have a vivid recollection of standing there at the end of one service. It was dark and cold outside, and everyone was putting on their coats and saying their goodbyes, before going home. As I stood and listened, I was for a moment very envious. I imagined those families going home, and snuggling on the sofa together in front of a nice warm fire. They would probably watch T.V. together, while they munched on hot buttered toast, and simply enjoy each other's company. I'd never felt it before, but in that instant, that was suddenly what I wanted. I'd spent all those years at boarding school, and now at university. A good deal of the time had been enjoyable, but family time was just the sort of thing I had missed out on all those years.

That first term seemed to be a conveyer belt of one problem after another. One of my subjects was English Literature and, as time went on, I was required to read a novel each week. This gave me more of a headache because I couldn't get the Braille books from the library sent to me quickly enough, which meant I fell far behind. By the time it got to Christmas, I was tired and thoroughly depressed. I really admire visually impaired students who managed to get a degree at that time or earlier, because things were really tough. In the days before the internet, and being able to download electronic copies of books, you had to pay other students to read to you. Now, things have really changed for the better, and life is so much easier in relation to studying. I, however, had simply had enough, and decided to leave the course. This wasn't a decision I made lightly. I spent hours laying on my bed in the evenings, wondering how I could help improve the situation. It seemed though, that the more I tried to engineer a way the worse it got. During one evening as I lay there, I experienced a feeling I'd never felt before. Everything felt dark and oppressive, like the world was closing in on me. I experienced a strong and deepening sense of doom, which really scared me. I was normally a happy optimistic kind of person. Over the years I'd negotiated my way through difficult situations, and been ok, but now this was different.

Gaz was fully aware of the difficulties I was grappling with, and was sympathetic. With the prospect of me leaving my course, I would also have to leave the accommodation. We discussed together what I would do next. I was faced with the dilemma of not knowing what to do. I knew I didn't want to stay at university, but I had no clue about what type of career I wanted. I just drew a complete blank. First things first though! The Christmas holidays were almost upon us, and how would I break the news to my parents. I came to the decision that it was better to tell them before I got home, and give them time to let the news sink in before I arrived. When I got home and walked into my bedroom, I found the bed freshly made, and covered in soft toys. Soft toys; what was all that about? As I mulled over the situation, I reached the conclusion, that Mum was fully expecting me to be coming home for good. Oh dear! Much as I love my parents, I knew at the time I had no plans to move back. It was important to me to keep my independence. It would have been too easy to just sink back into having everything done for me. No, I had already made plans but how was I going to tell them?

Gaz and I knew a gentleman who was the senior pastor of a church in Wolverhampton. He lived with his wife and two children in a large house with several rooms which he rented out to students. We made brief enquiries, and were very lucky to find that two of his rooms were vacant. We'd both had our fill of student accommodation. It was ok for a while, but the novelty soon wore off. I no longer wanted loud music at three a.m.; people running down the corridors shouting at all hours; not to mention the times when someone would knock on your door and wake you at different times of the night. We'd also experienced other interruptions during that term. Someone seemed to have a fascination for the fire alarm, or I suppose fire engines. Several times we were awoken and had to stand outside the building on a freezing cold night, waiting for the fire brigade to arrive and check out the building. After this happened several times, we were told that a fine would be imposed on all residents if it didn't stop.

For the most part, it was good fun in the hall, but there was one very sad occasion I will never forget. When one student wasn't seen for a couple of days, friends presumed that they had gone away for the weekend. However, they were surprised to find a couple of days later, they still hadn't returned. Then they became aware of an odour in the corridor, and the caretaker was called to investigate. We heard the devastating news, that this person had committed suicide and we were all in a state of shock. The usually happy, bustling busy place now fell silent, as everyone tried to take in the news. Virtually everyone went home the following weekend, and there was just a handful of us left in the entire building. The atmosphere was awful, but it must have been so much worse for the person's family.

I spent the Christmas of 1988 with Gaz's family. It was the first time I'd been away from my parents at that time of year, and it felt strange, although we had a great time in London. We went back up to Lancashire for the New Year, before I packed my things to return to Wolverhampton with Gaz. My Mum and Dad weren't particularly happy about it, but off I went. We moved into our new home in January 1989. Gaz had a room on the first floor, and mine was on the second floor. There were eight lodgers in total, some were students, and others were just single people who needed accommodation in the area. There was quite a mixture of different characters from different backgrounds, and my time there, can only be described as interesting.

Bob and Alex had devoted a large part of their married lives, to looking after others. While Bob was busy with the day to day running of the church, Alex took care of the large house, and the lodgers. They were a caring couple, who had made huge sacrifices in order to reach out and care for people. They had two young children of their own, and shared their family life with the rest of us. In the house were two living rooms. One was specifically for Bob and his family, and one for the lodgers. We each had our own rooms, and shared bathroom facilities. We payed rent on a weekly basis, which included some of our meals. Every evening, we would crowd around a large wooden table in the dining room, or "breakfast room" as it was known, to eat a meal together. Because there was so many of us, Alex would cook the food, but we all would take our turn to clear away and wash up afterwards. Gaz and I covered every Sunday lunch time, and as you can imagine, it seemed to take ages.

In the same way that you need to have a sense of humour when you have a disability, you also need one when you share a house with so many people. It took Alex quite a while to learn about what made us laugh, and one day without trying, I managed to cause offence. Gaz was washing, and I was drying after our meal, and things were going quite well. We had almost reached the end of our task, when Gaz

172

picked up a huge pile of plates, and walked toward the sink to wash them. I heard him, and rushed over to him shouting, "What the heck do you think you're doing? Are you blind? I've just dried them!" The place suddenly fell silent, then a huge burst of laughter rang out from Gaz and me. Alex couldn't believe it. She had been momentarily shocked. She had never expected someone to make a joke about their own disability, but eventually joined in with the laughter.

I had only been staying at the house for around two weeks when I awoke suddenly in the middle of the night. When I sat up in bed, I became aware of someone singing outside my window. I couldn't make out what they were singing, but I was concerned, because my room overlooked the back garden. Who was this, and how did they get into the garden? For a while I lay there wondering what to do, before I realised that the person was clearly drunk. Eventually the singing stopped, and I went back to sleep. I learned the following morning that it was one of the lodgers and I'm glad to say that it never happened again.

This wasn't the only time one of us would end up on the wrong side of a couple of drinks, on another occasion the fault lay with Gaz and I. We decided to wander down to the pub one Friday evening, when another guy from the house asked if he could join us. We had known him for a few months, and we both got on with him quite well, and so the three of us went off together. At the end of the evening he had only consumed two halves of lager, but unfortunately, he was as drunk as a skunk. It became apparent that we needed to get him home fast. Picture the scene, two blind people negotiating our way down the street after eleven in the evening, trying to find our own way, and assist someone who was clearly intoxicated, and blissfully unaware of what was happening. When we arrived home, he made so much noise, that he woke everyone, including Bob and Alex, who were furious. Gaz was instructed to take him to his room, but as they reached the top of the stairs on the second floor, he threw up everywhere, and Bob and Alex watched as chivalrous Gaz, manfully struggled to clear the mess. Earlier that evening, we had all eaten a meal which Alex called "bacon pie". It was a mixture of pieces of bacon, baked beans and mashed potato. Someone had renamed this "bacon splodge." Gaz often laughs as he remembers being on his hands and knees feeling around for the mess on the floor, and Alex exclaiming, "Ooh, there's a piece of bacon on the step!" The poor guy was so embarrassed the following day, that I don't think he spoke a word. Ah, student days!

21. Lessons in Life

We lodgers were quite a motley crew: people from different parts of the country, and different backgrounds, most of us having a certain amount of emotional baggage to a greater or lesser degree. I suppose it's fair to say that most people do. On the whole, we all got on pretty well together, although it wasn't always complete peace and harmony. One person decided that it would be a good idea to buy themselves a video recorder, which they would then rent out to other lodgers for a small fee, if they wanted to record or watch a TV programme. The person drew up an extremely formal document consisting of several pages, outlining rules, regulations and charges. This was printed out, and a copy was handed to everyone else. This wasn't a law student, but should have been. The result was that everyone took great offence and threw the paperwork back, all the while uttering their own words of displeasure. Feelings ran so high, that I felt quite sorry for the perpetrator, they had clearly not thought the process through, and certainly not anticipated such a negative reaction.

One day we were told that a female student was coming with her parents to look at a room, with the possibility of her joining our little crowd. Most of us were sitting in our lounge watching T.V. when she arrived, and was given a tour by Alex. Another lodger came in later, and related that the girl would not be joining us. Unfortunately, as she had walked through the dining room with her parents, someone had been seen randomly lying stretched out on the table. Oops, not a great advert then?

On another occasion, Gaz and I were studying, when we suddenly heard screaming. We were alarmed as we heard Alex shout, "Gaz, Jane, help!" We both ran down two flights of stairs to see what was happening, and when we reached the bottom, we heard the front door slam, and found someone standing in front of us. It was one of the other lodgers, and his hand was bleeding. Another of our group had been experiencing some deep emotional problems, and had, without any warning, gone chasing Alex around the house, armed with a knife. Just as we had arrived, they had both run out of the front door and Alex was screaming. I immediately rushed to the phone and rang Bob, telling him to get home straight away. The matter was dealt with, and I'm glad to say, no one was badly injured, but it's one of those moments in life I'll never forget.

Gaz and I weren't entirely without fault. We did our fair share of driving Bob and Alex up the wall. At that time, we got a liking for the

TV programme "Prisoner Cell Block H". This didn't usually begin until at least eleven in the evening, and sometimes after midnight. By that time, Gaz and I would have the munchies, and rush to the phone to order pizza. We would always ask the person at the take-away to tell the delivery guy to tap softly on the front window, and we would hear him. However, on numerous occasions, the message wouldn't get through, and there would be a loud knock on the front door. This would usually wake Bob and Alex, and they would stomp down the stairs, to voice their frustration and disapproval. There was to be one occasion, where we would both push Bob to the limit of his patience.

Gaz's long-time friend Chris, had come to visit us for the weekend. He had been given permission to sleep on the sofa in the lodgers' lounge, and then would come with us to church on Sunday. He arrived on the Friday evening, and we all walked down the road to enjoy a curry. Everything was going well and we were having a great time, until Saturday afternoon. I need to mention here, that Chris was a smoker. Smoking was not allowed in the house, so he would either have to go downstairs, or lean out of an open window. All three of us were in my room on the top floor, chatting and listening to music, when Chris decided it was time for a smoke. He asked if he could open my window, and I replied that it was ok, but to be careful, as it only opened on one side. Instead of checking properly, he simply reached out and tried to open the side which he located first. I was deep in conversation, when I heard Chris say, "Ooh, this window is a bit stiff!" To my horror, I then heard a terrible creaking sound as he applied pressure to the old wooden window frame. There was then a gasp, followed by "Oh no!" and a pregnant pause before we all heard a huge smash, as the whole window complete with frame crashed to the ground. A momentary stunned silence fell, before panic stations broke out. It was so lucky that no one was outside, or I dread to think what might have happened. I went to get help, and we cleared up the glass while we decided what we would do next. There was no one else in the house that day apart from the three of us, and one more person. I suppose it was a good thing as it gave us time to think about what we would say to Bob. When he did arrive, and we explained what had happened, he was furious. I'd never seen him like that before. It was clear that he was trying to stay calm, and he did a really good job, but it took several days I think, for him to forgive us. A piece of canvas type material was nailed to my hole in the wall, and it was quite chilly and rather noisy for the next few days until finally we paid for the work, and the window was replaced.

We did have our fill of laughs though. Once, we made some of the guys wear blindfolds and try to play us at chess and Othello, using our specially adapted games. They struggled much more than they had anticipated, and couldn't understand how we possibly managed. Then there was the day of the sudden earth tremor. I was in my room reading, when all of a sudden, I felt the whole house sway significantly to the right, and then back to the left again. I was on the top floor, and probably felt it more than the people on the lower floors, but everyone proceeded to dash out of their rooms, to talk about what had happened. It really was a strange experience.

Everyone has to get used to the idiosyncrasies of regional accents, and living in Wolverhampton, this was no exception. Instead of saying "spoon", it sounds more like "spoo-wn". This is the same with the word "town" or "tow-wn", which caused quite a misunderstanding one day. I heard Bob say that there had been some serious flooding in "tow-wn" or "town" to you. We were surprised, and wondered what had caused this to happen in Wolverhampton town centre. Later that day the mystery was solved. The flooding had happened in "Towyn" in Wales. "Ah, now I understand."

Gaz and I became friends with a couple who lived just a few doors away, and attended the same church. We would often visit them in the evening for a game of Trivial Pursuits. We always had guys versus girls, and it was great fun. One night, we were all doing quite well, but as we got toward the end of the game it was very close, and I got a question that had the potential to seal the game for the girls. As Max read out the question, I could hear the smile that crept across his face. It was a sport question, and I think he thought that girls never know the answers to sporting questions. He read out the question very slowly in a tone that confidently predicted my inability for sporting knowledge, and victory for the men. If I remember correctly, the question was asking the former career of the boxer Terry Marsh. My face fell, and I screwed up my eyes as I lowered my head and sighed. There were titters of laughter, and false sympathies as they smelled their impending win. I held the moment for a few seconds longer. Only a few days previously, and rather randomly, I'd heard the information on the T.V. when tuning in for some football results, but I sure wasn't going to let the boys know that! I was going to milk it for all it was worth. Eventually, I placed my head in my hands, and just as Max was about to reveal the answer, I shouted, "A fireman." Girl power!

I met many special people in Wolverhampton, including Archie. Archie was, I guess, in his early sixties, and his stature was as broad as his Black Country accent. He was as strong as an ox and I once witnessed him without a care, fill an old fashioned large dustbin full of rubble, sling it over his shoulder and carry it down the road to a truck, before repeating the same task several times. When the job was completed, he didn't seem at all tired; it seemed he could have carried on all day. Although he was physically strong, he was a gentle bloke, with a brilliant sense of humour. He had spent the majority of his life on the wrong side of the law but, in later life, had put all of that behind him. I really liked him, and one day, we sat together, with a hot drink as he related some stories of his past. I was shocked at the time, because to me, he was the perfect candidate for the part of Father Christmas. He told me the story of how he had once entered a night club, and after buying a drink, found somewhere to sit. A burley chap had approached him, and told him to move, as he was sitting in the chair of the leader of a well-known criminal gang. Archie's reaction, was to tell the chap that no one else was sitting there before, and he was staying where he was. As the conversation became more heated, several men began attacking him, but Archie, incredibly, fought each one of them off, and sat back down again. At the end of the evening, the gang leader approached him, and offered Archie the job of being his bodyguard.

Those days were now long gone, and he was a changed man. I didn't ever have any reason to fear him. He was just lovely. I don't know who made him his cup of tea on that day, because it certainly wasn't me. I am strictly a coffee maker. He wasn't however impressed with the beverage, because he said, "I can't drink this." I enquired why and he said "Because it's fortnight tea." I said, "What's that?" and he said, "Too weak!"

I admire Bob and Alex for their patience and compassion. Bob would receive phone calls from members of his congregation at all times of the day and night and would sometimes get out of bed and hurriedly get dressed in order to visit someone who needed his help. They often provided a few hours of respite care to the parents of a gentleman who had a learning disability. Ernie was in his mid-thirties, but had the mental age of, I would estimate, a five year old. He often spent time in the house, and kept us amused with the things he said. He would often come with us to church, where he gave us plenty to laugh about. During a service, Bob lay on the floor momentarily in an act of prayer, when suddenly in that quiet moment a loud voice rang around the building. It was Ernie, who said, "Is he dead?" In a different service, Bob announced, "Let's bow our heads in prayer," to which Ernie shouted, "Shan't!"

The funniest moment I can remember, also happened in church, during a service where several people were being baptised. Baptism in this case took the form of total immersion. Individuals would step down into a small pool of water slightly larger than a bath, and then be submerged momentarily under the water, before stepping outside again. There were limited resources to heat the water, and consequently it could be very cold. This day was no exception. As the first woman stepped forward and entered the water, we heard her let out a loud gasp, followed by "Oh, Jesus!" There was a pause, as I assume some onlookers were offended, and others were amused. I'm glad to say that there then followed a burst of laughter, as the woman stepped into the water and was lifted back up again, accompanied by a huge round of applause.

Unfortunately, my time spent in Wolverhampton wasn't the most fruitful and satisfying of times. I met many people who were lovely, but I was quite unhappy. After leaving university, I applied for several jobs, but it seemed that whenever prospective employers learned that I was blind, that was the end of the story. It left me feeling very despondent, and severely rocked my self-confidence. Without realising, I was on a downward slope. I spent most of my days mooching around the house, and staying up late into the night watching trash TV or chatting with other lodgers. Then I would sleep in bed until after two in the afternoon. I was poorly motivated, and pretty aimless. I had no idea of what I wanted to do, nor of how to set about finding out. Looking back, it was pretty grim.

Eventually, I made the decision to make an appointment with a careers officer to see if they could advise me or, at least, give me some ideas. Following several lengthy consultations, they decided that I should go back to university, and give it another go. They agreed that I had been let down in terms of the support level I had received, and that if I returned then things would be better. I however was dead against the idea. I didn't want to go back and was resolute in my protest. I was therefore shocked, when I was told that a meeting had taken place with university staff, and it had been arranged for me to attend a different course of study. I was baffled, how could this be arranged without my consent or co-operation. I wish I'd been more self-assertive, but unfortunately I wasn't, and so a few weeks later, I found myself in bed one evening, dreading the next day, which was the first day of my new course.

Things weren't different: they were just the same. This time however, instead of my frantically running around to try to make things work, I made very little effort. I cannot blame everything on the university. I was doing a course in which I had no interest, and in any case I didn't want to be there at all. It wasn't long before I simply walked out of the door and never returned. When the people responsible for arranging my place learned of what had happened, some were puzzled, and others were furious. I was summoned to a meeting, and it's a day I will never forget. It was like being court martialed. I sat in a room with several others who fired questions at me, and demanded answers concerning my decision to leave my course. After trying to explain for over an hour I was exhausted. I'd felt bad enough about myself after leaving the first time, and that was the reason I absolutely didn't want to go back, but now I'd done it again. My self-esteem had taken a beating, and now my self-confidence was at complete rock bottom. There came a point during that meeting when I simply fell silent. I'd had enough of explaining myself, and enough of people tearing strips off me. I wished they'd just leave me alone, and stop interfering. After the silence, one lady then made a comment about my being a Christian and going to church. I have no idea what the question she asked me was, but at the time I felt she was being utterly patronising, and this made me boil with anger. I refused to take the conversation any further, and left the building.

I realise that the people concerned had my best interests at heart, and that their intentions were good, but it was their method, in my opinion, that was wrong. Unfortunately it left me with a great deal of negative feelings toward myself. I felt a complete failure and I just wanted to hide away. I returned to my routine of late nights, and sleeping late in to the day. It's weird how sleep can become addictive. I'm pleased to say that I'd never experienced anything like that before, and never since. At that time however, I seemed to be able to almost sleep on demand. I wasn't getting a vast amount of exercise during the day, but I could sleep for hours on end. It was also strange to learn how I was seemingly masking my misery quite well to most people. One day, another of the lodgers surprised me when she said during a conversation, "I wish I was more like you Jane, you never seem to worry about anything!" I was flabbergasted! She couldn't have been further from the truth. I grinned as I thought to myself, "Maybe I should take up acting".

Every cloud has a silver lining, and it wasn't long before we reached December 1989, when my parents were making plans for my 21st birthday party. Gaz and I travelled up to Blackburn to meet with family, before my party, which was to take place on a Saturday evening. I wasn't aware at the time just how much fun the whole weekend would turn out to be. On the Saturday lunchtime, there was a sudden knock at the door. When I answered it, I couldn't believe my ears. There in front of me, were several of my friends from St. Vincent's. Mum and Dad had managed to track them down and invite them to the party. We all sat together and chatted excitedly, before there was another knock at the door. More friends; unbeknown to me, Mum and Dad were making trips backwards and forwards to the railway station to pick up more of my friends. It was fantastic, and a wonderful surprise.

By the time we reached early evening, the house was packed with people. I felt quite overwhelmed by the fact that so many of my friends had travelled such long journeys to come to the party. It was a wonderful idea on my parents' part, and I felt very blessed. Leah, my friend from Chorleywood had also joined me, and I knew we were all going to have a great evening. Family and friends kindly filled up their cars with guests, and we all made our way to the venue where my party would take place. I entered the building with Gaz at my side, and together with a group of friends we ordered a drink and found a seat. I welcomed a steady stream of other guests, and everything was going very well. From across the room I suddenly heard a familiar voice, and smiled. It was Josie. I was so glad she had been able to come and we exchanged a big hug. The lady who had once been my house parent at school, was now a trusted and precious friend. The party wouldn't have been the same without her. Irene, Dalton and his girlfriend Laura, had also travelled up from London, and it was great for our two families to get further acquainted. There was though, one other surprise to come.

There was a sudden tap on my shoulder, and from behind me I heard my Mum say, "Jane, there's a very special guest here who wants to speak with you!" Intrigued, I slowly turned round and immediately heard someone say, "Hello Jane." It took me a couple of seconds to process the voice, because it was one I hadn't heard for a while. I have to admit, it was more of a shock than a surprise. There in front of me larger than life stood Miss Woods, the headmistress of Chorleywood College. I was suddenly awash with a myriad of mixed emotions, but managed to keep my composure and greeted her in a shaky voice, which was not the result of the Jack Daniels I was holding in my hand, but more out of complete bemusement. Miss Woods mingled while I tingled with utter embarrassment and shame. If there had been a TV programme about embarrassing parents, then this was a candidate for the very top prize. I have to admit that inside I was utterly fuming. How many people share their 21st Birthday party with their former head mistress? How could they do this to me? What on earth would my friends think? Bad move Mum and Dad, very, very bad.

I pushed my irritation aside, and eased myself back into the party mood. Pondering what Miss Woods would make of the evening brought a wry smile to my face. Drinks flowed, and loud music filled the room, and soon, it was time for everyone to help themselves to the buffet. When I had filled my plate, I found a seat at one of the small tables, and chatted happily as I ate. I'll never forget what happened next. I had not realised that Miss Woods had taken a seat next to me, and as the music played, she leaned in toward me, and enquired, "Excuse me, but is this what they call rock and roll?" I smiled toward her and said, "Yes, that's right." In that moment I felt quite sorry for her. Her manner was quite timid, almost submissive, and I got the impression that all she wanted was to feel part of what was going on. I was sure that it was my Mum who had invited her, and she had graciously accepted. I was aware, that in recent years, following the closure of the college, she had experienced ongoing poor health, and she was not a young woman. Nevertheless, she had made the long journey up to Blackburn, and paid for her train journey, and accommodation for that weekend. At school, I had considered her to be a very fair person, although we saw very little of her, and she did at times seem very formidable. By then my initial embarrassment had ebbed away, and I genuinely hoped that she was enjoying herself. It was fantastic to have so many of my friends and family members together in the same room. The only problem was getting round everyone and spending quality time with them. Shortly before the end of the evening we all got together and did the conga around the room. It was a veritable mixture of the blind and the blind drunk, but I'm pleased to say that a good time was had by all.

The following morning a group of us, including my friends from St. Vincent's, Leah, Gaz's family and Miss Woods, gathered at my parent's house. We all jammed into the lounge, and drank coffee and laughed about the party. Miss Woods was very relaxed, and joined in with the conversation. She regaled us with many stories about Chorleywood College, and there was one in particular which had everyone in fits of laughter. A couple of times a year, staff members would take a small group of sixth form girls to visit the magistrates' court in order to sit in the public gallery, and listen to proceedings. Some students were interested in pursuing a career in law, and so it was considered that the trips would prove advantageous to their decision making in terms of a career. One morning, Miss Woods and the deputy head were having coffee in Miss Woods's office, when it came up in conversation, that the deputy head was taking a party of girls to the court on the following day. Miss Woods suddenly gasped, and nearly choked on her coffee. Rather sheepishly she told her colleague that she would have to postpone the trip. Miss Woods had committed a driving offence and was due to appear in court the following day. Imagine if that conversation had not taken place: the sixth form girls up in the gallery, while their head mistress was down below in the dock!

22. The importance of being Margaret

I heard that Baroness Thatcher died today, (8th April, 2013.) I immediately thought of another Margaret. Margaret Readfern, was Nanna Readfern to me, the mother of my dad. It wasn't long before my iPhone rang. It was my sister, and I announced, "I've been thinking about the two Margarets today. I can't get down to London to sign the book of condolence, but if I could, here's what I would write:

"Good on you Margaret! I'm sorry I wasn't old enough to appreciate you when you were Prime Minister, but you became a member of an exclusive club, you were a woman who had BALLS!"

My Nanna, who was known as Meg, had great admiration for Margaret Thatcher, and was an active member of the Conservative party for most of her adult life. She was passionate about politics, and every polling day, she would be there counting up the votes, after spending a good deal of time on the run up to that day, canvasing in her local area, drumming up support for her beloved party. Kirsten and I giggled during our telephone conversation, as we had both imagined Meg, standing waiting at the gates of heaven, smiling and enthusiastically waving her flag, and announcing, "Welcome Margaret, please allow me to show you around!"

Meg was the eldest of four children born to Tommy and Janie Readfern. She had two brothers, Fred, and Lewis. The youngest was her sister Jennie of whom I have already spoken. They lived in a small terraced house in the Mill Hill area of Blackburn, and although there were six of them in the family, I am assured that they never went short of anything. The family weren't particularly well off, but always managed to get by, and help others in the street who had less. Tommy was a plumber, and was often paid for his work in food items. His friends were a chimney sweep, a grocer, two publicans, and a butcher. Each year, one of his fellow tradesmen would give the family a large goose for their Christmas dinner. Tommy was also a very good singer, and would sing in the two pubs. Janie was a weaver. I have vague memories of a very warm friendly lady who was full of fun. During my teens, I learned that I was named after her. She was an extremely caring woman, and on a daily basis could be seen carrying heavy bags of vegetables home and would make enough food for her family, and also for several other less fortunate, struggling families in her street. On the occasions when she was lucky enough to acquire a large piece of meat, she would make a huge meat and potato pie and share it with her neighbours.

Life wasn't always easy. When she was pregnant with her youngest child, Jennie, she suffered from pernicious anaemia, and was advised to drink a glass of blood each day which she collected from the cattle market. I can't possibly imagine doing that. The thought of it makes me queasy. Her bravery paid off, and Jennie was born safe and sound. They all experienced a happy upbringing in a loving home, and had a lot of fun. When Janie died at the age of 79, the news appeared in the local paper, and this provoked a steady flow of people visiting the house to pay their respects, and to comment, that they thought her to be at least ten years younger than she really was.

Meg was certainly a woman who broke the mould. At the age of twenty-two, one day in August 1945, she suddenly told her mother that she wasn't well, and to call for the doctor. Following his visit, an ambulance was summoned and both Meg and Janie were rushed to hospital. A few hours later, Meg gave birth to a baby boy, (my father), much to the complete shock of her mother and the rest of the family. Everyone was sure Meg knew she was pregnant, but she had never told anyone. In those days, young mothers of illegitimate children were still being sent away, and it was considered to be a shameful act. When the news was broken to Tommy, his immediate reaction was "Yer' not bringin' 'Im 'ere lass!" but Janie was a strong woman and insisted that if the baby wasn't returning home with Meg, then she wasn't either. Janie always held the view, that this wasn't the first time that a young woman had ended up in this situation, and it certainly wouldn't be the last, and Tommy agreed. So little Kenneth was brought home with Meg, and the family all pulled together and rallied round.

Immediately after the birth, Meg was very ill and needed to spend a considerable time in hospital. Janie therefore took time off work to look after the new arrival. Auntie Jennie was sixteen when Kenneth was born. All their lives, Meg and Jennie had been made to share a bed, and this was still the case. When Meg returned home, there were three of them, and the baby slept in his cot, which was actually an old drawer beside their bed. Jennie often tells the story of how Meg would often have to work late into the night. At those times, she would take Kenneth from his cot and place him in bed with her. If Janie came and saw them, she would immediately put him back in his cot, but as soon as she had gone, Jennie would once more reach out and put him back with her.

Beyond the walls of that loving home, gossip was rife, but the family took it all in their stride, and didn't allow it to bother them. The possibility of adoption was never an issue, and everyone loved the new addition to their family, he was viewed as being special, and brought a great deal of joy to everyone. Several years later, when my Dad was just five years old, he began attending St. Aidens' Primary School. Meg was working full time, and Janie would walk him to School. So began a temporary ritual. Janie would walk to school with little Ken, and leave him in his classroom. She would then walk home, where she would find him sitting on the doorstep. When she enquired what he was doing there, my Dad would always say, "I don't like school, Gran. I'd rather stop at home with you!" She would then give my Dad a good telling off before returning him to St. Aiden's and find the headmaster. It was eventually decided after this happened several times, that someone would have to guard the school gate every morning, so he could no longer escape. This was done for many weeks until he settled down.

My Dad always speaks of having a happy childhood although this time was shortly after the end of the war. Rationing was still in force and imports were beginning to recover. His Uncle Fred, who had been on active service in the Navy, and after being abroad for a considerable time, returned with some strange gifts - bananas! My Dad had never seen one before. One day Janie took him out for a picnic, and gave him a banana to eat. As he tucked into that strange but delicious fruit, suddenly a greedy Swan from a nearby lake stole it from his grasp. Dad cried, and Janie was furious. It's a good job Swans are protected in this country, or it would probably have ended up on the table. Every year Dad was treated to a holiday with his Mum and Grandparents whether it be Ireland or Isle of Man. He was also taken for days out during School holidays by other Family members. Ken loved his mother, and also his grandmother, and this bond would be deepened when he reached the age of thirteen. As I stated earlier, Meg was an independent spirit. She decided that she wanted to go and work in Germany for several years, but would leave her son with his grandparents. I'm sure the family weren't enamoured of the idea, but Meg had made her decision, and off she went. My Dad missed his mother very much, and has often said that she left at a time when he really needed her. Janie once again stepped in and took over, doing her very best, and Dad was grateful. Meg kept in regular contact via letter, and finally returned three years later. She did not recognise the tall young man who came to meet her at the railway Station and brushed him to one side. It wasn't until the words, "Mum it's me Ken." were heard that the reunion was made. She immediately resumed her career in the retail industry, always taking a managerial role, and it seemed that things were getting back to normal.

By that time, Jennie was married, and living in a different house, with her husband Brian, not far from the family home. Approximately two years after Meg returned from Germany, another shock was in store for everyone. Not long before my Dad's eighteenth birthday, Jennie heard a knock at her door and went to answer it. She saw her Mother standing in front of her, and instinctively knew that something was wrong. Janie told her that Meg had been at home with her, when suddenly she had ordered a taxi and gone out. It turned out that the taxi had taken her to hospital, where she had given birth to another baby boy. During her first pregnancy, nobody had noticed any obvious signs. Jenny's husband Brian had, in recent months, aired his suspicions to Jennie that he strongly suspected that Meg was pregnant again. Jennie had not quizzed her sister, and didn't suspect anything. Nevertheless, it had happened again. History had repeated itself, and once again everyone provided all the support they could give. If my calculations are correct, Meg would have been thirty-nine when she had her second child. My Dad recalls being shocked at the idea of having a baby brother, but like everyone else, he would have to get used to it.

Meg was never particularly lucky in terms of romantic relationships. Both the fathers of her children disappeared when they heard of her pregnancies. One of them did provide financial support for a short while, but the relationship did not continue. Meg was a very hard worker, and provided well for her boys. All through his childhood, and well into his teens, Meg would take my Dad on holidays, and on regular day trips. Some were for pleasure, and others educational. She also taught him a great deal about social skills, taking him to a variety of different places and venues. Eating dinner in a high class restaurant in London was a world away from living in Mill Hill. Amidst this busy life, Meg had begun a relationship with a local gentleman. They were very happy, and it seems that the relationship could have blossomed if it were not for one problem. He was Catholic, and she was Protestant. Both families got on well together, but they were both dead against the two of them pursuing a serious relationship, and so they parted company. It's sad to think that such matters prevented what possibly could have been a long- standing relationship, but I never heard my Nan talk about it. I do, however, remember her spending much of her time with a gentleman from India. He was a well-respected doctor at the local Hospital, and they really enjoyed each other's company. Again, there were some whispers, but Meg never cared that people were talking about "the local woman who was dating a coloured man!"

The fact that Meg wasn't afraid to step away from the norm, didn't really bother any of her family. Her mother and father were both very proud of her. They never bore any grudge about the choices she made, and adored their grandchildren.

Over the years, the family home also accommodated a pet. Not long before Fred was sent abroad with the navy, he bought himself a dog. Fred apparently spent hours teaching the dog to perform various tricks, in response to different whistles. Fred and his dog were inseparable and, when he had to leave, the dog missed his owner greatly. Fred was away for two years, but early one morning, he returned on the train back to Mill hill. The little station was only a short distance away from his home, and as he began to walk, Fred whistled. The dog was out in the back yard, but heard the familiar sound. Before anyone knew what was happening, the animal turned, jumped straight through the closed living room window, and ran through the house on to the street. Moments later, Fred and his dog were reunited and very happy. Tommy however, wasn't impressed as he cleared up the glass, and had to get to work replacing the window. It's incredible that the dog suffered absolutely no injury whatsoever.

To me, my Nan was special. She was incredibly intelligent, and I adored her sense of humour. She was a laid back character, who could never be rushed. I remember endless journeys in the car, when Dad and I would travel over to her house to collect her and take her back to our house for Sunday lunch. If we needed her to be ready by eleven in the morning, we would simply tell her we would be arriving a ten. We would arrive at eleven, and then always had to wait for at least half an hour while she eventually got herself ready. My Dad used to get so frustrated, but nevertheless remained very patient. Back at home, we would sit together, and talk about what I'd been doing at school, and often she would read to me. During my mid-teens, we would often debate together, with me presenting my somewhat naive political views, but she would always listen patiently, and never made me feel silly. She was a loving, caring person, who wasn't afraid to show her feelings. She was never afraid to say, "I love you," and her family were precious to her.

We enjoyed many fun days out together, including the annual day out to Blackpool during the summer. Several of us including Kirsten and myself, Meg, Jennie and my other Nanna who lived with us, would crowd on to the train at Blackburn and travel to the coast. It was so exciting for us, as we were not used to travelling by train. We would spend hours on the beach, digging holes, making sand castles, and paddling in the sea. If there was time, we would visit the pleasure beach, and then find a cafe where we would tuck in to fish and chips followed by ice cream. Jennie and I still laugh about one incident. I remember during one of those days needing the toilet, and Auntie Jennie taking me to a public toilet block near the beach. She was shocked to learn that it would cost us ten pence each to have a wee. Jenny shouted, "10p to go for a wee? You should get Axminster carpet on the floor for that price!"

As the day drew to a close, we were all quite tired, but we couldn't leave before visiting a Blackpool rock shop. We then boarded the train home, clutching our bags of rock, buckets, spades and damp towels. The day once again had been a great success. However, it would be a week, at least, before we got rid of all the sand from our shoes!

It was as an adult that I became closer to my Nan. Even though I lived a considerable distance away from Lancashire, we spent many happy hours on the phone, doing crosswords together, debating political issues, or just chatting in general over the things we had done that day. There was always much laughter in our conversations, but it would always end with her telling me how much she loved me, and wished that we lived closer so we could spend more time with each other. I found her personality both captivating and inspiring, and even though it has been ten years since she died, I still miss her. She certainly had very strong views. She whole-heartedly agreed with Margaret Thatcher's policies and, in my Nan's eyes, she could do no wrong. I sometimes imagine what it would have been like if the two of them had met. The content of their conversation would have been a treat to behold.

In normal conversation, Meg spoke with her Lancashire accent, but regularly reverted to what we called her "Maggie Thatcher voice." One of the best examples of this happened on a memorable day. It was my other nan also named Irene who had her sixtieth birthday party on that particular evening. This was held at a venue in the town centre in Clitheroe. I remember travelling in the car with Meg and Jenny that evening. As we got out of the car, we were unsure exactly where the pub was situated. Meg approached a member of the public and in the aforementioned voice asked, "Excuse me, but could you tell me where the Castle Restaurant is?" The woman, adorned with a blank expression said in her broad Lancashire accent, "No luv, sorry." Suddenly, Jenny walked over to us and with a good deal of laughter in her voice said, "She means "cassle" luv!" Immediately, the penny dropped, and the woman lifted her hand to point, and replied, "Oh right, it's just down thurr luv."

Jennie and Meg were two sisters who loved each other to bits. They cared for each other, drove each other up the wall, but loved being together. My Auntie Jenny and Uncle Brian have always been a huge part of our family life. Jennie is a woman with a big voice, and both of them have even bigger hearts of gold. They were blessed with one child, a little girl named Janet, whom they both adored. The worst day of their lives was the day that Janet, then only twenty-eight was killed instantly in a car crash. Their young Grandson was also in the car and was seriously injured. For a while it was touch and go, but thankfully, after a long stretch in hospital, he pulled through. There's no way of saying it, other than Janet was an absolute super brain beyond compare when it came to writing computer code. In fact, when she died, the project she had been working on was so detailed and complex that nobody in the country was able to continue with her work.

Jennie and Brian were beyond devastated, and so followed one of the saddest periods in our recent family history. It was their strength of character and the strength of their marriage together with the support of family and friends that carried them through those dark days. I have no doubt that for them, the pain is just as deep today, thirty-two years later, but they have learned to live with it with unbounded dignity. When a young vibrant life, with so much potential is suddenly snatched away, the reason for it is unfathomable but Janet will never be forgotten. Her outgoing personality, good humour, tenacity, and amazing talent will remain as treasured memories in our hearts forever.

Meg was extremely proud of her family, like a lioness guarding her cubs. When we were growing up, if Kirsten and I won any certificates, or passed exams, the first person my Dad would ring to announce the good news was Meg. Nanna always wanted to keep in close contact to see what we were getting up to. Not long after leaving home, I decided to push the boat out and make myself some fruit scones. As I lifted them into the oven and waited patiently for them to cook, I suddenly panicked as it occurred to me that I had forgotten to add the sugar to the mixture. When I called Mum and Dad to tell them of my forgetfulness, guess who Dad then phoned to relate the news? Not long after, I answered the telephone. It was Nanna, who enquired in an impish yet loving voice, "Are you enjoying your diabetic scones Jane?"

Kirsten and I used to love playing Monopoly as kids, and often tried to cajole my Dad into playing with us, but it was no good, he hates the game. However, Meg would take the time to play. She was always so amusing. In every game, she aimed to purchase the electric company, and the waterworks, referring to them as "The twinkling lights," and "the drippin' tap." This never ceased to amuse us, and we still use those phrases now, whenever we play. The phrase we all remember her the most for though was her regular referral to her being "The head of the Readfern dynasty". During the speeches at my Mum and Dad's twenty-fifth wedding anniversary celebration, she stood up to make a speech in her Margaret Thatcher voice, and uttered those immortal words as she began. It really didn't matter though, we all loved her dearly. She was incredibly talented, amazingly articulate, phenomenally funny, and when it came to loving us all, we simply couldn't have asked for more. Even now, in recent months when I graduated at university with my teaching qualification, my Dad told me that he had instinctively rushed to the telephone, to tell his mother the good news, before replacing the handset and wishing he could enjoy that conversation.

Thank you, Margaret Readfern. Thanks for being brave and giving me the best Dad in the world. Thanks for never being ashamed, of just being who you were, and thanks for loving us, you were amazing, and we all loved you as much as you loved us.

23. The wanderers return

Gaz was doing a sandwich course at University and needed to find a placement for twelve months before returning to Wolverhampton for his final year at University. He was very lucky, because his tutor managed to secure employment for him for the year assisting in the speech lab with the Ministry of Defence in Malvern, just outside Worcester. We had not planned to go back there, but nevertheless when I heard the news, I was elated. I had enjoyed my time there, and was looking forward to going back. When we related our news to Eddie and Lin, they were very excited, and couldn't wait to spend more time with us. Eddie got to work straight away and managed to find a house for us to rent. It was on a small housing estate in Worcester, which meant that Gaz would have to commute to Malvern every day, but this didn't bother him. When we sat down with Bob and Alex to tell them our news, Bob in particular was very disappointed. We had both become heavily involved in church life in Wolverhampton, especially in the music group, and we would be missed. It seemed surprising to us, that Bob had assumed that we had pretty much made roots there, and the fact that we were leaving, seemed to come as a shock to him.

Arrangements started to take shape. Gaz made a visit to Malvern, and we both met up with Eddie in Worcester to take a tour of our prospective house. It seemed like there was a wealth of paperwork, and tasks to complete before we would be officially ready to move. Not only that, but we had to start packing. I didn't realise until I started, just how much stuff I'd managed to accumulate in just one room. Behind this seemingly arduous task was the huge incentive of returning to a city and people I loved very much. A further day trip to Worcester was required to sign documents for the house, and eventually the day arrived when we would be on our travels again.

Dad borrowed a van from work and drove down to meet us on a Saturday morning. We began running up and down several flights of stairs carrying all our possessions and loading them into the back of the van. I had in the past few months acquired a pair of very large waist high hi-fi speakers which sounded brilliant and I remember telling Dad to be really careful with them. Gaz had packed loads of his gear into my old trunk from Chorleywood, and he and Dad heaved it down the stairs. It was lifted into the van and Gaz and I sat on it surrounded by all our other stuff. I have such a clear memory of sitting on that trunk, as Dad and Bob chatted over to my right as it started to rain. We said our last goodbyes and Dad closed the van doors. We slowly drove away, and I was excited. The journey would only take around an hour, but I couldn't wait to get settled into the new house.

Eddie met us at the estate agent's to pick up the keys, and then we all drove over to our new home. We parked on the front drive of the three bedroomed property and unlocked the door before the process of carrying everything in there began. We had a small garage, and a garden at the back of the house. Downstairs was a lounge/diningroom, and a kitchen. Upstairs were three bedrooms, and a small bathroom. We also shared the house with an old friend from College, Tony, and we certainly had a lot of fun that year. Mum, Dad and Eddie left during late afternoon, and we got on with enjoying our new found freedom. Gaz chose the master bedroom, and Tony the room at the front of the house. I unfortunately was left with the smallest room, but I didn't really mind, and on the whole, we all got on incredibly well.

The strangest thing about those first few days, was being without a telephone in the house. We had to wait several days to get connected, but when we did, the phone certainly made up for it. It rang and rang relentlessly, and drove us up the wall. On the first day, someone rang, and asked if I could put them through to the meter reading department. I told them they had got the wrong number and thought nothing of it until several minutes later, when the phone rang again, and it was someone else asking to pay their bill. It turned out that our number was only one digit different from that of the electricity board, and in the next few weeks I really was bored of answering the telephone. I've always considered myself to be quite a patient person, but that incessant ringing meant that we practically begged the phone company to change the number. I'm glad to say that they heard our plea, and soon we had a completely different number.

So peace reigned for several weeks until the fateful night when the three of us returned from an evening at our local pub. Gaz started playing his keyboard, and was experimenting with some drum samples. Tony was trying to listen to the messages on the answering machine, and that gave me an idea. I suggested that we make up a rap for our answering machine message, for when people called us, and from nowhere, came up with this.

7, 6, 3 – 1, 4, 3.
Sorry we can't answer your enquiry.
Leave your name and number clearly after the tone.
We'll get back to you, soon as we get home.

Ok?

The guys fell about laughing and insisted that we record it immediately. The only problem was: could I keep a straight face? Gaz played the drums, I did the rap and Tony did the recording, and eventually following several attempts which ended up in me laughing and stopping in the middle, we finally nailed it. The recording came out really well and we played it back several times before leaving the message poised, ready for the first unsuspecting caller the next day.

It was brilliant! We laughed until we cried, when we heard several callers' reactions to the message. The irony of the situation was that nobody actually tried to leave a message. Most of the time, people would laugh down the phone, and often shout for a friend or partner to come and hear what they had heard. They would often ring a second time just to listen, or simply shouted stuff like, "That's brilliant!" In the end, we recorded over the tape because it just got silly, and there were times when we just wanted a simple message.

We were only a short walk away from the local pub, and would spend many an hour there. We would have a couple of drinks and sometimes a bar snack, before making our way home. On warm summer evenings we would sit outside, and enjoy the weather, and it was during one of those occasions, when another rather humorous event took place. Gaz and I were sitting at a picnic table when Tony joined us. He placed his pint on the table in front of him and stooped to sit down. Unfortunately, he caught the side of his glass with his chin and managed to cover himself in cider, and smash the glass on the floor. We both laughed, and Gaz shouted, "Chinned ya pint then Tony?"

Our Achilles' heel was pizza, and that was true for all three of us. We found a take-away which delivered to our home, which made the most wonderful Gringo pizza. This was a chili con carne pizza, complete with kidney beans, plus pepperoni and other toppings, and was fantastic. I have to say, that we ordered rather too often, but enjoyed every slice. Tony came up with the idea of saving the pizza boxes in the garage, and making a huge stack of them. If we could get the pile to reach the garage roof, then we should ask the restaurant for a free meal. We listened intently, and decided that it wasn't beyond the realms of possibility. So, several months later, we found that we had, indeed munched our way through a preposterous amount of pizza, and one evening, lifted the door of the garage for the manager to witness. The boys seemed quite proud of our achievement but, I have to admit, as everyone marveled at the pile of empty boxes, I cowered at the door rather sheepishly, feeling a tinge of remorse. Our reward was somewhat underwhelming; rather an anti-climax. We were sent a new pizza to try. A nine inch pizza to share between all three of us, topped with cheese and apple: yes, stewed apple, with a small tub of cream to place on the top. I was distinctly unimpressed at the gesture, but much more so with the pizza.

There was further retribution for our greed several weeks later. We kept telling ourselves that, one day, we would have to put the boxes outside to be collected by the bin men. No one actually said anything, but it was clear that we were all too embarrassed to confront the task. What would the neighbours think? Eventually we came up with a plan. We would remove the boxes, and stack them outside when it was dark, then they could be taken away before we emerged from the house the following morning. We executed the first part of the plan very well, keeping very quiet so as not to arouse anyone's curiosity. Weather conditions were not however kind to us the next day, and our secret was well and truly out for all to see. It turned out to be a very blustery day, and soon our little street was covered with cardboard cartons. Tony, who was partially sighted, furiously ran around trying to rescue the items from other people's properties, while we listened on shamefully. It was a considerable time before we ordered another pizza.

If we weren't eating pizza, I usually took care of making the meals. I had done O-Level food technology, and was pretty confident about cooking. I wasn't hugely adventurous, but usually managed to produce something the guys liked. I mainly made pasta dishes, or risotto and casseroles. One of our favourites was curry, and I also tried out a couple of Jamaican dishes. I suppose that many of you are wondering how it is possible for a blind person to cook, so I'll try to give you a little insight. It's fair to mention that most individuals who have been visually impaired from an early age, formulate the methods which work best for them, and these are often shared and exchanged within the network. When tackling the task of peeling and chopping veg, I prefer to use a peeler with a fixed blade, rather than the swivel ones. This is because I can control it better, and have a good idea of exactly where the peel is that I'm removing. When I have finished peeling a potato, I always rinse it under the cold water tap, because then it is much easier to feel around and detect the difference between the texture of the peeled area, and the places I might have missed, where skin still remains. Extra care needs to be taken when chopping vegetables, but this only means that it would take me a little longer than a sighted person, but the end result would be exactly the same.

The house we lived in was equipped with an electric cooker, and I learned how to use it. I have carried on using this method ever since, and still cook with electricity today. When I ordered the cooker, the manufacturer made me a panel for the front with raised markings around the controls that enable me to select the correct temperature. The rings on the top are solid fixed plates so that I can correctly align the pan before turning on the heat. It's not rocket science, just common sense, extra care, and allowing yourself time to find the method that best suits you.

One evening, Tony invited a friend to come over for dinner. He informed me that he would make the starter, and asked if I would cook a pasta dish for the main course. The friend he invited was someone he had known for several years and, in that time, she had often invited him around to her house for meals, acting as extended family to support him while at boarding school. For this reason, Tony was eager to impress, and really pushed the boat out. We welcomed our guest and enjoyed a pre-dinner drink before Tony asked us to take our places at the table. Both Gaz and I were somewhat perturbed to learn that the starter was smoked salmon with dill sauce. Not only did Gaz hate salmon, but he wouldn't even eat pizza if it was topped with dill sauce. I, however, would have happily slurped up the sauce if it meant I didn't have to grapple with, and grimace my way through, the dreaded smoked salmon. That didn't just require Chorleywood training, it called for the metal of S.A.S. endurance! I've never been so glad to see a plate of pasta! The rest of the evening went very well, unlike the rest of the smoked salmon, which went straight in the bin.

While making breakfast each morning, I fell into the routine of listening to a local radio station. I discovered that several times per week there was a competition where listeners were encouraged to ring in and give their answers. One day, we were given a riddle to solve, a kind of "Who done it?" scenario. We had to decide who committed the crime and why. I didn't know the answer, but thought that I would contribute some humour to the proceedings. I was put through to the studio, and one of the D.J.'s asked me for my answer. I said rather impishly, "It was the dustman. He knew where the house was because he'd bin there before!" To my surprise, everyone in the studio howled with laughter, and they decided that my answer was brilliant.

Eventually, someone did ring in with the correct answer, but there is a twist. At the end of the show, it was announced that I had won the prize, which was a huge pile of different kinds of books. The other listener only managed to secure the consolation prize which was two "Time Out" guides for Paris and New York, which were out of date. I never divulged to the radio station the irony of the situation. I won a pile of very expensive books, which I couldn't read, while the other person won a couple of out of date magazines they probably didn't want to read. Ah well, that's something else for the bin!

I'm glad to say that the books didn't go to waste. One in the collection was all about art, and contained several beautiful prints. I had a friend who was an artist, and when I presented her with it she was extremely grateful, even though I told her about the competition. My Uncle Brian loved his book all about Japanese history, and there were a couple of novels that another friend snapped up. It was rather uncanny. Every book seemed to perfectly suit the interests of one of my friends, and I got a great deal of enjoyment from seeing their pleasure. I'm not so sure I would have been as successful with those consolation prizes.

It was great that the three of us got on so well together. Tony had an interest in films, and would often cajole Gaz and myself into watching with him. The most memorable one for me that year was "Three Men And A Little Lady." It has remained one of my favourite films, and at the time, I have to admit to developing quite a liking for Tom Selleck. One evening stands out in my memory. I was sitting talking with Gaz, when Tony came home. We had been chatting about the previous evening when we had visited a friend, and she had been telling us about a game her children liked to play. It was called, "I've got a business!" This involved a group of people sitting together, and concocting a couple of lines to describe business, and creating a humorous punch-line. Let me give you a couple of examples:

"I've got a business!"
"What's your business?"
"I repair watches."
"How is business going?"
"Ticking over nicely, thank you."

"I've got a business!"
"What's your business?"

"I own a vineyard."
"How is business going?"
"Grape!"

"I've got a business!"
"What's your business?"
"I sell vacuum cleaners."
"How is business going?"
"Picking up nicely!"

That night we spent ages sitting around playing that game. It seems rather silly now, but there were some really good ones, and we laughed a great deal. Those are the type of evenings you never plan, but end up being some of the best times. They don't cost you a penny, and end up leaving priceless memories.

Amidst all the frivolity, I was still plagued by the fact that I didn't have a job. I had applied for basic admin type jobs, but never managed to secure one. It really bothered me, and I was desperate to get a chance to work. One thing that no one can ever say about me is that I am idle. Cleaning the house kept me busy, together with getting involved with church life. I learned all about the advantages and disadvantages of having your own house. During the time we lived there, the heating broke down many times. I think that the boiler was on its last legs and really needed replacing. It was unfortunate for us, that these breakdowns happened during the winter months and we were often reaching for that extra sweater. I think that the estate agent, and the owners of the house who lived abroad, got fed-up with the situation as they were called upon repeatedly to give permission for a plumber to visit us to repair the boiler. I once went downstairs early one morning, and suddenly felt a drop of water on my head. It startled me, and I raised my hand to see if it happened again. When it did, I had to find a bucket, and then spent ages, trying to put the bucket in the correct place on the floor to collect the drips, which by now were increasing in number. So followed another call to get help, and another repair bill for the owners. "Gosh!" I thought to myself. "You need an awful lot of money to buy a house and keep up with its maintenance."

We only lived at that address for a little under twelve months, but it was a really enjoyable time. I had the chance to develop my domestic skills, and had loads of fun in the process. During those months, my thoughts turned towards the prospect of applying for a guide dog. I had always loved dogs since the days of having Boo, and was spurred on by meeting a couple of friends who already had their own dog. I think it was around April 1991 when I made initial enquiries at my nearest training centre in Leamington Spa, and the process began. The first step required me to fill in several forms, and then visit my doctor to have a full medical. Once that was completed, I waited to be visited by a guide dog mobility instructor, otherwise referred to as a GDMI. Ever since those slightly scary days at St. Vincent's when I'd learned how to use a white cane, I'd managed quite well to get around independently but, somehow, I felt that I would manage better with a dog at my side.

I waited several weeks before receiving a phone call, informing me that someone would travel over to Worcester, to speak with me and explain a little about guide dog training. When the day arrived, I was excited. We spent a long time talking about what the training involved, and I was asked why I wanted a dog. So many factors must be taken into consideration: whether or not the applicant has any useful vision, their fitness level, walking speed, and whether they have any additional disabilities such as partial hearing loss. It is vital for the instructor to glean as much information as possible, in order to reach a decision about the person to decide when they are ready to embark upon the training programme. Shortly after the interview, I was pleased to receive a letter informing me that my name had been placed on the waiting list for a dog, and I would hear from them again soon.

Before the matching process could begin, I would require at least one other appointment with a GDMI. This took place in July, when further details were recorded: my height, weight and walking speed. There was also a discussion about my geographical surroundings, amongst other things. The Guide Dogs for the Blind Association, (GDBA), is meticulous in its attempts to match the right dog with the right person. Some dogs will require extra training if their prospective owner has a job which requires them to travel on a plane regularly. Some dogs prefer to work in quiet rural surroundings, while others thrive in a busy bustling environment. Some applicants have families with very young children, and others may already have a cat as a pet. It is vital to get all the information together when choosing the right dog for the right set of circumstances.

On the day of my visit, we exchanged relevant information, and then it was time to go outside for a walk. The instructor watched me walk a short distance with my cane, and then the fun began. I'm sure you are all aware that guide dogs wear a harness, which has a handle for the visually impaired owner to hold. On this occasion, there was the harness, but no dog. Now before you begin conjuring up ridiculous pictures of me holding the handle, with the instructor on his hands and knees in front of me, let me tell you that it did not happen! It was still pretty embarrassing, however. I held the handle, and my instructor held the front part where the dog would normally be, and we walked around the housing estate together. The GDMI wanted to assess how I coped with following him, and how easily I could detect when he turned. At certain points, he would lower the harness, trying to mimic the dog scavenging for some food from the pavement, and give me instructions on how to correct this behaviour. The whole experience was fascinating, but I hoped nobody who knew me saw what was happening.

When we returned to the house, he told me I had done really well, and that the process of searching for the right dog for me could begin. We had already discussed whether I had a preference for a specific breed of dog, and I had said I didn't mind, as long as the match was right. I did, however, add that in an ideal world, I would love to have a golden retriever. It was impossible to give me an idea of how many months I would have to wait until they found a dog. The waiting list was long, and I would have to be patient, but being patient wasn't easy for me in these circumstances. What type of dog would I get? What colour would it be? What would his or her name be? My head was full of questions and I found it hard to contain my excitement.

Around the same time, we received a letter informing us that our landlord intended to put the house on the market. We were given the option of renting on a month-to-month basis until the property was sold. The only snag was, we were given the task of showing prospective buyers around the property, and this didn't exactly fill us with enthusiasm. We were, however, very fair, and tried our best to keep the place as tidy as possible. Gaz was going back to Wolverhampton the following September, so he didn't have any accommodation worries. He had already made arrangements. Tony hadn't made any plans, but I decided to put my name down with the council and apply for a flat. It's strange the way things work out. When September arrived, Gaz went back to university, and Tony and I stayed in Worcester. It would be hard once more to only see Gaz at the weekend, but I preferred to stay where I was.

Out of the blue, I heard the news that the council had possibly found a flat for me just outside the town centre, and that I could view in the next few days. Tony then decided to move out and stay with a friend, so we gave a month's notice to the landlord. I remained in the house alone for the last few weeks. I was sad to be leaving, because I'd become rather attached to the place. I learned something about myself in those days, or should I say evenings. I liked my own company, but not for prolonged periods of time. In fact I found it to be very lonely. It made me wonder how I would manage alone in the flat. I was wandering around the house one morning, when the telephone rang. Much to my surprise, it was GDBA, and they announced the exciting news that they had potentially found a dog for me. Nothing was definite until they had watched me walk with the dog, and so a visit was arranged for the end of that week. The news came a great deal sooner than expected, but just at the right time. It really lifted my spirits, and the prospect of moving didn't seem quite so bad.

The first task in my diary though, did not fill me with the same amount of glee. I visited the flat, and wasn't greatly impressed. It was only a ten minute walk from the town centre which was great, but when I opened the door, and the housing officer showed me round, I needed a good deal of convincing. I had a small hall, with a large room straight ahead of me. This would be my lounge and bedroom. To the right was a small bathroom and, off to the left, a kitchen. The place was grimy and didn't smell great, but I was assured that, if I wanted the place, it would be cleaned, and given the obligatory magnolia walls before I moved in. In the kitchen was a cooker containing the remnants of a meal eaten by the previous occupant of the previous year. Something had to be done about that before I would go anywhere near the place again. I did want to stay in Worcester, and came to the conclusion that it was time for me to be brave, and get on with it. So I left after officially accepting the flat, and turned my thoughts to how I was possibly going to furnish the place! It would be a new chapter, and I would confront it head on, and I had something really special to look forward to at the end of the week.

24. "Right!" said Fred

"Right!" said Fred, "It's time you got a guide dog. That white cane is gonna have to go!"

Forgive me for my sudden outburst, but all will be revealed in due course. It was beautifully sunny that October morning when I awoke early. My thoughts immediately turned to the day ahead when I would meet my guide dog. I sprang out of bed, and hurried myself, getting ready, and tidying the house before my visitors arrived. I hadn't been given any information about the dog at all and, as I mulled over the situation, I tried to tell myself not to get too excited, because not all dogs are suitable. I didn't want to be disappointed but, hard as I tried to keep a level head, I really hoped that I would like the dog, and he or she would like me. I waited anxiously, for what seemed like hours, to hear a knock on the door, and paced around the house until, eventually, they arrived. Initially, I was surprised to find two representatives from the association, but there was no sign of a dog. I invited them in, and was pleased to learn that the dog was in the car, but it was necessary to have a chat first. On that day, I would once again be required to walk around the estate holding on to a harness, only this time, it would be attached to a real dog, which would possibly become my dog!

Eventually, one of the GDMI's went out to the car, and returned with a dog, which they introduced to me. Much to my delight, I reached out to find a very handsome, fluffy pedigree golden retriever called Fred. He was gorgeous both in appearance, and personality, and I fell in love with him straight away, but, despite my joy, I suddenly felt nervous. I needed to take a walk with him before it could be decided whether he was suitable for me. How would things go? Fred was fitted with his harness and lead, and I was shown how to hold them correctly, before going outside to take our first walk. I have never concentrated so hard in my life. Walking steadily, and trying my best to follow Fred as well as I could, feeling his movements, and listening to instructions from one of the GDMI's as they stood close by me. As the minutes passed, I became more relaxed, forgetting about any unnecessary pressure I had put on myself, and just enjoying the feeling of walking around with my new found Fred – sorry, I mean friend.

When we arrived home, we went to sit in the lounge. My instructor removed Fred's harness, and as I sat on the floor by my chair, I was so pleased to find that Fred came over and flopped on the floor beside me. He rested his head on my knee, and then turned and licked my hand. That was the beginning of a wonderful partnership. As I write this, I have to admit, that right now, tears are in my eyes as I recall that very special moment. A few seconds later, I was told that Fred and I were considered to be a great match, and that I could begin my guide dog training course at Leamington in November. I can't put into words, just how happy I was. The worst part of that day, was letting Fred leave to make the journey home, where he would receive the last couple of weeks of his training. As he jumped into the car, I reluctantly removed my hand from his fluffy coat, and told the GDMI's to make sure they took care of him until I arrived. They promised to do so, and drove away.

If I was excited before, now I was doubly so, having met Fred. That afternoon I travelled to Wolverhampton to tell Gaz the great news. Gaz has never been a big fan of dogs, but, nevertheless, he was pleased for me. I also met up with Bob and Alex, and told them all about Fred. Actually, in the days that followed, I probably became a rather large pain in the neck. I told everyone I met about him. I just couldn't stop myself. The following four weeks dragged by, and I simply couldn't wait to make the journey to Leamington to begin my training. There were still lots of other jobs to be done. I had to sign more paperwork before receiving the keys to my flat, and then there was all the rest of my packing to be done and the house needed cleaning before finally returning the keys to the estate agent. I remember the day I left that house. When we had lived there it had been a busy place, full of music, laughter and fun, but now it was empty and silent. It seemed strange to be leaving, and as I reluctantly closed the door for the last time, I felt quite sad. We'd had some great times there, and I wished we could stay. Lin drove me to drop the keys off, and then we went back to her house. My new flat had been decorated, but that was all. I needed to get a carpet for the main room, and somehow acquire some furniture before I could move in. With everything else going on, and Christmas not being too far away, Eddie and Lin had very kindly offered to let me stay with them until everything was ready.

It was very wet and dreary that Friday lunch time, as I travelled to Leamington Spa to begin my training at the guide dog centre. I arrived around four in the afternoon, and was immediately shown the way upstairs to the room where I would be staying for the next four weeks. I unpacked my things, and then made my way down to the large lounge where others had gathered. There were ten people on the course, the youngest person was in his late teens, and the eldest was a gentleman in his early seventies. Eight of us had come to be trained with our first guide dog, while two people had come to train with a new dog after their previous one had retired. On that Friday evening, it was all about learning our way around the building, meeting our GDMI's and getting to know the other people on the course. We were sad to learn that we would have a full days training the following day, but wouldn't actually meet our dogs until Sunday afternoon.

That evening, we ate a meal together in the large dining room, and spent some time in the bar before retiring to our rooms to get a good night's sleep. After breakfast on the Saturday morning, we received a talk about caring for our dogs, including feeding and grooming. In the afternoon, we spent time walking around the grounds, once again holding on to the handle of a guide dog harness with an instructor taking the role of the dog, in order to give us more practice before the real thing the next day. By Saturday night we were all quite tired. There had been a lot of information to take in. As the evening wore on, an air of tension could be detected. We were very anxious to meet our dogs and get started with the training. I climbed into bed with a head full of thoughts. I just couldn't wait to see Fred. As I lay there, I could see the light in the corridor shining through the small glass panel in the top of my door, and wished I could get to sleep. I lay there for hours and hours just waiting for the morning to arrive. I felt Fred was so close to me, and yet so far away.

When Sunday morning arrived, we ate breakfast, before doing yet more walks around the grounds. At lunch time, we sat at our tables, but I don't think that any of us were particularly hungry. We knew it was nearly time for the big moment. When we had finished, we were taken in to the lounge, where an instructor told us what was going to happen next. We were asked to go and sit in our rooms, and our dogs would be brought from their kennels to meet us. We would then be left for around an hour to spend time getting to know the dogs in our rooms. I remember sitting on a chair opposite my bed, and listening as instructors knocked on people's doors. Suddenly, it was my turn, and in front of me was the friend I'd longed to meet again. I reached out my hand to find Fred, who was just as fluffy and adorable as I remembered.

It takes time and patience for a dog to bond with its new owner. While they are in training, dogs become very attached to their instructors, and it takes a while for them to transfer their affections to their new owners. As my GDMI proceeded down the corridor, Fred would hear her voice, walk to the door and whine. Luckily, we had been warned about this possibility, so it didn't bother me too much. At the end of the hour, we were asked to put leads on our dogs, and make our way back down to the lounge, where we could all spend some time becoming acquainted once more. We were given another talk about handling, and taught some basic obedience commands, such as getting the dog to sit, or lie down beside us.

In contrast with the previous evening, that night I slept very well. Fred had his dog bed beside me, and settled down with no problems. The only thing I remember was momentarily waking up a couple of times after hearing an unfamiliar sound. As I sat up, I suddenly remembered. Oh yes, of course that was Fred. When my alarm went off the next morning, I got an extra wake-up call, a very cold wet nose on my hand and then on my face.

On the Monday morning, we experienced our first taste of pounding the pavements with our new dogs. It takes a good deal of both physical and mental energy to get through the course. Our days were very well organised and structured, with time shared between working outside, or back at the centre, learning how to groom our dogs, and how to care for them correctly. On that first day, I realised just how much information we were required to take in and commit to memory. As I began my first walk, I realised that the time ahead over the next few weeks would be all about me getting to know Fred, and him me. We attempted a tentative, but successful walk, and when I had finished, I knew I had made the right decision in applying for a guide dog.

When working outside during that first week, we spent most of our time walking around a quiet residential area. Each session would last around forty five minutes, and we gradually built up our confidence. By the end of the first week, we were all very tired, but beginning to relax more while working our dogs. Unfortunately, because it was November, it would often be raining hard when we were out, and we'd return feeling quite cold, but there was always a hot drink and plenty of biscuits waiting for us back at the centre. The afternoon sessions would take a similar format to that of the morning. After lunch, we would split into two groups. One would go out in the minibus to walk the streets of Leamington, while the other group would be back at the centre, grooming their dogs, or doing some obedience training. Then the process would be reversed when the other group returned. At the start of the training, when we were out and about, our instructors would walk close behind us, but as the days and weeks moved on, and we grew in confidence and ability, they would follow further behind.

In order for a guide dog and its owner to work together effectively, it is necessary to learn a combination of foot positions, hand signals, and verbal commands. A dog will always sit when he or she reaches a down kerb at a road side, indicating the step, and then will wait for a command as to what to do next. This could be a simple instruction to go forward", or possibly to turn left or right. It is a complete myth that a dog can be asked by its owner to be taken to the bank or anywhere else for that matter. The handler must have a mental picture of where they want to go, and issue appropriate commands. The dog does, inevitably, become used to familiar routes, but they are trained to work following instruction from their owner. Dogs are, however, trained to use their initiative. Only today, I was walking round the busy town centre, when my dog stopped in the middle of the pavement and refused to go forward. I learned that this happened because some scaffolding, which wasn't normally there, was now in the way. Unaware of that, I gave him the command to go forward, but he just sat still. This was my cue to realise that there was some kind of obstacle in front of me and I was able to allow him to guide me around it and get back to our normal route.

After a full days training, we would all spend the evenings socialising in the bar, or sometimes have a quiz in the lounge area. There were a couple of pay phones, so we could keep in touch with our families, and let them know how we were getting on. There were always lots of people around if we required any help, and we got to know many of the staff who worked in the building. We would often see other dogs who were still being trained, and I will always remember one of them. I was walking through the bar area, when a dog's very waggy tail brushed my hand. I noticed that the dog had a bandage on his tail and feeling sympathy for him, I enquired as to what had happened. I was told that the dog insisted on wagging his tail vigorously, and often. He had in fact wagged it so hard that it had started to bleed, and a bandage was required. Nevertheless, the dog was still wagging seemingly unaware of his injury. I felt sorry for him. He was so sweet, but at the same time, I found it rather amusing.

Fred was a real character. He was as I said before, extremely handsome, and he knew it. He was what we used to call "a poser." Whenever anyone stopped to tell him so, he would lift his nose high in the air and wag his tail. Fred's tail had a natural kink in it, which meant that it made the shape of a letter C. While at the training centre, one of the GDMI's commented that he had quite a regal look about him and maybe he should be knighted. So one morning, the ceremony took place, with Fred sitting patiently. Instead of a sword, a butter knife was used. Yes, there were some rather crazy, hilarious moments during that month of training. It was great fun. We tackled the busy town centre, travelled on the train, and avoided countless obstacles, as we learned to be competent guide dog owners.

It is important to give your dog at least one opportunity per week to be able to run freely and play. So one day, we all went over to a local park to allow them to let off some steam. The dog wears a special "play collar" on these occasions, which has a bell so that they can be heard while running around. They are trained to return as soon as they hear their owners blow a whistle, and call their names. This sounds quite straight forward, and normally works fine, but what about when there are ten dogs all at the same time? Picture the scene. Ten blind people stand in a line, and at the same time allow their dogs to go freely running around the park. Several minutes later, we are told to blow our whistles and call them back. I'm sure we could have sold tickets that day. Ten dogs suddenly ran in the same direction, and ten people leant forward to reach for their dog but, in the melee, none necessarily finding the right one. It was hilarious. I however didn't have a problem as there was no mistaking Fred's fluffy coat, and long floppy ears, not to mention that rather distinctive tail.

One Sunday morning, towards the end of our training, we all piled on to a minibus and took a trip out into the country. As we left the busy streets, and entered those narrow lanes with open fields on either side, suddenly the noise began. The dogs had no trouble realising where they were, and certainly let us know. It began with a little whine and whimper, then they began to twitch and fidget. They became so excited that the bus was then filled with a barking rabble. We put into practice the obedience training we had been given, and moments later, there was relative calm, but those dogs struggled to contain their excitement, before finally being allowed to get out of the bus and enjoy their surroundings. There was a treat in store for us too; a well-earned drink in a country pub.

At meal times, our dogs were trained to sit patiently under the table until we had finished. Guide dogs are given a well-balanced diet, to keep them fit and healthy, and maintain a steady weight. Unhealthy treats such as biscuits or crisps are strictly forbidden. Adhering to this advice is greatly beneficial to the dogs, and probably the reason why Fred lived until he was fourteen. It is my opinion that during one of these times several of the dogs had their own conversation, and cooked up a mischievous plan. I was woken at four in the morning, by a cold wet nose and a whimper. With a yawn and a stretch, I decided that it was time for me to put on my dressing gown and take Fred downstairs to the spending pen for a wee. I did my best to be as quiet as possible so as not to disturb anyone else, but was surprised to find that when I reached the door, there were already two people taking their dogs for a wee. As we giggled about the coincidence, others appeared, and it seemed that for some strange reason, just on this one night, every dog had needed a wee at the same time. Talk about being led astray! I once heard someone say that when making a comparison with a dog's sense of smell to ours the easiest way of doing this would be to compare the size of a stamp, with the size of a standard envelope. (Ours is the stamp, and theirs is the envelope.) It must be so difficult to smell all that lovely food your owner is eating, while you sit patiently on the floor, so maybe this was their rebellious response.

On a busy afternoon in the centre of town, I walked with Fred, closely followed by my instructor. Suddenly, my right shoulder brushed a sign that was sticking out, and my GDMI stopped me. She told me that in that situation, I was to gently flick the handle attached to Fred's harness, and give the command "watch", to indicate to the dog that I had detected an obstacle. I paused and pondered the information. It left me feeling a little uncomfortable as I pictured different scenes in my head. As I issued the instruction to watch, I imagined pedestrians walking toward me and hearing me assuming it was aimed toward them. Some would scuttle away quickly and submissively, while others would issue me with the filthiest of offended looks. As I explained these reservations to my instructor, she couldn't stop laughing, and said she had never thought about it like that before. That was just one of many times we spent standing on a pavement unable to control our giggling.

I only had one week left of my training when I received some sad news. My godfather, Uncle Eric had died. When his wife, my Auntie Annie rang me, she was so apologetic when telling me that unfortunately the funeral would take place on my birthday, but I was more upset to have lost such a kind, fun-loving person from my life, and felt terrible about being unable to attend the funeral. Auntie was adamant. I must complete the training, and bring Fred home to meet her. During that final week, we were driven into the town centre, and told to walk to Dale Street, where our GDMI's would be waiting for us. It was an area we had walked around several times, and so we should all have been fairly confident about completing the task. Unfortunately, I managed to get myself completely lost. I suddenly thought to myself, "This doesn't seem right." However, I'd had plenty of mobility training over the years, and this situation didn't cause me to panic. I stopped the next member of the public who walked by me, and asked directions. I was able to get myself back on track, and make my way to the meeting point. The thought never entered my head that anyone would be worried.

Back at Dale Street, when it was realised that I had strayed from the pack, the GDMI's became anxious. Everyone else was loaded back on the bus, while they began the search on foot. I must have only been a few minutes late, but nevertheless they were concerned for my safety. As I sauntered up to the minibus moments later, one of the instructors shouted, "Here she comes with a smile on her face, not a care in the world, as if nothing has happened. There was great relief among the group, as if I'd been gone for hours, and I was left wondering what all the fuss was about. The following day, several of my fellow students questioned me about what had happened. If there was just me around, they would ask me if I was scared, and how did I find my way back, always adding that they were glad it didn't happen to them, because they definitely would have been thrown into a state of panic. I suppose all those years of tapping along the streets with my cane at St. Vincent's and Chorleywood served me well.

Our final day's training was my birthday. I spent a good deal of time thinking about Auntie Annie and Uncle Eric, but I knew that neither of them would want me to be miserable and tried to push those thoughts aside. We went out to do our final walk, and I'm pleased to say that I didn't get lost. I strode out confidently and it was a brilliant feeling. When dog and handler have learned to work together, the sense of freedom and independence a blind person experiences is absolutely priceless. Because we had all done so well, we were told that we would be going out for a meal that evening before going home the following day. As we gathered in the lounge around seven o'clock, there was another surprise in store for me. Suddenly everyone began to sing "Happy Birthday", and in front of me was a huge cake covered in candles. It was a lovely gesture on behalf of the staff at the centre, and that night we went to bed stuffed full with curry and cake. My parents came to collect me the following day and I proudly introduced them to Sir Fred. That month had been hard work, but well worth it, and now I was leaving with a dog who was an absolute dream. I simply couldn't thank the staff enough. Guide dog mobility instructors are some of the most dedicated, knowledgeable, and caring people I have ever met. They work tirelessly, in all weathers, and often very long hours, to give us remarkable dogs that provide us with so much independence and joy. If you've ever donated to the Guide Dogs for the Blind Association, many, many thanks, and thanks to everyone at GDBA. Keep up the good work.

25. Me 'N' Thee

I left Leamington, and travelled up to my parent's house to spend Christmas with them. Gaz joined us a couple of days later, and we all had a great time. Wherever we went, Fred was the star of the show, and all the family loved him. My GDMI made a couple of trips to see how we were getting on, and taught us a few routes around the area so I could give Fred a good long walk. We had already become inseparable, and I couldn't possibly calculate the miles we clocked up together over the years that followed. Wherever I went, Fred went too. He didn't like being separated from me, especially during those early days. I remember one particular afternoon when I left Fred lying in the lounge, and went to use the bathroom. I'd only been gone for a minute, when outside the door I heard Fred whining. He was such a softy.

Fred was extremely vocal, and it always made me laugh. Each morning when I got up to let him go outside, he developed what I always referred to as his "good morning growl." When I called his name, he would dash toward me with a growl that wasn't at all aggressive, but had almost a kind of melody behind it. His tail would wag vigorously, and he would always, in true retriever style, carry a toy in his mouth and present it to me. Fred loved being outdoors, where he would spend hours chasing after a ball, before returning and dropping it at my feet. He would then dance around, willing me to throw it once again. Sometimes, it seemed he would never tire but, eventually, I would take him back inside, where he would lie on the floor, sounding like a steam train. I filled his dish with fresh water, and he would look over at it, not knowing whether to drink, or carry on panting. He was excellent at catching a ball too. I would throw it up in the air, and he would jump and catch it nearly every time. When he did so, he would growl, proudly announcing his victory, before dropping the ball in my lap, and barking until I threw it up again.

When the festive season was over, it was time for Gaz to return to Wolverhampton. I travelled back to Worcester, and stayed with Eddie and Lin until my flat was ready. My GDMI made further visits and we learned a few routes around the City centre. Around that time, I heard the good news that Leah was also about to attend her guide dog training centre in the North West, to get her first dog. When she called me, she had just had her matching visit, and was due to train with a Labrador whose name was Jasper. Leah sounded just as excited about the prospect as I had several weeks earlier. I was very pleased for her, and we chatted about what the next few weeks would involve.

By the end of January my flat was ready. Emotionally, I don't think I was quite ready to move in, but I kept my feelings to myself. It was time to bight the bullet, and stand on my own too feet. I thought about those four weeks I had spent alone in our previous house when Gaz and Tony had moved out. During the days it had been ok, but the evenings always seemed long and lonely on my own. This time, it was slightly different. I had Fred to keep me company. My flat was in a block with six others, and in those first few days, I learned that we were a mishmash of rather interesting characters. I was regularly a captive audience to nocturnal shenanigans as one lady entertained her regular gentlemen visitors. During the day, I would often play my guitar and sing. I hadn't had any complaints in the past, but now this would often be brought to an abrupt end when the gentleman who lived above me would thump his foot on my ceiling, and command me to be quiet, using the most colourful language. Surprisingly, I found this shocking from an elderly person.

Location-wise, my flat was great. It was a ten minute walk away from the city centre, and only two minutes away, there were several shops. Every day, I would spend at least an hour walking with Fred to ensure he had plenty of exercise. On one occasion, not long after moving, we were out one day and I was crossing a quiet road. Instead of crossing in a straight line, Fred veered quite far over to the right. I stood on the opposite side of the road feeling perplexed. I was still obviously quite inexperienced and wondered why this had happened. As I stood there, a member of the public approached me, and asked, "Are you ok?" I replied that I was fine and turned to go on my way. As I did so, the person stopped me and said, "Did you know your dog just lead you around a big hole in the road?" There was my answer. Fred had done his job, and I had been completely oblivious to his good work. I bent down, gave him a pat and told him what a good dog he was. I was so pleased with his ability to use his initiative, and felt quite guilty that I had doubted him.

With each trip out, it seemed that more and more people were stopping to admire Fred. I decided one day, that I would count how many people commented or asked if they could stroke him. In the space of one hour, fourteen people approached me, and it became apparent that it probably would have taken me less time to get my errands done if I'd have used my white cane instead. There was no chance of that happening though. Fred was amazing, and even better, he was mine! However, I did find one little chink in Fred's armour, or

211

should I say fur? He hated the rain. I learned that one morning as we made our way into town to catch the bus over to Eddie and Lin's house. Half way between home and the bus station it suddenly started to rain, and when I say rain, I mean very hard. Fred suddenly stopped and sat down. First I gently encouraged him to continue, then I commanded him, but to no avail. Retrievers are known for having a stubborn streak, and Fred was certainly no exception. He lay on the ground and refused to move. I pleaded with him, and even bribed him with his favourite dog treats, but nothing worked. I stood there, frustrated, and soaked to the skin. I felt so embarrassed as a few people who walked past tried to coax him into moving, and eventually he stood up. By that time I had missed my bus over to Lin's house, and they only ran every two hours, so a rather bedraggled woman and her dog returned home to get warm and dry. My flat smelled of damp dog for the rest of the day, and I was left with a huge pile of towels to wash.

Talking about washing, it was a good few weeks before I got the money together to buy myself a washing machine. At first I had to hand wash some stuff, and take the rest to the launderette which wasn't an easy task. I was positively ecstatic when Eddie came over to install my washing machine. When he had gone, I loaded it, and sat for the next hour just listening to it do its work. It sounds rather pathetic now, but at the time I was so grateful to have it. At weekends, Gaz would come over to see me, and we always spent the time staying at Eddie and Lin's house. We loved those weekends, which have left us with many precious memories. On Saturday evenings, Lin would often hold a dinner party for several friends, and we were also invited. We enjoyed fantastic food, and equally good company. It was so generous of them to include us in their family life, and we loved them both very much. The four of us attended the church in their village. Gaz played keyboard, I played my flute, and Lin sang with us. She has always been an excellent singer, and we enjoyed hour upon hour at their house singing in three part harmony, as Eddie listened, and often made recordings. The church service was held on Sunday evening, and so the morning would often find us walking round the village with Fred and their two dogs. Upon our return, Lin would busily make lunch, but would insist on Gaz and I going into the large front hall to play the piano and sing to her while she cooked. Eddie often joined us, and occasionally we would coax him into playing the piano. When lunch was served, we always tucked into a wonderful Sunday roast, followed by the main event of the day, the dessert. Lin was fully aware of my passion for chocolate, and took it upon herself to create me a different chocolate dessert every weekend. As I tucked in, always complimenting her on her achievement, she would say, "Oh Jane, you're so predictable!" and we would all laugh.

After church in the evening, a few of us would go back to the house, where we would crowd around the breakfast bar in the kitchen and munch on cheese on toast, while Gaz would bombard the church pastor with interesting theological questions. It was during one of these eventful weekends that we experienced a moment I will never forget.

Eddie, Lin, Gaz and I were making breakfast, when Eddie spilled his bowl of cornflakes on the kitchen work top. He was a very laid back kind of guy, and simply proceeded to sweep them back in to his bowl, before adding milk and eating them. As he was finishing, Lin came over and asked, "Have you seen a couple of tablets on the work top?" Eddie replied that he hadn't seen anything, and asked what kind of tablets they were. Lin explained that she had just prepared food for their pet cat, and had left two tablets out ready to add to his meal. Suddenly the penny dropped, and Eddie laughed, as he told Lin that he had probably eaten them when he shovelled his cereal into the bowl. We all expressed our concern, and then I enquired, "Tell meow you're feline Eddie?" Everyone laughed uncontrollably, to the point where we cried, before Lin went to get more medication for the cat.

Eddie was an extremely hard working and successful businessman who sometimes worked very long hours. At home, however, he was one of the most laid back, good humoured people I have ever met. Many people gave him a lighthearted ribbing about how shall we say, "careful" he was with his money, but in mine and Gaz's experience, he was one of the most generous people I have ever known. I consider myself very blessed, because I have extremely loving and supportive parents, but in addition, Lin and Eddie were like a second set of parents to Gaz and me. Eddie would always leave the house early in the morning to go the his office in Worcester. On Mondays Gaz would need to return to Wolverhampton, and so would grab a lift with him. I would sometimes join them if I wanted to get home early too. These mornings would often find us rushing around to be ready on time, grabbing some kind of breakfast to take with us in the car. Eddie had an interesting choice on those occasions, he would make himself a marmalade and banana sandwich, which he would put on to a large plate, accompanied by a mug of coffee. This he would place very carefully on his lap, and actually manage to drive without spilling a drop. Eddie also got a lot of stick about the state of the inside of his car. We would usually find ourselves surrounded by newspapers, empty coffee cups, and sweet wrappers, to mention just a few. We didn't care, Eddie was a star, and we wouldn't have wanted to change him for the world.

As I opened the door of my silent flat, it seemed a world away from those fun weekends, full of chat and laughter. I still felt tormented by the fact that I didn't have a job, and was very glad when one day shortly after moving in, I received a call from the guide dog centre. The regional fund raising manager asked if he and a colleague could meet up with me for lunch, as they had something to discuss with me. I was excited to find that they wanted me to be responsible for giving talks on how guide dogs are trained, and what it is like working together. This would only be on a voluntary basis, but my travel expenses would be reimbursed. I was given information to read and listen too, including relevant facts and figures, and also advice about giving talks from others already doing the job in other geographical areas. I was the only guide dog owner covering Hereford and Worcester, and after only a few weeks of being involved, I was very busy.

I suppose you could say that I was thrown in at the deep end, because one of my first tasks was to give a talk to a large group of students at a comprehensive school. They had raised a considerable amount of money for GDBA, and I was to give a talk followed by a short speech thanking pupils and staff for their tremendous efforts. Reporters from the local press were also present, and I had my photo taken accepting the cheque. Being a speaker for GDBA kept me relatively busy over the months that followed. From young farmers societies, to the Women's Institute, Fred was adored and admired. It was however in schools that he elicited the biggest "Ah's" of wonder and delight. It didn't matter whether it was an infant school or a grammar school, Fred was always the star, and took it all in his stride. I would often be invited to return for additional visits, and following my regular talk, would be asked to visit all the classrooms to allow the children more time to ask questions and spend time with Fred.

It was during my visit to a private school that I faced one of my biggest challenges. At the end of the morning, the principal said that she would be extremely grateful if I would consider staying for lunch, and then visiting the pre-school children, to speak to them. Not wishing to appear uncooperative, I agreed, but inside, I wondered how I could keep the attention of several two, three and four year old infants for even five minutes! Lucky for me, and them, I had lunch time to try to work out a strategy. When two o'clock arrived, and I stood at the front of the small hall, I introduced myself, then Fred, and then sat on the floor with everyone else. Surprisingly, I filled the next twenty minutes, with questions to the children, asking them things like, "What is it like when you go out to the shops with your Mummy or Daddy? Is it quiet, or is it noisy?" I would then wait for their excited answers, and explain how my special dog needed to walk past noisy busses and cars, and help me even though sometimes it might be a little scary. This stratagem of asking them questions, meant that most of them became engaged and I was surprised how quickly the time went before I had to leave. Giving those talks was a good deal of fun, and taught me about public speaking. It also was a worthwhile exercise in confidence-building for me personally.

My days were quite busy, but again it was the evenings that seemed to drag. I would make frequent visits up the road to my old college, to meet up with friends I had known while I was there as a student. We would have some great times, but when I returned home around eleven in the evening, my flat was quiet and lonely. I experienced a couple of unnerving incidents which caused some rather worrying and broken night's sleep. Once, I awoke around two in the morning to hear footsteps outside the front of my flat. The main room which was both my living room and my bedroom was around eighteen feet long, and I could hear the footsteps walk up and down the length outside, which went on for several minutes. I lay in bed feeling quite scared, and wondering what to do. Eventually, the person went away, but it was several hours before I got back to sleep.

A couple of days later, I returned home after taking Fred for a walk. I approached my back door, and as I reached my kitchen window just before the door, I became aware that there was someone standing in front of my window, looking through it. I knew this because, as soon as he heard me, the man swung around and in a rather flustered voice, said, "Good afternoon, how are you?" I recognised his voice as being a man who often visited the elderly lady who lived next door to me. I have to admit that I didn't feel entirely comfortable in his presence and didn't hang around to make conversation. Not long after, I was making my way to the chip shop around tea time, when two ladies approached me. They rather politely, but tentatively introduced themselves, and told me that they were concerned about me, because they had seen a man peeking through a tiny gap in my curtains the evening before, and wanted to let me know. From then on I was very careful about making sure my curtains were fully closed, I always kept my door locked, and sometimes slept with my lamp on beside my bed. I like my own time and space, but I wasn't the best person when it came to living on my own.

Guide dogs aren't trained to be guard dogs, but around that time, I experienced something quite strange. I was walking along a street not far from my flat when I heard two people talking and walking toward me. I thought nothing of it, but as they were around eight feet away from me, Fred suddenly lowered his head, and let out a very low menacing growl, that went on until the people crossed the road and continued on the other side. Nothing like that had ever happened before, and I have absolutely no explanation for why it happened, but Fred seemed very sure about what he wanted. I've heard some people say that dogs have a sixth sense and maybe it's true. In all the years we worked together, this never happened again, but, whatever his reasons, I'm glad Fred was with me at the time. I simply couldn't have wished for a better dog. We virtually spent every minute together over those few months and he was almost perfect in his work, unconditionally faithful, and it was my utter joy and my privilege that he was mine.

26. Wedding Bells

In March 1992, my parents celebrated their twenty-fifth wedding anniversary. Eddie and Lin were sent an invitation to attend the party, and this sparked off a significant discussion between Lin, Gaz, me and a couple of our mutual friends. The question was posed about when Gaz and I were finally going to get married. By that time, we had been together for over five years, and had always planned to marry once we had both left university, but we still hadn't been able to save enough money to cover the cost. It wasn't long before some of the girls, who went to the same church as we did, suggested that our friends could get together to help keep costs down, so we could have the ceremony, and have a great party afterwards.

Less than an hour later, we had spoken with the senior pastor of our church, a date had been set, and several plans had been put into place. I spent the rest of the day feeling a little bemused, but very excited. The only problem now though was how I was going to break the news to Mum and Dad.

The news filtered around church members very quickly, and everyone seemed just as excited as we were. We were to be married at St. Paul's Church in Worcester on the fourth of July, and then have the reception in the grounds of Eddie and Lin's manor house in a small village just outside Worcester. We were completely overwhelmed by the kindness of our friends. A team of ladies got together to organise the catering, and another to organise the flowers. Someone offered to drive Dad and myself to church in their rather expensive car, and another gentleman offered to play the piano during the reception. People just kept coming forward with offers of help, and we were continually amazed by their generosity.

When I plucked up the courage to break the news to my parents, they weren't exactly jumping for joy. I think they had always expected me to get married in my home town, rather than in Worcester, but that was where most of our friends were, and it made sense because it was half way between Gaz's family and mine. I appreciate that it can't have been easy for them though. Poor Dad had already paid out a huge sum of money for their silver wedding celebration, and now they would feel obliged to contribute toward the wedding only four months later. Nevertheless, we continued with our plans, including making a guest list, and sending all the invitations. Eddie was meticulous in compiling several detailed lists. I simply don't know how we would have managed without his, and Lin's boundless energy and kindness. I had no problem in choosing my bridesmaids, that job would go to Kirsten and Leah. Leah had great fun trying on loads of different dresses, but as usual, I wasn't quite as enthusiastic. Gaz had more of a dilemma when deciding on his best man. Chris, his best friend from school was at the top of his list, but so was Eddie. In the end, it was decided that the two of them would take on the task together. Unconventional, yes, but it worked really well.

The Manor house became the wedding headquarters, and as the day drew closer its bustling busyness increased. Mum came down a week early to stay with Lin and help with all the last minute errands. On the Thursday afternoon before the big day, I went over there. As I entered the kitchen, I witnessed a plethora of ladies all furiously chopping vegetables, and preparing food. Outside, others were erecting a huge marquee on one of the lawns. One lady had made a beautiful linen lining for the inside and as I listened to everything going on around me, I felt quite overcome with emotion. These people were so incredibly generous.

The day before the wedding, I left my flat and walked into town with Fred. I wanted to buy a special gift for Gaz, which ended up being a rather expensive wallet. As we made our way home, and I walked past the church where the ceremony would take place, someone approached me to say hello. It turned out to be a lady from the church whom I had not known for very long. As our conversation drew to a close, she said, "I must dash, there's a big wedding on at church tomorrow, and I'm helping with the flowers." She had no idea it was my wedding, and as we parted I said, "I'm sure you'll do a great job."

That afternoon, Mum collected Leah from the railway station, and we all travelled over to Eddie and Lin's house where many guests had gathered. Guest houses in the area did very well that weekend, because so many people travelled to celebrate with us. There were four pubs in the village, and that evening, we all congregated in the largest one to eat together before the main party began. Eddie had everything planned. The girls would frequent all of the four pubs that evening travelling in one direction, while the guys did the same but the opposite way round. We went out to party, and party, we did! I recall that we girls gave a particularly rowdy rendition of "Delilah" as I held a rather large glass of Bacardi and coke in my hand. At the end of the evening I was told that Gaz had been tied to a large anchor outside one of the pubs. It was rather late when Leah and I got into bed in the room we shared back at Lin's house, but it had been a fantastic evening.

I slept very well that night, until we were both woken up around seven the next morning. I've never been the best at getting up early, and that morning was no exception. As my Mum urged us to get up, I hid under my duvet. The only wedding present I wanted in that moment, was an extra hour in bed. Before eight a.m. my Mum, Kirsten, Leah and I were walking up a long wooden staircase, and into a salon, to have our hair done. As my new hair style took shape, I sat and pondered on how the day would go. Would all the guests arrive? Would the weather be good? How was Gaz feeling? Luckily, I had the girls around me to keep me from being overly concerned. Once every strand of hair was perfectly placed, we took a short walk over to one of the village pubs, where we enjoyed breakfast together. I was highly amused after learning that Gaz's family had only arrived at six o'clock that morning. Instead of arriving for dinner the previous evening, they had been delayed, and travelled through the night. Well, they were on Jamaican time I suppose!

We enjoyed a long leisurely breakfast, before returning to the manor house to get ready for the ceremony which was scheduled to begin at two o'clock. Seeing Leah get so much enjoyment from having her make-up on and wearing her bridesmaid dress really brought a grin to my face too. She loved all that girly stuff. As for me, I just wanted to get to the church and get on with it. I think my Mum must have hatched a little devious plan weeks previously, because as we girls entered one of the large bedrooms to start getting changed, she appeared with a large bottle of expensive champagne. For years, she had endured my irritation at having to get dressed up, and today would be no exception. Maybe, she thought that if she could ply me with copious amounts of champers, I wouldn't be bothered about my wedding dress. On that day there would definitely be no protest from me, however, I wasn't going to tell Mum that. Could you refill my glass please?

Lin joined us as we continued to get ready. There was a great deal of chat, laughter, and a few tears, as Mum and Lin told us how beautiful we looked, and took some photographs. Several times my thoughts turned to Gaz, as I wondered what he was doing and how he was feeling, but I was sure that Chris and Eddie had everything in hand. Moments later, we heard someone running down the corridor outside, and then there was a knock at our door. Eddie appeared looking rather flustered. He immediately composed himself, gave me a big hug, and commented on how lovely we all looked. He then turned, and dashed out of the door, and with a cheeky little giggle, exclaiming, "Got to go, I Can't find Gaz!" "Can't find Gaz?" I thought, "I think it's time for another glass of champagne." I learned later, that Gaz had been whisked away by his brother to have a last minute haircut.

Eventually, we were ready, and the girls got into the car and off to church. I made my way downstairs, sat with my Dad, and had some more photographs taken with him. I then took Dad's arm, and followed him out to our waiting car. The weather wasn't as good as we'd hoped, but at least it wasn't raining. We made the twenty minute journey into Worcester city centre, and over to the church. As I stepped out of the car and on to the pavement, trying not to get tangled in the wealth of material in my dress, I felt rather nervous. As we walked through the door, Mum, Kirsten and Leah were waiting for us. We had a brief conversation before taking a final deep breath, and then my Dad and I walked into the main part of the church, and down the aisle. The service was everything I'd hoped for, except for a slight hitch when Gaz tried putting the wedding ring on my finger, and it got stuck. Our pastor laughed and asked the congregation, "Does anyone have any soap?" In a split second though, it slid on my finger, and we continued with proceedings.

The congregation was in fine voice as we sang through our chosen hymns and songs. We had invited around one hundred and fifty guests to the church, but I was to find out during the service, that there were many more present. During the signing of the register, Lin sang a song for us. It was extremely beautiful and very moving, but then again Lin's voice always does sound very beautiful. One of the most memorable moments of that day was when the pastor announced us "now being man and wife together." There was a thunderous roar of cheers, and applause which really surprised but pleased us, and sounded as if there were several hundred people in the building. We often laugh about it and are still not sure whether it was affirmation, or whether they were actually saying "About time too!" As Gaz and I walked down the aisle together and outside to greet our friends and family, we were both very happy, the day had finally come, Mr and Mrs Readfern-Gray, what a great team, even though I say it myself!

We spent a long time outside the church, greeting friends, and having photos. So many people had travelled considerable distances to share our day. From London to Lancashire, and Birmingham to

Liverpool, they were all there including of course Josie. We wanted to try and greet as many guests as possible and spend time with them before we all drove back to the manor house for the reception. The large marquee had been filled with long tables and chairs where everyone would sit to enjoy a meal. Each table had a beautiful flower arrangement, and the menu was simply amazing. When it came to dessert, I wasn't sure how I would manage to eat it, but then I learned that Lin had made homemade chocolate roulade just for me, and banoffee pie for Gaz and we were left with no doubt that we'd find room. There were several speeches, including one from my Dad, one from Eddie and one from Chris which had us all in fits of laughter. In the evening we had a disco, and Gaz and I took the opportunity to chill out with some of our friends from college. It was a very special day, shared with our very special friends, and we will never forget what fun it was and how kind our friends were toward us. If you were there, and especially if you were part of the huge team who helped out, let me now say a huge heartfelt thank you to every single one of you. You are all incredibly generous people.

We spent our honeymoon in Wales, where we went on a cable car, tobogganed down the Great Orme, and rode the waves in a speedboat. The hotel where we stayed was quite small, and we got to know some of the other guests. Gaz's Mum had made our wedding cake, and there was so much of it that we took some with us and shared it with the other guests. Irene's home made fruit cake was indeed a cake to be reckoned with. I think the alcohol content was greater than the rest of the ingredients put together, but it was amazingly good. I remember one particularly eventful breakfast time after having shared our cake the previous night. One couple, from Liverpool, asked another couple, "Did you 'ave some of their cake last night? You could have got bevied off that!" It made us laugh, and I suppose they were right. That same day, someone approached our table, handed Gaz a telegram, and enquired whether Gaz would like it to be read out to him. He thanked the lady concerned, and she began to read:

Hi Mike,
I hope you are enjoying your week away with the lads. Me and the kids all miss you very much. Can't wait to see you next week.
Loads of love,
Mavis x x

The dining room was quite small, and other diners had heard the contents of the telegram. There was a silent pause, before Gaz and I started to laugh, and Gaz shouted, "I bet that was your Dad!" We found out later that day, that it was actually my Mum who had sent it, but don't think you're getting away with it, Dad; I'm sure you had plenty to do with it.

One of our favourite places to visit during that week, was an expensive hotel on the seafront, which had a bar where you could listen to a live jazz artist or band. On several evenings, we put on our best outfits, and entered the room, where we sat on rather plush sofas and worked our way through their extensive cocktail menu. It was simply the best venue to relax and chat, while listening to some cool jazz. One evening, we got rather more than we'd bargained for. As we sipped our cocktails, we were suddenly interrupted by a loud confident voice. A gentleman and his wife pulled chairs over to our table, and as they sat down he announced in a broad Scottish accent, "Can I buy you two independent bu***rs a drink?" Feeling a little embarrassed, we accepted, and Bob went to the bar and returned with a tray of drinks for the four of us. He was certainly a guy who liked to chat, but very friendly. We offered to buy the next round of drinks, but it was clear that Bob was having none of it, especially when he learned that we were on our honeymoon. Halfway through the evening, there was an interval so the band could take a break, and people walked around the room selling raffle tickets. When the person reached our table, I reached for my bag, but Bob was insistent. He was paying for the tickets. He handed Gaz and I a strip of tickets each, and bought some for himself and his wife, and we then waited for the draw.

When the number for first prize was called out, it turned out to be one of Bob's tickets. He walked on to the stage, and was handed a bottle of Champagne. Instead of returning to his seat though, he took the liberty of walking centre stage, taking one of the microphones, and announcing, "I'd like to give this to the blind couple over there who are here on their honeymoon!" There was a rapturous round of applause, as Bob strode across the room and presented Gaz with the large bottle. We both felt it was a kind gesture, but we were a little embarrassed.

The second ticket was then drawn, and this time it wasn't for Bob. The winner went to collect their prize, and we thought nothing of it until we heard an elderly gentleman with a soft voice speaking into the microphone. "I'd like to give these chocolates to the blind lady who is here on her honeymoon." He walked over, gave me the chocolates, and I thanked him warmly. People were very kind to us on that evening, but sometimes despite your disability, you just want to mingle into the crowd and not stand out. The final blow was when the third ticket was pulled out of the box, and it was mine. Everyone began to laugh, and I shouted, "Please draw another one!" We've never been brave enough to go back to that hotel.

That week flew by so quickly, and before we knew it, we were travelling home. We went straight over to Eddie and Lin's house, where Fred was waiting for me. Lin had kindly offered to look after him while I was away, and I knew she would look after him very well. He was used to spending time at her house, and got on well with her two pet dogs. It was clear though that he had missed me, as I had him. Lin told me of how the two of them had been having a great time together for the first few days, but she was rather miffed when in the middle of the week, he had gone upstairs to one of the bedrooms, and lay by the bed where I had slept during visits over the past few months. We stayed with Lin and Eddie for a couple of nights, before the three of us returned to my little studio flat. Loads of our gear had to be stored at Eddie's house, as there simply wasn't room for it in the flat. It was quite a squeeze, and we continued to go and spend the weekends at the manor house. My godmother had bought us a double bed for our wedding present, but just how we squeezed it into that place was a miracle. We were so pleased when a couple of months after getting married, we found a one bedroom flat to move into and got to work packing our stuff. As we put everything into bags, suitcases and boxes, another chapter was beginning, but we were happy, and looking forward to what the future would bring.

27. Ups and Downs

Once again, Lin and Eddie rallied the troops from our church, and we filled a van with our stuff to move to our new abode. It was only a one-bedroomed ground floor flat, but it was much more spacious than our previous home. There was a large grassy area out at the front for Fred to run around on, and a concreted area at the back with several washing lines. Because it was over the other side of the city, we needed to learn our way around our local area, but thankfully it didn't take very long. There was a bus stop only a few paces from the flat, and it took around five minutes to walk to a parade of shops, where, among others, there was a news agent's, a chemist, and a small supermarket.

Once we had moved all the furniture and boxes into the flat, we all sat down to enjoy a cup of tea or coffee. Everyone turned, when we heard something drop through the letterbox. It was a large card from our new neighbours upstairs. We hadn't met, but nevertheless, they wanted to wish us well in our new home, and we were soon great friends. Bridie lived with her partner, and two young sons. She was always so cheerful, welcoming, and ready to help if we needed her. Above her lived Sheila and George, a retired couple, who, again, were very friendly. Sheila loved baking, and she was excellent at it. Wonderful smells of fresh bread and cakes would often waft down the stairs, making us all very hungry and very envious. On regular occasions, there would be a knock at the door, and there she would be, with a tray of biscuits or cake, and they were totally delicious.

We soon got to know lots of people in our community: Bev, who worked in the supermarket and helped us get our shopping, Trevor the butcher, Chris who owned the chip shop, and Squib who owned the bakery. I had a surprise when I went in there one day to buy some lunch. A young gentleman served me, and I was puzzled. His voice sounded strangely familiar, but I just couldn't work out where I had heard it before. Moments later, his mother came out from the back of the shop, and I learned that the young gentleman in question played the part of John Archer in the Radio 4 serial "The Archers." You see, I knew I'd heard that voice before.

At the end of the row of shops, was a pub called "The Glover's Needle." On Tuesday evenings, there was a live band or artist, so Gaz and I often walked down there to have a pint and listen. The acts were usually very good, and we would round the evening off by calling at the chip shop on the way home. Chris would always see us, and call over, even before we'd entered the shop. I have to admit, it was a very good chippy, and I missed it years later when we moved away. So, all in all, we settled in to our new environment very well, and made many new friends.

Life was pretty good in Warndon, except for one single incident which left me a little shaken. Gaz and I had made arrangements to meet our friend Tim in our local pub one evening, but Gaz had to change his plans because someone wanted him to play his bass guitar for a musical event. I asked him if he would mind if I met Tim for a short while in the evening and he was quite happy for us to meet. I walked down the road with Fred, and into the pub. It was quite busy, and I walked over to the bar, bought myself a drink and waited for Tim to arrive. I found a seat on an empty table next to the bar, but was surprised to find that over fifteen minutes later there was no sign of our friend. I started to feel a little uncomfortable being on my own, and decided to finish my drink and walk home.

As I was about to get up to leave, a guy put his drink down on the table and took a seat next to me. He began talking in a friendly manner, but my discomfort increased. Not wishing to appear rude, I engaged in the conversation, all the time desperately hoping that Tim would turn up soon. He continued to ply me with the usual questions such as did I go there often, and when I told him I was waiting for a friend, I'm sure he wasn't convinced. At one point, he placed his hand on my wrist and told me that he would walk me home. I immediately told him that my friend would walk me home, but suddenly, his grip on my wrist tightened. I tried to pull away, but he gripped even tighter, and he leaned in very close and in rather a dominant voice said, "I'm taking you home tonight."

I kept my cool, put a smile on my face, and began a new conversation with him, but inside I was full of panic, and my brain was doing somersaults. As we talked, I was hatching my plan of escape. I would offer him a drink, go to the bar, and make a phone call. I would call my friend who was our regular taxi driver, and ask him to come in to the pub to collect me. We would then drive around in the opposite direction, so that this guy would have no idea in which direction I lived. A second later, I jumped, as I felt a tap on my shoulder, it was Tim. I'd never been so relieved in my life to meet him, and he took a seat next to me. Immediately, the other guy left, and later I told Tim what had happened. I've never been in a pub on my own since, and I'm so glad that Tim turned up when he did.

225

I had been used to walking into the City centre, but after making our move, it was much too far to continue, and I would need to travel on the bus. As I've already stated, it only took a matter of seconds to get from our front door to the bus stop, so journeys into town happened several times per week. Fred always accompanied me, and he was well behaved on the bus. I remember one return journey that always makes me laugh. Gaz, Fred and I got on to the bus, and asked the driver if he would tell us when we got to Cranham Drive. We took our seats, and chatted happily, as the bus drove through the Worcester streets. Suddenly our conversation was interrupted, as Fred stood up which was not normal. I realised that we had been so engrossed in conversation, that I'd not been taking any notice of our route. Although I couldn't see enough to look through the window for any landmarks, I usually timed the journey and reminded the driver nearer the time of the stop I wanted. When Fred stood it prompted me to ask the driver, who had forgotten but, amazingly, Fred had stood up, just before the stop we needed. I must stress, that guide dogs are not trained to prompt their owners at their required bus stops, but on this occasion, Fred had obviously taken the initiative. Both Gaz and I were completely flummoxed, but very proud of him, and very grateful. As the driver stopped, and we stepped off the bus, I heard two elderly ladies behind me saying, "You know, if it wasn't for that dog, they would have missed their stop." They were right, well done Fred.

Although I have always been quite an independent traveller, most of you will probably be pleased to know that, as yet, I have not managed to perfect the art of driving a car. I did get very close one evening. Gaz and I had attended a concert in Birmingham on Saturday with one of Gaz's old friends from college, and Lin had joined us, providing our transport. We all stayed at Eddie and Lin's house that weekend, and on the way home, Lin parked the car for a few minutes outside the village hall to wish a friend a happy birthday, as she had been unable to attend the party. As the three of us, all visually impaired, sat waiting patiently in the car, a gentleman approached us.

He stuck his head through the open driver's window and in a rather terse voice, said, "Excuse me, could you move your car?" Gaz explained that the driver was in the village hall, and would return shortly. Without hesitation, he then said, in a manner that was impatient, irritable and incredibly rude, "Can't you move it!" Now he wasn't the only one who was feeling somewhat irritated, so I answered him in a confident voice, "Of course, sir. Just give me a moment to attach my guide dog to the bonnet."

Shortly after moving house, we made enquiries about having some home help, with basic cleaning duties. The first day our home help lady was due to arrive, we were both a little nervous. We hoped that we would like her, and she would like us. I'm pleased to say that our fears were soon dispelled when another lady called Linn knocked at our door. Linn is one of the loveliest, most cheerful people I have had the pleasure to meet. She is warm, friendly, caring, and a pleasure to have around, as well as being brilliant at her job. I always looked forward to her visits because she always cheered me up. It was completely impossible to be miserable when Linn was around, and we had loads of laughs. Whenever she visited us, I would insist that she take a tea break, and we would chat as we drank our coffee, and ate our chockie biscuits - only the best for our Linn! Several years later, when we had to move from Worcester, she was one of the people that I wanted to pack in my suitcase and take with me. After we moved, we really missed her. There simply wasn't anyone else who could replace her. Since then, we have kept in contact by phone. Whenever we speak, it only takes seconds before Linn has me giggling. Thanks Linn for all you did for us. You are one of the best! Keep on spreading the joy, girl.

For one of our wedding presents, we had been given a rather nice mahogany coffee table, together with a matching nest of tables. We were very pleased with them and proudly placed the long coffee table in the middle of the sitting room. It wasn't long before we realised that there was a snag. Fred's letter C shaped tail was both unique and beautiful. It was also wonderful when it fanned you on a hot day, but it wasn't in favour when he started swiping cups of coffee and glasses of red wine off the table and across the room. We realized, disappointedly, that maybe the coffee table wasn't such a great idea.

Despite the red wine stain on my carpet, Fred was still the star of the show. Several times a year, we would make the journey up to Lancashire to visit my family. In 1993, Mum, Dad, and Nanna moved from Blackburn, to a village in the Ribble valley called Whalley. Sometimes we'd travel by train, and on other occasions Dad would drive down and take us back in the car. Fred was so funny, because as we drove along a stretch of road just before we entered their village, Fred would sniff the air, and start to whine. This always seemed to begin at exactly the same place. His whines would turn to excited

227

howls as we finally drove on to the drive and then he would jump out of the car. Fred loved the countryside, and he also adored my Dad, who would take him out for long walks.

Mum and Dad worked full time, but Nanna was always at home during the day. Each evening, Fred would suddenly rush to the front window, and put his front paws on the window sill. The first time it happened, we didn't have a clue what was going on, but Fred knew. Seconds later, my Dad drove up the drive and Fred rushed to the front door. Fred always knew when Dad was on the way home long before we did, and it was so funny to watch. He was such an incredibly intelligent dog. At one end of their living room, my parents had a patio door, which opened out on to the garden. Fred would often lie on the carpet in the sunshine. One day, Dad had opened the door, and we stood outside talking. He called Fred to come out, but he stayed where he was. After calling him several times, we were puzzled as to why he just stood there and didn't move. When I finally called him, Fred tentatively inched slightly forward and then lifted his front paw rather cautiously. After seeing this it quickly dawned on my Dad that Fred was obviously confused, not understanding about when the door was open or closed. Yes, Fred was an amazing dog.

Every guide dog is amazing in its own way. Shortly after I got Fred, Leah got a guide dog called Jasper. He was a feisty character who loved his food. Our mutual friend Jessica, who had worked at Chorleywood, had warned me all about him after they had been to visit her for a few days. Unfortunately, not long after arriving at her flat, Jasper had been violently sick, and Leah and Jessica had the task of clearing up. I remember Jessica saying, "I'm sure that Jasper must have eaten the entire contents of a Blackpool dustbin before travelling down to visit me."

Jasper's passion for his food was confirmed when I went up to visit Leah in the summer of 1994. Gaz had been doing a foundational maths course with the Open University, and needed to attend a summer school for the week, so I took the opportunity to stay with Leah. On the first evening, when it was time to feed our dogs, we decided to feed them separately. Of course, Jasper went first. As Leah put the food into his bowl, Jasper sat across the room salivating. I will never forget what happened next. Leah shouted, "Jasper, yum yums!" In a nanosecond, Jasper flew across the carpet and over to his bowl. It was like a scene out of a cartoon, or as if someone had attached a rope to his collar, and in one tug, had dragged him across the room. How he moved that quickly I will never know, but it was hilarious.

My favourite and most memorable time during my stay, happened one afternoon, when Leah decided that we should take a walk along the prom, and onto the beach. It was a hot sunny day, and it would be great for the dogs to run on the beach. When we arrived, the beach was full of families having a great time, playing ball games, and making sand castles. We made our way through the crowds, and as the tide was far out walked a fair distance away from everyone. The sand was compact under our feet, and we could feel the lines the waves had left. Eventually, the sound of the people was far behind us, in fact, we couldn't hear much of anything. We put the play collars on the dogs which contained their bells so we could hear where they were and removed their leads and harnesses so they could run free. In fact, we all ran free. There was nothing to bang into, and nothing to trip over. We could run in any direction we wanted without fear of falling and it was brilliant. We chased after the dogs and the dogs chased after us. We laughed and ran, and ran and laughed. Such a feeling of freedom is priceless, and we savoured every moment. We ran and ran until we could run no more and fell in a heap on the sand.

Once we'd got our breath back, we put the harnesses back on the dogs and wondered as to which direction we should take. Note to guide dog owners, do not under any circumstances attempt the same thing either at home or on holiday without sighted assistance. If my GDMI reads this, I'm going to be in a whole heap of trouble. So, we simply put our trust in our dogs and let them lead the way. I'm pleased to say that, without hesitation, they faithfully lead us back to the top end of the beach where everyone else was still enjoying themselves. On our arrival, our first stop was at a cafe, where Leah and I had an ice-cream, and the dogs enjoyed a large bowl of water. I've never forgotten that day. It was a spontaneous decision, that ended up being amazing fun. Thanks Leah, and thanks, Fred and Jasper, that was brilliant.

Round about the same time as my parents moved house, Gaz managed to get some consultancy work, and worked from home. I however had not managed to find employment. After attending several interviews, I decided to explore the possibility of going back to college to acquire more academic qualifications. The process of securing a place, and funding took several months, but in October 1994, I finally began a course at the Royal National College for the Blind in

Hereford. The majority of the students had residential places, but as the journey from Worcester only took an hour, it was convenient for me to travel home each day.

With the onset of my course, my daily routine changed dramatically. I got up at five thirty, and by six o'clock, I would be standing at the bus stop. The usually busy road was silent, and it was dark; actually it was pitch black, and the silence was eerie. I was glad to have Fred with me. I was always glad when the silence was broken by the bus arriving to take me into the city centre. On my first journey, I was surprised to find that there were several people on the bus, even at six in the morning. I had expected to be the only one, but was glad I wasn't. Fifteen minutes later, I would arrive in the middle of town, and then walk the short distance to the station. On this route, there were two significant roads to cross, and in one instance I was left in a state of disbelief at the stupidity of one member of the public. I was crossing a road, and as I reached the middle, someone was walking toward me from the other side. Without a thought she stopped, and began to make a fuss of Fred. I'm not in the habit of giving people dirty looks, but I made an exception on that occasion. I urged Fred to cross safely to the other side, and we carried on with our route. Let me add, that there were cars on the road and, in my opinion, this person had no excuse for potentially placing us in danger. They sure do walk among us!

Once we were safely aboard the train, I would spend the next hour listening to music or reading, while I watched the darkness turn to daylight. The train was usually quite busy, and I was glad when I arrived at college to begin my day. I enjoyed my time there, and made several new friends. The staff I came into contact with were excellent, and I realised quickly that I had chosen the right place to study, despite the long journey. At four o'clock, I made my way back to the station, to get the train back to Worcester. On the way home, I watched the day turn to darkness. I had just stepped off the train and was walking to the bus station to go home one evening, when I met Eddie. We stood and chatted for a while before Eddie told me to be careful not to turn into a vampire, as it would be several weeks before I saw Worcester in daylight again.

I had underestimated just how tiring my new schedule was going to be. After a couple of weeks, I would arrive home, and after a brief conversation with Gaz, I would fall fast asleep on the sofa. Initially, we both agreed that as time went on I would get used to the daily commute, and not be so tired. The situation, however, grew worse and Gaz grew more concerned. I had noticed some other changes, too, and, if I was right, our lives were about to change in a big way.

28. Change is here to stay!

As I sat on the train, one dark November evening travelling from Hereford to Worcester, I contemplated what the future would bring. I knew that when I arrived home, the first thing I needed to do was ring my doctor, for some test results. Would this be the last time I would be making this journey, or would I be continuing with the course? As I walked from the railway station to the bus station, the air was cold, and I just couldn't stop myself from thinking about those test results. When I arrived home, Gaz wasn't around, but this didn't stop me from grabbing the phone and dialing the number for the surgery. I didn't know when he'd be back, and I couldn't wait. Seconds later, I was given some good news, and as I replaced the receiver, I smiled to myself. While my hand was still on the telephone, I suddenly had a thought. I'd better make a call to my college. Feeling rather sheepish, I asked to speak to my tutor, explaining that I would be unable to complete my course, as I was now expecting a baby.

Gaz was thrilled when I gave him the news, as were many of our friends. I recall sitting around the table in the kitchen of the manor house with Lin and Eddie, and when they heard our news, Lin grinned and said, "Oh boy, your lives are really going to change." Lin was referring to our routines both day and night. Most people viewed the prospect of us being parents as a great thing, and said things like, "You'll cope very well," and "It's going to be great." While others asked, "Are you going to have a carer live with you now that you're going to have a baby?" The latter comment is the type that makes me so angry. Yes, I'm blind, but my brain is in full working order. When confronted with a new situation, you don't just acquire a carer, you adapt. I do value my independence, but I've never been afraid, or too proud to ask for help when I need it.

Linn was so excited when we told her. So many times over the months that followed, she would giggle, and say, "I just can't wait to see this baby!" Bridie, too, was thrilled for us, and immediately said, "If you ever need a baby sitter, you know where I am." The pregnancy went very well on the whole. I didn't have a hint of morning sickness, but there were a few occasions when, if I stood still in one place for too long, I felt rather faint. One evening I was chopping some peppers for our evening meal, when suddenly I felt rather sick and faint. I needed to go outside for some fresh air, and I think that at the time Gaz wondered what was going on. This was all new to us.

A few months in to my pregnancy, I developed a serious craving for Weetabix with hot milk. I'm not really a cereal person, in fact, I'm not really much of a breakfast person, but at that time I could have eaten it for every meal, and on some days, that's exactly what I did. Gaz had to resort to buying boxes of forty-eight at a time to keep me going. It's really rather strange, but a couple of years later when my sister was expecting a baby, she had cravings for exactly the same thing. We made regular visits to the hospital for antenatal appointments and scans, and also went to antenatal classes. It was the last few weeks which proved to be the most difficult.

Unfortunately, I managed to pick up an infection, and shivered in my bed beneath a thick duvet, even though it was the middle of a hot summer. It took me a few days to recover, but by then I just wanted our baby to arrive. You know that feeling, ladies, when you've had enough of being pregnant, and just want to meet your child for the first time. As the due date drew closer, we grew more excited, and more impatient. On the day itself, we waited and waited, but there was no sign of anything happening. Three days after my due date, we had a scheduled appointment at the hospital. I was examined, and told that everything was fine, but if nothing happened in the next few days, they would consider inducing me.

Following the appointment, we took a trip into the city centre, and did some shopping. The day was very hot, and I felt quite weary. As we got in to a taxi to make our way home with all the shopping, a friend saw me and ran over shouting, "Have you not had that baby yet?" It was around five o'clock when we got back to the flat, and I went to have a lie down. Not long after, I felt a pain, but as a second one didn't materialise, I thought nothing of it. My thoughts were averted, when there was a knock at the door, and it was Lin. I joined her and Gaz in the living room, and it was during that time, that I began to wonder if our baby was soon to make an appearance.

When Lin had gone, I told Gaz, who suddenly flew into a panic. I managed to calm him down, reminding him that on many occasions, the midwives had told us not to arrive at the hospital until we felt it was necessary. The pains weren't particularly bad, and it could be hours yet, so I decided to have a small snack, and see how things progressed. On reflection, that wasn't the best judgement I have made, because within half an hour, I can remember standing in our bathroom, pressing my hands hard against the wall, while breathing deeply as another rather testing pain challenged my ability to stay calm and not wonder how bad this could get.

By this time, it was around eight o'clock and I told Gaz it was definitely time to get to the hospital. While he called our friend to give us a lift, I lay on the bed. I remember thinking, that this labour stuff is certainly not a barrel of laughs. it seemed that every time another pain washed over me it was saying, "Come on, this time I'm gonna make you scream." I had always thought I had a pretty high pain threshold, but this really was tough stuff. I managed to get myself in to the car, and sat gritting my teeth as we drove to the hospital. By that time, I was struggling, but I was surprised to find that Gaz and his friend were quite calm. So calm in fact, that they casually discussed the cricket together." Cricket!!!" I thought, "Right now, if I had a cricket bat, I know what I'd be hitting, and it wouldn't be a cricket ball."

When we arrived at the hospital, I was taken to a side room, where I lay on a bed. It wasn't long after when the pain got so bad that I gave in. I turned on my side, gripped the side of the bed, and cried out. A woman heard me and walked by. I have no idea whether she was a midwife, or a nurse, but she seemed distinctly unimpressed. Her manner gave me the impression that she was thinking, "Whatever, I've seen it all before." Eventually, a rather nice midwife approached me, and asked if she could examine me. When she did so, she learned that I hadn't been making a fuss over nothing. In fact, I was already eight centimetres dilated, and it really wouldn't be long before we would finally meet our baby. I was immediately taken to the delivery suite, where at 10.50 in the evening, Joshua was born.

Our little man weighed six pounds and two ounces, and already had masses of black hair. During the latter weeks of my pregnancy, I'd experienced a great deal of heart burn, and I was amused when so many people told me, that it meant that the baby would be born with loads of hair. At the time I thought it was daft, but they turned out to be correct. Words can never describe fully the emotions one feels when your first child is born. Pure joy and elation, meet with feelings of responsibility, and the need to nurture and protect. I recall as we made our way to the ward, wheeling Joshua in his little cot, feeling so happy, but at the same time the thought of now being someone's parent was quite daunting.

I didn't sleep a wink that night. My head was full of so many thoughts. It was so hot in the ward, and every few minutes, another baby cried. However, I was so happy with my little man, that nothing bothered me. In truth, I couldn't wait for him to wake up so I could give him a cuddle. Josh was a very chilled out, contented baby. The only thing I experienced some difficulty with during the first couple of days, was getting used to breast- feeding. However, I persevered, and got the hang of it. My parents travelled down from Lancashire to meet their first grandchild, and Josie came to meet him too. In fact, over the next few days, Gaz and I were so blessed with the number of good wishes, and visits to the hospital. The wife of one of our teachers from college, who was a nurse, visited us, and my bed was completely surrounded with flowers and cards. One gentleman who owned a coffee shop in Worcester which we frequented, came to visit us, and when my Dad's video camera developed some problems, he lent him his camcorder to continue taking film of Josh. The list of visitors was endless, Lin and Eddie, Bridie, Sheila, and Marilyn who used to work at the college, to mention but a few. They all helped in making those days in hospital much more cheery.

During that time, Josh had his eyes examined, and we were pleased to learn that the doctors didn't have any concerns about his sight. They would, however, continue to make regular checks. I'm pleased to say that his eyes turned out to be fine. It wasn't all plain sailing, however. My bed was right at the end of the ward, at the furthest point away from the corridor where the bathrooms were. The staff insisted that I should press my buzzer when I required the toilet, or a shower, but it is a fact that staff are very busy. When I had to wait so long just to get to the toilet, I got very uncomfortable, and very frustrated, although I did keep my cool. Eventually I was moved to the bed nearest to the door, when someone was discharged. It meant I could see to myself and not be dependent upon anyone when I needed the bathroom, and it made a world of difference to me.

I got to know a few of the other mums on the ward. I would often chat to the mum in the next bed to me, and I remember an occasion when I was glad that we'd become friends. A number of us had gathered around the dining table at the far end of the ward for Sunday lunch. We talked quite happily, until the moment when a baby started crying. I knew it was Josh, and said, "I've almost finished. I will go and get him in a moment." The conversation suddenly tailed off, and I could tell that most of the ladies were feeling uncomfortable, and wondering if it was their baby. My friend however, sat quite relaxed, and said, "Jane knows what Josh sounds like, so she's probably right." Seconds later, all the mums except for her, left the table to check their babies. They returned one by one looking rather sheepish, and exclaiming as they took their seats, "It is Josh." As I left my seat to attend to Josh, I heard my friend say, "Told you, but you didn't believe me."

On the day we were discharged to go home, Lin came to pick us up. She arrived very excited, with the car seat we had bought ready for Josh. I was so glad to be going home. My stay in hospital had been ok. I had met with the usual mixture of views, some a great deal more positive than others at the prospect of two blind people having a baby, but I didn't let it bother me. Gaz, Joshua and I would be just fine. I wasn't under any illusions that this would be without its challenges, but I was ready to give it my best, and thankfully, we had plenty of friends and family around us to give us support. I clearly remember carrying Josh in his car seat along the path and into our flat, I was so pleased to be home. Not long after we arrived, Josh needed his nappy changing, and I laid him gently on his mat. Lin observed quietly as I changed him, and when I'd finished, I remember her saying, "I can see you're going to be a natural at all of this."

This reminds me of a question someone once asked me several years later. A good friend of our family, who had had four children himself, said "Jane, how does a blind person change a child's nappy?" I knew his question was a genuine enquiry, and I paused for a moment. I then turned toward him and with a grin said, "Carefully." We both laughed, and I know it is a story he has related to others on several occasions. When you have a disability, you have to learn to be adaptable. One method of doing something may work for one person with a visual impairment, but it may not necessarily suit another. The important thing is that each individual finds a method which works for them and produces a successful result. It doesn't matter if the method is unconventional, and it doesn't matter if it takes them longer, all that matters is that it works.

When I changed my son's nappy, I always put the large padded changing mat on the floor, and never used a high changing unit for fear he may roll off it. Before beginning, I always gathered everything around me that I would need before I began the process. I didn't want to leave him unattended while I dashed to grab a nappy sack or cream, so made sure I had everything ready beforehand. You don't have to be a superstar to be a visually impaired parent, you just have to be a little more organised and give thought to planning tasks.

On that first evening, I felt a little nervous. I no longer had the reassurance of having a midwife or nurse on hand, but everything went quite smoothly. I did however have Bridie upstairs who I knew would be more than happy to help if I needed her. Bridie was so kind, during the first week, she knocked on our door one evening and presented Gaz and I with a meal that she had cooked for us. It was such a blessing at the time, and a really kind thought. One of the things that stands out in my mind over those first few weeks, was feeding Josh during the night. The weather was still very hot. I would sit up in bed, with my back pressed firmly against the cold wall behind me, partly to try and stay cool, and partly in the hope that it would keep me awake. On occasions, I am sure that I was on the point of falling asleep while feeding him, because, my head would suddenly fall forward. I have to say that, at the time, it seemed really hard work. Gaz was so supportive however, and would often talk to me as I fed Josh to help me stay awake.

When he was around ten days old, Gaz and I took Josh for his first trip to our local shops. I felt very proud as I walked beside Gaz, both of us holding on to the pram. We were lucky, as Gaz had enough sight to be able to push the pram. Everyone was delighted to see our little boy, and it was great to see how happy they were for us. Something that pleased me was getting my first unbroken night of sleep. I couldn't believe it when I suddenly awoke and realised the time. I dashed out of bed, immediately worried that there must be something wrong with Josh, but no, he was sound asleep. What was more surprising, was that he was only eight weeks old, but from that point on, he continued to sleep right through the night.

People have often asked me, "Isn't it very difficult caring for a young baby?" In fact my answer is always that it is much easier looking after a baby than a toddler. When they are babies and not particularly mobile, you can place them in their Moses basket, or pram, and they will stay where you have put them. You always know where they are, and you don't have to worry about what they might be getting up to. However, as they get older, and start crawling, or walking, then that's where the fun begins.

When Josh was only four months old, a local housing association offered us the chance to rent one of their new two bed houses. We were so excited, as the three of us together with Fred in that flat had been feeling rather cramped. Once again the faithful troops helped us move, and we felt so blessed in our new home. Downstairs we had a living room at the front of the house, and a kitchen at the back which was huge. In fact, it was larger than the living room. Upstairs, we had a bathroom, and two good-sized bedrooms. We loved the place, and the added bonus was that it was only down the road from our old flat, so we already knew our way around the area. Another advantage was the fact that we were only a five-minute walk away from a large Sainsbury's supermarket. I hadn't realised before how close it was to where we lived, but now I knew, I often visited much to the frustration of Gaz. The staff there were always very helpful, and willing to escort me around the store and help me pick my shopping. I would often exit the store with Fred on my left, and in my right hand would be several bags of shopping. One morning, I walked out of the store laden with bags, and turned to walk across the car park, ready to make my way home, when a lady suddenly rushed over to me. She said, "Hello, I saw you on the bus yesterday, are you ok?" I replied that I was, and was about to walk on, when she said, "Oh let me give you a hand, I'd be happy to help you carry your bags to your car!" I paused, looked toward her, and then down at my guide dog, and again toward her before smiling and saying, "Thank you, but I'm walking home today."

Only a few weeks after moving house, the Christmas period was upon us. We had barely finished emptying all our boxes, when it was time to pack our things and make the trip up to my parent's house where we would all be spending the holiday together. By then, Josh was six months old. One of the most memorable moments occurred on Christmas Eve. We were all busy in the living room, wrapping presents for family and friends when Josh began squealing with delight. He had already perfected the art of rolling from one side of the room to the other, but now he was doing it, while grabbing out at all the brightly coloured paper which he crinkled in his tiny hands. He thought it was great fun, and we got a great deal of pleasure just watching him having such a great time.

It wasn't long before the rolling transitioned to crawling. When he had been a baby, as I mentioned earlier, I could put him in his pram or baby chair and leave him for a couple of minutes knowing he would be perfectly safe, if I needed to make a drink, or answer the telephone. Now however, came the next stage. I would always have to be in the same room and stay pretty close to him in order to make sure he was safe, and not touching or picking up anything that had the potential to harm him. I remember when he was at the crawling stage, and Gaz and I took him to a friend's house for the day. We were sitting in their lounge and having a drink together and Josh was crawling around on the carpet observed by my friend's neighbour. I suddenly heard a sound, and knew immediately that there was something wrong. My friend gasped, and picked up Josh who by now was making sounds as if he were choking. My friend suddenly said, "I think he has picked up some pot pouri, and put it in his mouth." I immediately rushed over to her, as people around me panicked. I don't know how I managed to keep my cool, but I simply laid Josh over my lap on his tummy, and slapped him on the back twice. Thankfully, the item dislodged itself and the crisis was averted. Josh cried, and I gave him a cuddle, but I was so grateful that he was ok.

That was the first of several occasions when Josh got himself into a difficult situation. Another time, when he was around six years old, we were again at a friend's house when Josh had been playing with a large round tin of Lego. Instead of constructing a model, Josh had decided that it would be much more fun to wear the tin on his head. So he tipped it upside down and wore it like a hat. This wasn't a problem until he decided to remove it. I was in the kitchen, when I heard a good deal of noise, and went to investigate. Josh was running around the room, pursued by a number of adults and children who had been trying to remove the tin from his head, but without success. By that time, Josh was very distressed. I sat him down on my knee, and calmed him down, telling him not to worry about the silly tin, and that we'd sort it out later. During our conversation, he calmed down, and as we talked, I asked him to count to ten for me. He began counting, and before he knew it, I put my hands either side of the pretend hat, and gave a quick firm tug. In an instant, the tin was removed, and my little man was happy again.

So, what does a visually impaired parent do, when their child is well into the crawling stage, but she needs to leave him for a moment so they can use the bathroom? Well, my secret weapon, and, quite frankly a godsend, was a playpen. It was wonderful, and I don't know how I would have survived without mine. If I was playing with Josh and someone knocked at the door, I could put him in the playpen, and have peace of mind knowing that he was safe. He was quite happy in there for short periods of time with his favourite toys, and it gave me the freedom to do little chores like loading the washing machine.

Another challenge for me was when Josh began the weaning process. This was another potentially sticky mess requiring a degree of planning. I quickly learned that it was more practical to use the type of

239

bib that is like a small wrap around gown, than just a small bib that fastens around the baby's neck. That way all his clothes were covered, and if he chose to wipe his hands anywhere, then his clothes underneath would still be clean. I would sit him in the high chair, and always keep a clean damp cloth on the corner of his tray, to quickly wipe up any spillages, and mine or Josh's hands. I developed my own method. I would gently cup his chin in one hand, and then guide the spoon to his mouth with the other. With the passage of time, this process, which began as a very messy procedure, soon became more efficient. It's quite amazing, how quickly a small child will learn the art of leaning toward the spoon and taking the food, rather than just opening his mouth, and waiting for the food to arrive. I have talked with many other visually impaired parents, who have related similar stories. Sadly, things don't always run as smoothly as chocolate and banana pudding - down the hatch, no problem. When baby decides he doesn't want anything to do with chicken casserole, then the chicken casserole can end up everywhere except for their mouth. Oh the joys!

That first year flew by so quickly. Before we knew it, we were planning his first birthday party. We had a small gathering of children at our home, and Josh loved his present, a large red car, which he could sit in, and push himself around the house with his feet. We still have a picture of him, grabbing on to the table cloth, as he peered from under the table, on which sat his large birthday cake. Around that time, Gaz and I took Josh on a day trip to Birmingham. It was only a short train journey away from Worcester, and Gaz needed to buy an item from a music shop there. Once that task was completed, we took Josh to choose a gift from a large toy shop nearby. When we left the shop, we made our way toward the shopping centre, which was just above the railway station. As we walked, we heard the sound of someone playing a harmonica. As we passed the busker, he suddenly stopped. We then heard him say in his distinctive Brummy accent, "Hey are you blind?" Gaz answered, "Yes." He then directed the same question at me in rather a morose tone. I replied "Yes." He continued his enquiries asking, "Is that your kid?" We both said "yes." He then paused, and exclaimed, "Oh, poor kid!" I bit my lip very hard, all the time wanting to reply, "We may be blind, but our vision for our son amounts to more than playing a harmonica!"

The way in which individuals respond to meeting someone with a disability is diverse. While some are completely unfazed, and respond quite naturally, others just don't have the first clue about how to cope.

I once attended a conference with some friends, and was standing, waiting to complete a registration form, when one of the administrators approached us. Instead of speaking directly to me, she persisted in initiating her questions with, "Could you ask the blind lady..." or, "Could you tell the blind lady..." My two friends who were with me were exasperated, so just imagine how I felt! I didn't feel it was the correct time or place to confront her, so simply took my seat. Sometimes, it's better to let things go. As we sat down a friend turned to me and said, "You must have to have so much graciousness when faced with some people's behaviour and attitudes. It was true that I had refrained from confronting the issue, but all the time I had wanted to say in rather a loud voice, "Could you please tell the lady with the particularly severe speech impediment that I am perfectly capable of engaging in a sensible conversation if she would have the courtesy to address me."

By the time he was fourteen months old, Josh had taken his first steps, and received his first pair of shoes. He was a very active, inquisitive child, who didn't like sitting still for long. During one visit to church on a Sunday morning, we sat on the front row, and Josh sat beside me in his little chair. At the end a woman came to the front, and another lady began praying for her. What I didn't realise until afterwards, was that as the lady stood praying, Josh was furiously tugging on the bottom of her skirt. It's a wonder there wasn't an extremely embarrassing moment. On the way home, we couldn't stop laughing. That little mischevious streak continued. When, one day, I went to the washing machine to load it up, for some reason, instead of just pushing all the clothes in, I first put my hand in there to feel around. To my surprise, there were onions in the washing machine! Josh had obviously emptied my vegetable rack, and filled the machine. Not wishing to know what a load of machine washed onions would turn out like, I removed them, put in the clothes, and decided to stick with good old fashioned washing powder.

It is a well-known fact that children who have at least one parent who is visually impaired, adapt quickly and easily to their circumstances. Their speech often develops quicker, as pointing at something they want is not an option. When it came to making his needs known, Josh was never a child for holding back. We walked out of church one morning, with our friend James, who was also visually impaired, and were intending to make our way to a friend's car to get a lift home. Josh however had different plans. He tugged hard on

James's arm leading him in a different direction. James was inquisitive, and so were we. We all followed to see what Josh wanted. He led James along the side of the building and on to a street. He then walked a few paces down the road, and into a small shop. We were all giggling, because, none of us had any clue that the shop even existed until that point, but Josh knew. Furthermore, he took James to a shelf, and placed his hand on an object, and even though he could only say a few words, shouted triumphantly, "banana!" It was another side splittingly hilarious moment. Needless to say, Josh got his banana, but now we had to find our way back to the car park, but Josh wasn't particularly concerned about that now he'd got what he wanted.

While we're on the subject of locating things, it reminds me of when Josh was around eighteen months old. Gaz had looked after him while I went to do some shopping. I returned with several bags and began to unpack them and place them in cupboards. Josh was determined to help, and so we put the items away together, or so I thought. The following breakfast time, I was puzzled to find that I couldn't find the Weetabix I had bought the previous day. I searched and searched, until I suddenly realized I couldn't actually remember unpacking and putting it away. I concluded that I must have left it on the checkout and made something different for breakfast. The following day, I opened the freezer to retrieve some ice cream, and the first thing I touched was a cardboard box. Not recognising it, I pulled it out to investigate. It didn't take me long to discover that it was the missing Weetabix. Josh must have put it there while he was helping me: thanks Josh.

Just before Josh's second birthday, we took a holiday in Portugal. As well as the three of us, there was Mum, Dad and Kirsten with her husband plus their nine month old daughter. I don't think we had a single drop of rain the whole two weeks we were over there and had a brilliant time. It was during that holiday, that I strongly suspected that I was pregnant again, but kept my suspicions to myself. The day before we flew home, it was Joshua's second birthday, and as we all enjoyed his party, neither Gaz nor I were aware of the changes that would happen over the weeks that would follow.

29. Moving On

Just before our holiday, Gaz had attended an interview for a job with the Royal National Institute of the blind in Peterborough. He had been working as a consultant computer programmer, but really wanted a job with a regular monthly income. Not long after returning from Portugal, we received the news that he had been offered the job. We discussed the situation. It would, indeed, be a huge change for us if we were to move to Peterborough. I hated the thought of leaving Worcester. It felt like home to me, and even worse, was the thought of leaving Lin and Eddie. Once again I found myself calling the doctor who confirmed that I was pregnant again. We were both overjoyed at the news, but now the decision about whether to accept the job offer would take a great deal of thought and consideration.

We did eventually decide to make the move to Cambridgeshire, and it was then that everything escalated. We had to make several trips down to Peterborough to find a house to rent, and then we would have the task of learning our way around our new neighbourhood. There was so much to take in, and I felt a mixture of emotions. A good deal of sadness at leaving our friends in Worcester, but at least a little excitement about what the future would hold. Lin helped us with our packing, and helped us find a good removal firm. There were so many people that I would miss terribly: Eddie and Lin, Bridie, Lynne, and a number of friends from our church.

Very early one Saturday morning, in September 1997, Mum and Dad drove to meet us and Lin and Eddie came to spend our last morning in Worcester with us. A few hours later, a large removal van arrived and loaded up all our possessions. I vividly remember standing on our front drive. My parents were getting Josh into his seat in their car whilst Gaz and I hugged Lin and Eddie while wishing we didn't have to leave. As Gaz and I got into my parents' car, and drove away from our house for the last time, my mind wandered to all the things we had experienced in Worcester: the good times, including our wedding, and having Joshua; the difficult times, including the days we had both been desperate to find a job. I remembered standing at the bus stop one day. It was a Wednesday, and we had paid all our weekly bills, but Gaz had five pounds in his pocket, and that was all we had to spend until the following Monday. I'd had a good deal of growing up to do during my time in Worcester. I had been a pretty care-free student there for two years, but then had to take on the responsibility of living on my own and renting a flat. I felt the weight of responsibility, or growing up for the first time, when faced with the harsh reality of having to spend my own precious cash on nothing other than a new toilet seat! A toilet seat? I would actually have to spend my money on a toilet seat!!! That was a tough thing to swallow - not the toilet seat, but having to pay for it myself. The cheapest one I could find cost me twenty-five pounds, and I still say today, that was the day I was finally forced into accepting that I now had to become a responsible adult.

I pondered over those embarrassing incidents, that still make me cringe. One day, I wanted to make a phone call while in the city centre. In the middle of the high street was a cluster of around six phone boxes. I decided that I would sidle up to the first one, and listen to see if there was anyone in there, and as I listened I heard a voice in conversation, so I moved on to the next one. Eventually I stood outside one booth, and after a few seconds heard no sound, so decided it must be empty. I opened the door, and put my hand out to lift the telephone receiver, but unfortunately, there was someone in there, and I managed to place my hand firmly on their shoulder. In a split second, I had made my retreat, with a rather red face, and probably leaving the other person rather confused.

Another time, I stood at the counter in the post office, and was asked to sign a form. I trailed my hand across the counter, until I found a piece of string, which I assumed was tied to the pen I needed. Without a thought, I tugged on the string hoping to find the pen. To my horror, I discovered that a lady standing next to me was using it. I felt so bad. I apologised, as I considered that I must have drawn a line across the unsuspecting woman's paper, as she wrote. The lady however was very gracious and said, "Oh no, you use it. I've been standing here for ages, please, you use it." I signed my document quickly, and gave the pen back, before leaving, again with a very red face.

It was clear that I certainly needed no help in getting myself into embarrassing situations, but when Josh came along, the two of us definitely meant trouble. During our time in Worcester, the old bus station in the centre of the city was renovated. On our first visit there after the work was completed, we noticed that there was now a shop opposite the bay where we waited for our bus. The three of us went in, to get some refreshments while we waited. Well, two of us made a purchase. After leaving the shop, we stood at the bus stop, and as Gaz and I chatted, I heard someone in the queue lean down to Josh in his pushchair and say, "Is that your juice darling?" Puzzled, I reached out toward Josh to investigate. To my surprise, I found that he had two small cartons of juice, one in each hand. To be perfectly honest, I didn't know whether to feel horrified, or to laugh. I went straight back to the shop, paid for the items and I'm glad to say that the manager understood, and that was the end of the matter.

Coincidently, I was also standing at the bus stop one afternoon, when I discovered that Josh had a small chocolate bar in his hand. We had been shopping in Woolworths, and I suspect that he had taken it from the pick-n-mix section. I walked all the way back to the shop, and stood in a long queue waiting to pay for the item. When it was finally my turn, I explained apologetically what had happened. There was a stunned silence, and I suppose a strange look from the check-out lady, as she said in rather a weary voice, "Eight pence please." It was a ten minute walk back to the bus station, but my conscience was clear. For a long time after that, whenever we went out shopping, I would check Josh every time we left a shop. I'm very glad to say, that he grew out of his need to help himself when shopping.

There were a couple of scary times that I certainly wouldn't like to repeat. The first was the time I described earlier, in my local pub. The second was when I was travelling to give one of my talks for the Guide Dogs Association. Because the area I covered was pretty extensive, I often relied on the kindness of the people who organised the events to give me a lift in their cars. These were usually people I had never met before, and had only spoken to, when arranging dates and times. There was normally no problem at all until one afternoon when Josh was about two months old. I had been asked to give a talk in the city, and I knew he would be ok with Gaz for a couple of hours. I had no reason to worry as I got in to the car, with the gentleman who was to drive me to the venue, but several minutes later, I was growing rather anxious. I knew that our destination was a good ten minutes drive away, but was puzzled to find that we were on what sounded like a motorway. I was sure that we didn't need to use the motorway to get to our destination, and felt rather perplexed.

Usually, when making the journey to give a talk, my driver would engage in conversation about my dog and how often I gave talks about guide dogs. On this occasion however, the man began talking about cars. It isn't a subject I know much about, but I didn't need to in this case, as he was happy to make all of the conversation. I sat listening to him, and the sound of the traffic. The journey seemed to go on forever, and I was seriously panicking. I kept thinking about little Josh at home, and just where this man was taking me. If ever there was a time for a silent prayer, it was then. I was extremely relieved, when the car slowed down, and I heard a voice from the street, and someone leant through the car window. They were attending my talk, and as they spoke, it became clear, that we would soon arrive at the hall. In those few moments before I was taken to the room where the talk would take place, I had just enough time to compose myself, and get my thoughts together. I'm pleased to say that everything went well, and the journey home was much quicker than the outward one. I never found out about why we took so long to get to the venue, but I didn't really care. I was just glad to get home.

Possibly the worst thing about living in Worcester for us, was the question that we would be asked by members of the public on regular occasions. It was a question that we laughed about at first, but eventually, we became extremely irritated by it. That question was, "Are you at the college then?" It didn't matter what age we were, people seemed to assume that if you lived in Worcester and were blind, then you must be residing at the "blind college" as it was often called. I could understand the enquiry before we had a child, but afterwards, when we were pushing him around in his pram.

I'll never forget the day we both took Joshua for his first set of injections. When we had seen the nurse, we approached the receptionist to ask if she would kindly order a taxi for us to get home. She didn't ask where we were going, but as she talked on the phone, I heard her say, "They're going to the blind college!" I grimaced, and sighed. When our regular taxi driver arrived, we got into the car, and as we strapped Josh safely in his seat, he said, "Hiya Gaz and Jane, off to the blind college?" and then burst out laughing. The questioning continued and I became increasingly irritated. While walking in town one afternoon, with Josh, someone asked the dreaded question and the touch paper had been lit. I turned to Gaz and in an exasperated tone said, "If anyone else asks us that, I'm going to say, "Yes, of course, didn't you know that they are doing an experiment in breeding child slaves for blind parents?"

Now the Worcester chapter was closing, and the Peterborough one beginning. The church we had attended in Worcester, had links with people who knew about a large church in Peterborough, and before moving, Gaz and I had visited a couple of times. We had made some new friends, and they were very kind, visiting us during the weekend we moved, and offering to help if we needed anything. We also got back in contact with a couple with whom Gaz and I had been at College. They, too, had married, and lived in Peterborough. In fact they worked at the same charity where Gaz had just got his new job. They were also very kind to us. On our first day, there was a knock on the door, and it was a taxi, the driver explained that he had several items which our friends had sent as a welcome present. Mum and Dad stayed for the weekend, helping us unpack, and teaching us some local routes around our home, including the way to the small shopping centre nearby. On Monday morning, my parents travelled home, and Gaz started his new day at work, and that's when reality hit, and life started to get tough for me.

In previous months, Gaz had worked from home. I hadn't spent much time with him during the day, but now he was at work all day, it felt very strange. I didn't know the area very well, and couldn't venture far on my own. Looking after a two-year-old while not knowing many people to chat with, made for what seemed like very long days. By that time I was four months pregnant, and everything was going well, but I had other worries. Fred had been experiencing some health problems. He had been given several tests, and nothing serious had been detected, but his symptoms persisted, as did my concern for him. I felt very lonely, and have to admit, that I cried every day for the first six months. I remember saying to poor Gaz, "I just want to go home." I missed Eddie and Lin terribly, but I also understood that Gaz had taken the job for all the right reasons, and accepted the fact that I needed to be patient.

Because of our move, I was visited regularly by a guide dog mobility instructor. Fred seemed to be working ok, but he was sometimes a little distracted. One morning while walking in the shopping centre, another dog suddenly jumped out at him. The dog was growling furiously, and I struggled to pull Fred to safety. I'm not sure whether it knocked his confidence, but shortly after, I had to have a difficult conversation with my GDMI. Fred was still experiencing health issues, and in the end, I was advised that it may be better to allow Fred to have an early retirement. The fact that I had moved house several times since having him probably didn't help, and I'd also had a baby. Fred wasn't at all jealous, in fact he was wonderful with Josh, but he just seemed like he'd had enough of working. He had been the most wonderful, faithful dog anyone could have wished for, and I really didn't want him to retire, but this wasn't about me, it was about what was right for Fred.

When I had trained with Fred at the guide dog training centre, his puppy walkers had visited me and said that, when he retired, they would like to care for him. When guide dogs retire, the owner is allowed to keep them as pets if they have room for them and their new guide dog. If they are not able to keep the dog, then they can arrange for a family member or friend to adopt them. Often this will be a person who lives close by so that the previous owner can still visit the dog regularly. I really didn't want to let Fred go, but I knew I was being selfish. His puppy walkers lived in a large house with an extensive garden. Fred loved to run around, and it would be perfect for him. In the end, I made the painful choice to let him go.

It was a sad day for me when I had to pack all of Fred's things, and Ken came to pick him up and drive him back to Oxfordshire. He brought his camcorder and took some video, before loading everything into the car. He promised that they would make regular visits, so that I could still see Fred, and off they went. Kleenex tissues had an extra boost to their profits that day, but I knew I'd made the right choice. In any case, it was only a matter of weeks until my baby was due, and it was much better for everyone that everything was settled before then.

My second pregnancy had gone well, apart from one incident. I had left the house with Fred and Joshua to go to the shops, but wasn't aware that it was icy outside. There was a large patch of ice directly in front of our house, and I went flying. I know my name is Jane, but Torville is not my surname, and so I ended up in a sorry heap upon the floor. Worried about the baby, I called Gaz, and then called a taxi to take me to the hospital. After routine tests, it was discovered that everything was fine, and I was sent home. Once again, someone was watching over me, and I was very thankful. I didn't have a craving for Weetabix with my second baby, but I did have one for Jaffa Cakes. I'm not sure how many boxes I got through, but every time I had to be weighed, I wondered how much was baby, and how much was Jaffa Cakes.

Prospective parents can spend hours discussing and deciding upon the right name for their baby. I recall sharing my thoughts about names with Irene, my mother-in-law. For a girl, one of the names I liked was Georgia. I was surprised at how horrified Irene was at the idea. She said rather anxiously, "Ya can't call 'er Georgia. Georgia is di place where all di poor people live!" I don't know whether the above statement is actually true, but I found her outburst amusing.

On a cold evening in February, Gaz and I found ourselves once more in a labour suite, waiting for the arrival of our second child. She was born at four minutes past one, and weighed six pounds and six ounces. We felt so blessed to have a little boy, and a little girl, and I have to say that Rosanna was a wonderfully contented baby. My stay in hospital was very different from when I had Josh. This time, I was pleased to find I had been given a room of my own. However, it wasn't all plain sailing. I was so happy as we wheeled Rosanna's cot back to my room, and I snuggled down in my bed to get a well-earned sleep. A midwife informed me that the buzzer by my bed wasn't working properly. If I needed help, I was to ring the bell a second time if no one came. When I did ring the next morning, nobody came after five minutes, so I rang again. Shortly after, another midwife came bustling in, and gave me some short sharp stern words for having rung my bell twice. This left me feeling distinctly uncomfortable, and I was reluctant to ask for help after that. Indeed, I missed a couple of meals because nobody came to help me to the dining room, and I didn't know where to find them. Luckily, Gaz brought food in for me, and I just couldn't wait to get home.

Mum and dad had travelled down to visit us, and looked after Josh . They all came to see me the afternoon after the birth. I had a present prepared for Josh, which I said was from his new baby sister. I had bought him a back-pack bearing a picture of one of his favourite T.V. characters, and filled it with paper, crayons and other goodies. He was very pleased, and took an instant shine to his sister.

During my second, and final night's stay, I got up during the night to visit the bathroom. When I returned, I was startled to find that there was someone in my room. As I entered, she said to me, "Are you going home tomorrow?" I answered "Yes." She then said, "I think that would be best," and left. It took me a while to get back to sleep, because I couldn't stop thinking about what the member of staff had said. I wasn't aware that I'd caused any problems, indeed, I hadn't had much to do with anyone, and all I wanted was to go home. By lunch time the following day, we had been given our final medical checks, and the taxi arrived to take us home. I longed for my own surroundings, and my own bed; oh, and a decent cup of coffee.

Several weeks before Rosanna was born, Joshua began attending pre-school. He loved it! He was always a very fun loving and active child. One day Gaz picked him up from pre-School and brought him home. Josh ran through the house and stood in front of me. He lifted up his top, and said in a very proud and happy voice, "Look Mummy, I've got chicken spots!" Of course he meant chicken pox, and my first thought was, "I hope your feeling just as happy about them tomorrow son." As I suspected, his glee didn't last long. He hated the calamine lotion, and would cry and say, "Don't put the white thing on me Mummy." My Doctor also gave me a remedy to put in the bath, which resembled pieces of green foliage, and Josh hated it. When we tried to put him in the bath he screamed. I'm glad to say that he recovered after a couple of weeks, but then guess what? We had taken a trip to stay with my parents and I was changing a nappy, when I noticed something. I suspected that Rosanna had chicken pox. Ironically, even though I was staying in a house full of sighted people, I was the first to notice her spots. I was very concerned, as she was only four months old, but surprisingly, she sailed through it without much trouble or discomfort.

From a very early age, Rosanna was a child who knew her own mind, and certainly made her feelings known. She was very placid and quiet, but if she took a dislike to anyone, they would be on the receiving end of a very stern look. The fact that she wasn't able to speak didn't matter; all it took was the look. She was very affectionate to those close to her. She went through a stage at around twelve months old of leaning over, as she was being held, and rub your back with her tiny hand, in a comforting way. It was so sweet, and when others saw it, they found it quite moving. As with Josh, Rosanna also got herself into a few tricky situations. She seemed to be playing happily in her playpen one afternoon, when I went over to get her out to give her a cuddle. I wasn't quite ready for the mess that greeted me. Rather foolishly, I must have left an open pot of cream close by from when I last changed her. Rosanna had emptied the cream everywhere. It was in her hair, all over her clothes, and all over her toys, and all over the playpen. Mums, you know the consistency of that stuff; it's sticky, greasy, and a nightmare to get off everything. It took me hours to get her and everything else clean, and I never made the same mistake again.

Rosanna had a good appetite until she was roughly twelve months old. Suddenly she seemed to decide that food wasn't really for her. Consequently, for a number of years, meal times became a tedious experience for all the family. I was once cleaning the lounge, and

250

decided to pull out the sofa to vacuum behind it, when I found an unexpected item. It was a cold baked potato. We had eaten baked potatoes the previous evening. As I picked it up and threw it away, I thought to myself, "The things your kids get up to, and get away with, when they have two blind parents!" This however was not an isolated incident. I was tidying Rosanna's bedroom, when I moved her wardrobe, and found that she had hidden a slice of pizza underneath. After that, we made sure that nobody left the table until all plates had been thoroughly checked. I also took the opportunity to employ a cleaner.

30. Coincidence, or just weird?

Have you ever been in the position where someone has mistaken you for someone else? At Chorleywood College, on the few occasions I did come into contact with the head mistress, she would refer to me as "Shelley", who was another girl from my year. This didn't particularly bother me, but during my adult life, this seemed to get a whole lot worse. When living in Worcester, one shop keeper in particular whom I saw on a regular basis was convinced that I had been a supporter of the city's football team, and had frequently visited the ground. He would often relate this to other customers in the shop at the time, and ask me if I would be going to the match. Not wishing to embarrass him, for the seven years that this continued, I simply went along with it and never had the courage to put him straight.

After moving to Peterborough, for several months, I noticed that certain assistants in supermarkets or shops in the city centre began referring to me as "Kate." Initially, I couldn't understand it. I had one blind friend named Kate, but she had dark hair, and didn't have a guide dog, so why were they getting us mixed up? It wasn't till several months later, after being constantly referred to as Kate, that I finally met the lady in question. She had spent the previous few months being called "Jane" and was beginning to get as exasperated as I was. She had the same hair colour as me, and we both had guide dogs who looked very similar. So, mystery solved, but everyone continued to mix us up. I was never Jane, and she was never Kate.

If that was weird, then the next incident is positively spooky. I was walking through my local shopping centre, when I heard someone running behind me. A rather breathless woman then shouted, "Hello there, I'm so glad to have met you. We've all really missed you since you moved from Melton Mowbray. How is Josh, and your little girl? Your dog seems to be working well!" The lady continued chatting as she stood in front of me, and I was sure that at some point she would realise that I wasn't the person she thought me to be, but no. The closest I've got to Melton Mowbray is eating a pork pie, and I had no idea of who the woman was. It was very strange to think that, somewhere, there was a blind woman with a guide dog, a son called Josh, and a little girl, who had recently moved to Peterborough. If there was, I never met her.

Silly coincidences do happen. One morning, I was on the bus, and a few stops down the road, a friend of mine got on with his guide dog. He sat next to me and we carried on with our journey. At the next stop, a woman got on, and sat opposite us, and struck up a conversation about our dogs. When we arrived in the town centre, we all got off at the same stop, just outside Asda, where we parted company and got on with our day. A couple of hours later, I went to a different bus stop to catch a bus home. I was surprised to find that all three of us had congregated at the same bus stop, to go home at the same time. When the bus arrived, we boarded, and sat in the same seats where we had been on our outward journey, and once again, we chatted about our dogs. How does that sort of stuff happen?

That reminds me of another strange happening on a bus. Again, I was making my way into town, when a woman boarded. When she saw me, she immediately approached me, embraced me, and in rather an emotional voice said, "Thank you so much for everything you have done for my Anthony." I was rather taken aback, not having any idea what or who she was talking about. I just smiled, as she took her seat. "Well" I thought to myself. "I haven't got a clue who Anthony is, but I'm very glad he's doing so well!"

31. The little darlings!

If I had a pound for every time someone said to Gaz and me, "Oh those children will be such a help to you both when they're older!" I'd be a multi-millionaire by now. I can honestly say that, they often are very helpful. However, just like any other children, they can be anything but, at times. When Gaz and I first talked about the possibility of having children, we came to the conclusion that if we didn't have them, then we would get along just fine. If, however, we did decide to be parents, we were adamant that our children should be brought up having a happy childhood, and be allowed to be kids, and certainly not be our carers.

The thing about small children is that they are extremely adaptable. We often wondered how they would view our disability, and desperately wanted to do everything we could to be the best parents that we could be. As I touched upon earlier, it's simply a case of adapting and learning together. When Josh needed Calpol when he was teething, I was pleased to learn that I could administer that myself by using a 5ml oral syringe, instead of struggling with a spoon. If I needed to go out on my own, I would carry him in a backpack style baby carrier. If my children were a little off colour, apart from obvious signs like feeling their tummies and knowing they have a temperature, I found that they all had a distinctive smell on their breath when they weren't well. It wasn't an unpleasant smell, but definitely different when they were ill.

However you're feeling, there's nothing like cuddling up together and reading a good story. My kids loved bedtime stories, in fact any time stories for that matter. I learned about an organisation called Clearvision, which has a lending library for parents who have a visual impairment. Books are adapted by taking them apart, and inserting clear plastic sheets between the pages containing the story in Braille. Because the plastic sheets are clear, they do not obscure the pictures so the children can still see the pages, while the blind parent is reading the story. It's brilliant. We read stories about "The Rainbow Fish' and "Barney the Dinosaur", but the absolute favourite was always "The Giant Jam Sandwich." That was a story I knew off by heart.

When the children were toddlers, people repeatedly commented about how advanced their speech was. I am quite sure that this was a result of not being able to point at what they wanted. If they needed something, then they had to let us know, and were never shy about it. Not long after we moved to Peterborough, we were exploring the city centre, with Josh in his buggy. He was just turned two years old at the time. He liked the TV programme, "Teletubbies" although it wasn't my favourite. As we walked through a small shopping centre, Josh suddenly shouted, "Mummy, Teletubbies balloon." Our reaction was "Oh wow, Josh, where is it?" He leaned over to his right, and stretched out his arm saying "Over there!" We followed his instruction, and found a shop which sold party wear. He had seen a large helium balloon, and we were both so impressed that Josh got what he wanted on that occasion.

Josh certainly knew what he wanted, and this was definitely true the day a friend came to visit us. Josh was three at the time, and after the event, I didn't know whether to laugh or be slightly concerned. As we sat chatting, Josh pulled a small pewter dish from my friend's bag. I told him not to touch, but Chrissie said he could play with it. For the first few minutes, he had great fun rolling it on its side, up and down the carpet. Then, Josh had another idea. We were interrupted by a little voice saying "Money for Jesus?" as he held out the dish toward us. We paused, and then realised that he was copying the collection or offering as part of our regular church service. There were a couple of "Ah's" and a few giggles, before we both began placing a few coins in his bowl. He carried them over to the other side of the room, and spent ages tipping the coins out on to the carpet, and then putting them back one by one. When it was time for Chrissie to leave, she needed to collect her dish and so went over to get it from Josh. As they tipped the coins on to the floor, I said, "Oh Josh, is that your money for Jesus?" Without hesitation, and in a firm voice his reply was, "No, it's my ice-cream money!"

Similarly, there were times when I cringed while travelling on the bus. As we sat together on the front seat, a woman walked past us, and Josh shouted, "Mummy, that lady has got chicken spots!" My reaction was, "Josh, can you see any red cars out of the window?" On another journey, Josh realised that there was a bell that made a wonderful sound. I am presuming he found it wonderful from the number of times he pressed it. Of course, at first, I didn't see him leaning forward to reach it. I also thought that other passengers were pressing for their stops, but no, it was Josh. A woman sitting behind me politely informed me, and after that, I made sure I held his hand for the rest of the journey. The bus driver was not very happy, but when he realised the situation, I think he found it rather amusing.

Rosanna was quite capable of getting up to her own little tricks. I would often shop at my local Asda supermarket, where the same member of staff would help me push the trolley around and pick the items on my list. Rosanna was always very patient, sitting in the trolley until the job was done. One morning, she sat quietly as we ran through the shopping list. One of the items was a large bag of grapes, which the assistant had placed in the front next to Rosanna so they wouldn't get squashed. When we arrived at the check-out, I was astonished to find that my darling daughter had eaten the entire bag of grapes. I remember putting my hand in the bag, feeling the stalk, and saying, "Well, how are we going to weigh and pay for those?"

There were several occasions when I would be putting all my shopping away, and come across an item I didn't recognise. It would often turn out to be something that one of the children had randomly picked off a shelf and thrown in to the trolley. One day my shopping was significantly more expensive than I had intended. This time Josh was in the trolley, and it was a few weeks before the Christmas period. My friendly Asda assistant suddenly burst out laughing. Josh had reached out, and taken a rather large soft toy from a shelf. It was a pure white polar bear, wearing a red scarf. He picked it up and sat it in the trolley next to him. I have to admit, it did look very comical. As we continued around the store, many people stopped and laughed. By the time we were ready to pay, so many had approached me saying how lovely it looked, that I had no choice. Josh had one arm around the polar bear, and clung on for all he was worth. So he came home with us, after my shopping had cost me an extra ten pounds.

All too quickly came the momentous day when Josh started school. He had only just turned four, and I was concerned about how well he would settle in. He, however, was more ready to go than I was to let go. He settled in quickly, and so began the daily routine of the school run. The school we had chosen was a twenty-five minute walk away from where we lived, but it had a good reputation, and anyway, the walk would be good for us. I had some mobility lessons, to teach me the route so, by the time the term started, I felt quite confident. A friend of mine who is also blind, had told me about an adapted pram she had bought for her daughter, and we met up so I could try it out. I was so impressed, that I also ordered one, and it was well worth the money. It was a three-wheeler; the heavy terrain type with chunky tyres. I simply turned it around, walked with my white cane in front of me in my right hand, and pulled the pram behind with my left.

Rosanna was quite safe, and the method worked very well. I asked a rehabilitation officer to accompany me as I took a stroll one day to assess for safety, and she was confident that I would be fine.

I have to admit to feeling a little reticent about going to school. I had heard stories from other blind parents about their experiences of standing on their own in a crowded playground, listening to all the sounds of the children running around, and parents conversing, but feeling quite isolated as they stood alone waiting to meet their child. I had plenty of friends from my church, but didn't know many people in my neighbourhood. I consider myself very blessed, because, after just a few days, I was making friends with other mums. It was fantastic the way things worked out. A group of us would meet together as we walked to school. Sometimes the group was larger, but in general, there were four of us, who would walk together and have a good old chinwag, as they say in Lancashire.

Liz, Jenny and Nicky were brilliant friends to me. As I strode out on the cycle track, I would often hear a voice shouting from behind me, "Jane, wait for me!" It was Liz, and she would say, "Get that pram turned round, I need something to lean on." This however, was a friendly excuse to give me a hand pushing the pram so we could chat as we walked. She was great, and would always make me laugh. At Easter time, Liz helped me make a wonderful Easter bonnet for Rosanna, She had four children, and knew exactly what to do when it came around to making costumes, and had all sorts of stuff that we needed for school projects. She was a godsend: I don't know how I would have managed without her. One day I went to her house to have a coffee and she said "Jane you can come to my house any time you like, because I know you are the only one who doesn't come for a nosy, and won't make judgement if my house isn't tidy." That made me laugh! Liz was often amused when Rosanna, leaning as far forward in her pram as she could, shook her fists and called out to Josh, who was walking in front of us with his friends, with a loud "Josh-eee-aah!"

The start of one morning proved somewhat anxious for Liz and me. As we walked the usual route, Josh was walking slightly in front with his friends. Moments later, Liz noticed that he was nowhere to be seen. We increased our pace, but still couldn't locate him. Feeling rather anxious, we came to the conclusion that he had probably run off ahead to school. When we arrived and found him, I was extremely relieved, but furious. I decided not to say much to him, as I had to leave him at school, but that evening we sat down together and had a talk. I wasn't angry with him, but he needed to know that he mustn't run away from my side again, and so I had to decide on an appropriate punishment. For the following week, Josh wasn't allowed to watch any TV, and he wasn't allowed to have any dessert after dinner. It wasn't easy to enforce; there were certainly times when I was tempted to give in, but I did stick with it. One of the other Mums said to me that she couldn't have persevered. I did, however, and Josh never did anything like that again, thank goodness.

By the time he was about seven, Josh began to ask if he could play with his friends on the open grassy area just opposite our house. I was uneasy and needed to come up with a plan. I bought a set of walkie-talkies so that we could keep in touch, and that worked really well. In addition, we had a fifteen minute rule. Every fifteen minutes, Josh would have to pop his head around the door to show he was ok, and as he got older we increased the time gradually. I wanted him to enjoy himself, but I wanted to know he was safe.

Josh always knew how to give me the run around regarding where he was. Once, I stood in the playground waiting for him to come out of his classroom and run over to me at the end of the day. I waited, but no sign of my boy. Suddenly, I heard someone shout, "Jane, he's hiding behind you!" He repeated this little trick on several occasions, but, remember "Those kids will be such a help to you when they are older!"

Before I knew it, it was time for Rosanna to start school. I certainly clocked up the miles during those first couple of weeks, because Josh was there full time, but Rosanna only had to attend in the afternoons. I would walk there and back in the morning to drop Josh off, and then repeat the process at eleven thirty to take Rosanna. Finally, I returned to pick them both up just after three in the afternoon. During one of those journeys to school with Rosanna, it started raining very hard. We stopped to shelter for a while in the underpass just by the school, and I could hear the rain leaking through a part of the roof. Rosanna rather randomly said, "Can you hear that Mummy?" I said "Yes." She then said, "Do you know what that is? It's poisoned soup, one sip of that and you're a gonner!" What a strange comment for a four year old to make! It really made me laugh, despite the miserable day.

Head lice! Nits! I don't know what you call them, but I call them a complete pain in the bum! I can see you scratching already. If I were to be asked what is the worst thing about being a blind parent? most people would probably expect me to say something like, not being able to see the faces of my children. Yes, I do miss that, but it has never moved me to tears, whereas head lice...

At the end of each school day, I would have to check their book bags to see if they had been given any letters. If head lice had been detected in the class, then the note would always appear on a long thin strip of paper. I dreaded putting my hand in the book bag and finding that piece of paper, it always spelled trouble. How does a blind person cope with head lice? The answer is, in my experience, not very well. Not having any family around meant that I had to rely on the kindness of friends or a health visitor to check the kids. If they had them, then it was off to the chemist to get those smelly lotions. It always seemed to happen just after I'd paid a considerable sum to have my hair done, and then it would be completely ruined by having to dunk my hair in the same stuff.

Even worse, were the endless hours of combing. I could never be sure I'd got rid of everything, and so had to always find someone to check again. I spent a fortune on different combs, and products to try to reduce frequency with which the kids were infected, and even bought a special comb that supposedly made a bleeping sound if it detected any of the little blighters. People gave me all kinds of advice like putting hair spray on the kids every day, and using tea tree oil, but nothing was ever that great. At one stage I went through a period of around twelve months when they seemed to have them constantly, and I used to find a quiet corner and cry tears of absolute frustration. It was bad, and I completely sympathise with other visually impaired parents who have gone through or are going through the same. Now you can stop scratching!

Let's move on to happier times, like going out to the local pub for Sunday lunch. The four of us sat around a table enjoying a pre-dinner drink, and engaging in pleasant family conversation. When it came to choosing what we wanted to eat, I casually said, "Mmm, I don't know what I fancy." A split second later, Rosanna shouted at the top of her voice, "I know what you fancy Mummy. You fancy Daddy!"

32. Train Travail

Not being able to see, means that one is completely reliant on public transport for travel. For many years, I have travelled on trains, and I could probably write a book about those experiences, so here are just a few. Sit back and enjoy the ride. Sorry, the *read*!

A couple of years ago, I was elated to learn that I had won two tickets to go to see a well-known gospel artist who has been one of my favourite singers for many years. I was looking forward to the day with eager anticipation. Best of all was the added bonus that before the concert, we would have a chance to meet and chat with the artist. As the time grew closer, I became more and more excited and couldn't wait for the day to arrive. My parents were staying with us that weekend, so Gaz and I would be able to travel together while Mum and Dad took care of the kids.

The journey from Peterborough to London only takes around one hour if you take the quickest route, and we made sure we had left extra time to arrive in Kings Cross, and take the tube to the venue. On our arrival at the station, we were concerned to find that, because of an accident, the train had been cancelled. We had to wait an extra half hour for another train. We finally embarked, and then our problems started. Several passengers had transferred from other trains which meant that we were packed on like sardines. People were squashed in the aisles nose to nose, and it was extremely uncomfortable. If I hadn't been going to the concert, I would have abandoned my journey there and then. However, this was an opportunity I really didn't want to miss, so we decided to proceed.

When the train left the station, I was relieved to be on my way, and hoped we wouldn't meet any further delays, but I was to be disappointed. Standing all the time, in such cramped conditions meant that we all grew very hot, and when the train was forced to stop at a station because the broken down train had still not been removed from the track, some were glad to just get some fresh air. We took the opportunity to sit for a while on the seats that had been vacated. At that point, the journey which should have taken around twenty minutes had actually taken us over an hour. I was then further exasperated when someone hit the emergency button. The alarm went off continually, and staff struggled to find out who had done it. One hour later, the alarm was still going off, and the perpetrator had not been identified. As the time ticked on, I came to the realisation that this day might not end up being what I had hoped for.

Eventually, we left the station, but didn't arrive in London until just after seven pm. An hour's journey, had turned into three. We arrived feeling hot, weary and disappointed. As we got in to a taxi, we were both determined that we should at least hear some of the concert. We arrived just as the support act had finished, and took our seats. We did enjoy a very good concert, but sadly, never got to meet the artist. The meet and greet had taken place before the gig, and though we tried to plead our case to staff at the venue, we left very disappointed.

Now all there was left to do, was go home. We arrived at the station to learn that we had just missed our train, and would have to wait for an hour for the next one. There were still problems on the line because of the earlier breakdown, and we were told that our journey would again be a long one. Having time to kill, we bought burgers, and ate them in disappointed, dejected silence. One thing I've learned over the years, is that whatever life throws at you, it's better if you can just find at least something to laugh about. When the train finally arrived, we found a seat, and as the train pulled away, we began talking with a retired couple sitting opposite us. We shared our experiences of travel trauma that day, and I joked about the fact that it was all probably our fault, we often experienced unexpected events when travelling on the train. At the time, I had no idea what the next couple of hours were to bring.

The conversation stopped suddenly when the train reduced in speed, and began to crawl for several minutes. We had no idea what was going on. Not long after, a sense of normality resumed when we picked up speed and were seemingly continuing with our journey. This situation was short lived. All of a sudden, the train suddenly slowed again. Without warning, the engine stopped, and then all the lighting went off except for the emergency lighting. All the passengers were wondering what was happening, when all the lighting went off completely. There were shouts and screams of panic all around us, but I calmly turned to Gaz and said, "Oh well, looks like we're in charge now!" Yes, amidst the screams and the darkness, there were two blind people sitting together laughing. It was one of those moments when you wonder what else in your day can go wrong? Then you conclude that you have absolutely no control, so it's probably best to find something to laugh about.

It was only a matter of seconds before the lights came back on, and calm was restored--for a short while. As we approached a station, passengers prepared to get off, but were again sent into a state of panic when the train went through the station without stopping. As exasperated travellers reached for their phones, we suddenly slowed, reversed, and crawled back into the station. How we wished it was our stop. After that, the train was relatively quiet apart from the couple we were talking to, and a few others. As our new found friends prepared to get off at the next stop, we wished them well and shook their hands. This we were to learn was a somewhat premature farewell. Once again, the train sailed through the station without stopping, and made no attempt to reverse.

By this time, my earlier comment was no longer a joke. The gentleman took his phone and began calling rail enquiries for some helpful information. His tone became increasingly irritated as the call went on, and who could blame him. We were all losing the will to live when the person at the call centre announced, "Sir I have an electronic map in front of me and I can assure you that the train is just about to stop at your station." Our friend retorted, "Well, I am sitting on that train right now, and I can absolutely assure you that we have left the station without stopping." It became apparent, that pleading our case with the person on the other end of the phone was futile. We were getting nowhere. In fact we were on our way to Peterborough, but that was no comfort for our friends. We did advise them to stay on until Peterborough as it would be easier to find overnight accommodation at two thirty in the morning, but they just wanted to get off that "ghost train" and, at the next stop, that's just what they did. I was concerned for them, as it was an unmanned station, and I sincerely hoped that they could call a taxi which would arrive soon. Eventually, we did pull into our station, and arrived home some time after three a.m., not wanting to see another train for a while.

The railway network in this country has a system for assisting disabled travellers. Journeys can be planned in advance with just a telephone call to the relevant company. Passengers can be met at the station, and helped to their seat on the train. At their destination, they will be met by a member of staff and taken to a taxi, or to a pre-arranged point to be met by friends or family members. This system can work well, but on occasions, things may not go as planned. On one occasion, we were travelling home to Worcester, when we ran into problems. Instead of making a straight-through journey from Birmingham to Worcester, we were informed that we would have to make a change due to engineering work. We disembarked from the train, and were surprised to find that we couldn't find anyone at the station. No staff, or passengers.

We didn't want to venture far for reasons of safety, but waited, hoping that someone would soon arrive. We were glad when we heard a voice, and approached the member of rail staff for help to get to our platform. Unfortunately, help wasn't forthcoming. He led us to a lift, then reached his hand in to press a button, and left us as the doors closed. When we stopped, we walked out of the lift, and waited for him to arrive. With all that waiting, I was sure we'd probably miss our train. Nobody turned up to offer any help, and by that time, my blood pressure was rising, I was six months pregnant with Josh, and really didn't need the stress. Gaz left me to see if he could find his way to the platform and came back to help me, accompanied by a very helpful member of the public. We eventually got our train, and arrived home safely, but as for the member of station staff, he was never seen again, at least not by us!

I have to say, that over the years, I have come into contact with many friendly and helpful people who work at railway stations. This was certainly the case, during a journey between Worcester and Peterborough. Again, we were making a change at Birmingham New Street, and were met by a lady and a gentleman who introduced themselves. It was nice to be greeted by two members of staff, and we thought we were getting VIP treatment, having the luxury of a guide each. They helpfully showed us on to our train, and wished us well as they left us to continue our journey.

A few minutes after the train had left the station we heard an announcement that certainly got our attention, "Welcome passengers to the 17.36 to London Euston..." Oh no, here we go again! How two sighted members of rail staff managed to put us both on the wrong train I'll never know, but it was true. We were lucky to find that the first stop was at Birmingham international, and as soon as those doors opened, we got off to try and find a train back to New Street. When we got back, all I can say is that we had words with someone, and made sure we were put on the correct train the second time around.

Poor old New Street, you do seem to get all the flack where I'm concerned, because it was also there that a potentially more serious incident occurred. Gaz and I were returning from a weekend break at the coast and, again, needed to change trains at Birmingham. I had my guide dog with me, and we were met by a member of staff. As we approached the door of our carriage, Gaz was led on to the train with me following. The gentleman guiding, informed us that there was a high step on to the train but he failed to tell us that there was also a wide gap between the platform and the step on to the train. My dog must have noticed the gap, because she suddenly jumped up the high step. Unfortunately, I was unaware of what was happening, and felt a heavy tug on the lead as I stepped forward. The force pulled me and unfortunately I fell through the gap between the train and the platform. The first thing I was aware of, was the scream of someone behind me, and then arms around my waist, as I was hoisted to safety. I was understandably shocked, as well as being very bruised, and bleeding from several lacerations to my legs. In a state of perplexity, I was helped into the carriage by the lady behind me, and, as the train prepared to leave, the staff member made a quick exit without enquiring about my wellbeing.

If two of us travelling together does have its hazards, add young children to the equation! I can hear you groaning already! Having one set of parents living in London, and the other in Lancashire, meant that the presence of a blind couple on trains with a child or two, a guide dog, luggage and a travel cot, was not unheard of. I look back now sometimes and wonder how we had the courage to do it. Actually, it probably wasn't courage so much as madness. Just getting on to the train, finding seats, somewhere to put all our luggage, not to mention a space for a guide dog, was a colossal conundrum of MENSA proportions in itself.

When Joshua was a baby he certainly knew how to make an journey eventful. I remember the time he decided to bless us, and the rest of the passengers with the smelliest nappy ever created. I've never seen such a mass exodus toward the doors. If they thought they had anything to complain about though, then they should have tried changing that nappy while being squashed into the small space that is the bathroom. Another time, we were returning home from London when Josh was sick everywhere. It just so happened that he was sitting on my knee, and I was baptised in a substance that made me want to add to the pile. Soon, a chain of passengers was passing me tissues, napkins, and anything else they could pull from bags and pockets. As for the smell, unfortunately there was nothing I could do.

On another jaunt to London, the ride was surprisingly uneventful, and we were actually starting to relax for once, when suddenly, Josh began calling out, "Grandma! Grandma!" A Jamaican lady had just got on to the train, and our son was convinced it was Gaz's Mum. It took a good deal of explaining and a visit from the lady before he could be convinced. He was always a very friendly little chap, making friends with other travellers whether they liked it or not, and, on numerous occasions, offering them things, including our lunch.

If it's difficult getting everyone and everything on to the train, getting off is just as problematic. We had made the three hour journey from Peterborough through to Manchester, where Mum and Dad were waiting for us on the platform. I am always quite obsessive about getting our things together early, and not having to make a mad rush when we reach our destination. As the train stopped, we made our way down the aisle carrying all manner of suitcases and bags. Everything was going well, until a passenger, who was still seated, decided that it would be the perfect time to become acquainted with my guide dog. As you can imagine, the dog was more than happy to oblige, and as I urged him forward, he refused to move. As I gave him the command to go forward once again in rather an exasperated voice, Gaz shouted from behind me to get a move on. As I tried to move forward, I heard a sound. It was the doors closing, and the train moving on.

At the time, Josh was around eight, and Rosanna five years old. Seeing Nanna and Granddad disappear as the train pulled away from the platform sent them into panic, and they both stood there in floods of tears. Gaz made an attempt to calm them down and reassure them, while I approached the guard. I'm sorry to say that he wasn't in the least sympathetic. His manner was rather disgruntled, and he seemed not to care one bit about the children's distress. In rather a brusque manner, he told us that we would have to stay on the train till the next stop and then take one back to Manchester. The next stop was around twenty minutes away, and I knew that my parents would be worried. Luckily, when we did reach the station and explained our predicament, they were a good deal more sympathetic, and offered to call Manchester to let Mum and Dad know what was happening. We did, eventually, reach our destination safely, and all was well, but I'd had enough of trains for that day.

On a lighter note, there have been at least a few moments that have made me giggle. At one time, my parents owned a caravan near Settle in Yorkshire, which they used at the weekend. During school holidays we would visit them. As we travelled up to Yorkshire, we found ourselves sitting at a table opposite a group of four young people. They were on their way to a music festival, and were having a drink and a good time in general, but they weren't at all rowdy, and most considerate toward other passengers. During the journey they struck up a conversation with us, and then came the moment. One of the guys asked me, "Would you mind taking a photograph of me and my friends?" and handed me his camera. I smiled, and wondered how I could explain this one without causing him embarrassment. I said, "I'm really sorry I can't see, but I'm sure my son wouldn't mind taking one." There was an awkward pause, so I just went for it. I smiled and said, "Ah mate, your friends are gonna give you such a ribbin' when you get off this train, you'll never live this one down will you?" The tension suddenly lifted and everyone started laughing including the young man who'd asked me to take the photo. I regaled them with some of the stories you have already heard, and once they understood my sense of humour, all was forgotten and no one needed to feel bad. Ironically, today there are plenty of blind people taking photos with their mobile phones. There is even an ap on the IPhone which allows you to take a picture, and then voiceover, built-in speech on the phone, describes what the picture is.

Finally, on another journey up to Settle, we made a change at Leeds, and a very nice member of staff helped us to get our connection. As we walked, he asked where I was going, and on hearing my destination, said, "If you're going up to Settle, you'll be near to Carlisle. You should go there because there's some lovely scenery!" I smiled to myself, and then turned to him saying, "Thank you for that, I really must look in to it!"

33. Stevie's story

Just before my daughter started Primary School, I began training with my second guide dog. Once Rosanna had reached three years old, I began considering the possibility. Fred had retired when I was eight months pregnant, and I had put off the idea of having another dog because I wanted to wait until Rosanna was old enough to be able to understand a little about looking after dogs, and that they sometimes need their own space to relax. I suppose that the way the story unfolded is quite ironic. I trained with a Labrador retriever who was initially a good worker, and I was glad to have her around. However, things very soon turned difficult.

It became apparent that she was a one person dog, and didn't like having children around. With Fred, we had bonded quickly, but in this case, the process never really happened. I tried extremely hard to make things work, but after a period of around three months, I reached the conclusion that I would have to let her go. The instructors at GDBA were extremely supportive, and reassured me I hadn't done anything wrong.

On the day when a guide dog mobility instructor was due to come and collect my dog and take her back to one of the training centres. I found myself sitting at the top of the stairs crying. I had wanted things to work out so much, but I knew it was best to let her go. I had become very nervous one day when Josh and Rosie had returned from a few days holiday with their grandparents and, on their return, she had growled at them. After she had gone, I found myself weeping again, but at that time, I wasn't aware of just how quickly a replacement dog would be found.

Only a few days later, I had just returned from school with the children when the phone rang. It was exciting news. A prospective dog had been found for me, and he was a golden Labrador called Stevie. I couldn't wait to meet him and hoped he would like everyone in our family. From the moment I met him, I fell in love with Stevie. Words cannot describe just how wonderful he was. He was affectionate, faithful, fun-loving, and the consistency of his work was top notch. Our three week training course went like a dream, and several years later, my instructor remarked, "I didn't really have anything to do. You two took to each other straight away, and all I had to do was observe how well you worked together."

I first met super Stevie the day after his second birthday. He sat down next to me, and rested his nose on my knee. I rubbed his soft fur, and as soon as I stopped, I immediately felt his nose push under my arm as if to say, "Hang on a minute, why have you stopped? I was enjoying that!" This trait lasted for the rest of his life. I had bruised wrists or arms on several occasions after he nudged my arm when it was under the table, and I banged it. It really didn't matter: he was just fantastic.

My guide dog mobility instructor explained to me that Stevie would probably like to be where I was, and I shouldn't be surprised if he always came to sit where I was sitting. I quickly learned that this was right. It didn't matter where I sat, Stevie would come and sit at my feet. If I got up, then he would get up, and follow me wherever I went. I was warned to be careful when opening cupboards and doing other general tasks, because I would have to consider the fact that Stevie would be there too. I soon got used to having a shadow. This was part of Stevie's personality, he just wanted to be loved, and he was more than worth it.

Everyone who came into contact with Stevie loved him. It was impossible not to. He was always happy. Nothing ever seemed to get him down, or stress him out. He didn't care what the weather was like: rain, sun, snow, he just loved to be outside working or having a free run. I clearly recall the first time he saw snow. He jumped around, kicking it about, and barking with delight. He rolled around and ate the stuff, before shaking himself all over me. His love for snow did on occasions give me a few problems, especially on school days. The poor dog found it very hard to concentrate on guiding me, instead of playing.

One morning when the snow was thick on the ground, I got the children ready for school, and, kitted out in warm coats, boots, hat and gloves, we ventured outside for the journey. Stevie did more playing and eating the snow than guiding me, but eventually we made it to the playground. The air was full of the sounds of children running, screeching with delight and shouts as some were pelted with snowballs. I dropped Rosanna off at her classroom, and then Josh and I walked to his door. As I turned to leave, Josh could see that I was struggling to get Stevie under control, and to concentrate. It's fair to say that I was a little frustrated, and my pride slightly dented, when, in the end, I had to approach one of the teachers in the playground and ask if Josh could walk me home because, clearly, this was one occasion when Stevie's mind was on other things.

Stevie was also a true Labrador: his appetite was bigger than he was, and it gave me a few causes for concern. The first Christmas we had Stevie, we attended a concert at the children's school. Stevie came with us, and after it was over, we visited some friends who lived nearby to exchange Christmas presents. There were wrapped gifts for the children, and another specially wrapped present for Stevie. We walked home, and put the presents under the tree before settling Stevie in his bed and turning in for the night. I really hadn't given it a second thought, but in the morning I had quite a shock. I opened the lounge door to find that Stevie had taken both the children's presents, which turned out to be selection boxes, and ripped into them. He had eaten all of the chocolate bars, complete with some of the wrappings, but not attempted to touch his own gift. Obviously, he had decided that his present should wait until Christmas day! Instead of greeting me with his jovial doggy song, Stevie sat rather solemnly in his bed. The floor was littered with vomit and pieces of chocolate bar wrappers. That meant an immediate trip to the vets and, unfortunately the cleaning up would have to wait. I returned later that morning with a more perky looking dog, only to learn that Rosanna had been sent home from school feeling unwell.

Gaz went off to work, and it was time for me to roll up my sleeves. I made sure that Rosie was tucked up in bed, gave her a drink, and took a deep breath as I considered my next task in the living room. The next couple of hours was just like an episode of "Mr. Bean." I couldn't see where each pile of dog vomit was, and the smell filled the whole room, so that was no help. I knelt down with my large bowl of disinfectant, and floor cloth, and tentatively reached out to see what I would find. I seemed to be doing quite well, until the moment when Rosie called me from upstairs. I ran into the downstairs toilet, shouting, "I'm coming darling. I just need to wash my hands." When I reached her room, she told me that she had been sick. I didn't say anything, but in my mind I was saying, "You really didn't need to tell me that, I could smell it before I opened the door." Oh well, in for a penny. I cleaned up the bedroom carpet and changed the bedding and Rosie's nightwear before settling her down, this time with a bowl just in case. Then I took a very large deep breath before returning to the lounge. It wasn't until a couple of hours later, when the house smelled considerably sweeter, and I had managed to get a friend to check that I had successfully completed the job, that a rather exhausted Mummy could get a coffee and some lunch. Actually, by that time, I just stuck to the coffee; I wasn't exactly feeling very hungry!

After Christmas came Easter, and we were to learn another lesson. The children had received several Easter eggs that they had to keep until Easter Sunday. We left quite early on the Sunday morning to go to church. I had told the children to leave their eggs in their bedrooms so that Stevie couldn't get to them and we thought that all would be well. How wrong could we be? Indeed the Easter eggs were left in the bedrooms, but the kids had forgotten to close their doors. When we returned, we found that the majority of the eggs had gone. Incredibly, Stevie hadn't been sick, but as soon as everyone got into the house, I was calling a taxi to take Stevie and me to see the vet again. He was given an injection to make him sick, and I was told that following that, he certainly looked a good deal better. Chocolate can be very dangerous for dogs, and in some cases can prove fatal, so it was imperative to ensure that he didn't digest any. Once again I took Stevie home and wished that chocolate didn't exist - for at least a couple of hours!

I'm pleased to say that there were no more chocolate incidents, but there were other food related episodes. One evening, Josh and Rosie had a friend round for tea. One of the items I had cooked was Rosie's favourite, chicken satay. This type was a small cocktail stick containing three pieces of chicken. Everything was going well until someone dropped one of their satays on the floor. In a flash, Stevie dived and devoured the lot, including the cocktail stick. I was horrified. I hadn't realised that Stevie had left his bed, and had sat under the dining table in eager anticipation of any crumbs. All I could think of was that cocktail stick inside my precious dog, and what damage it might do. In quite a fluster, I rang the vet. As you can imagine, she said, with what sounded like a wry smile on her face, "Ah it's Stevie again! What has he been up to this time?"

The vet managed to alleviate my immediate concerns, about him needing emergency surgery. She advised me to feed him a full loaf of bread in order to help him pass the cocktail stick naturally. Everyone in the family thought it was very funny, especially as guide dogs are kept to a strict diet. Here I was breaking all the rules by feeding him an entire loaf, when he was a greedy little blighter already. I was always astonished by how quickly he would wolf down the food which he was given twice a day, and sometimes would end the process by letting out a huge burp. Now he had found a way to scavenge AND reward himself by getting a large loaf of bread.

Stevie's need for food was not confined to the family home, although in the following situation, I couldn't really blame him. We were walking through our local shopping centre one afternoon, on the way to collect the kids from school. A young mum was walking towards me, pushing her toddler in a buggy. What I didn't realise was that the child was holding a roll in her hand. I guess that as far as Stevie was concerned, food was there right in front of him at his eye level. It was fair game, and he took advantage of the situation. The first thing I knew was hearing a rather irate mother shouting at me. "Your dog has just stolen a roll from my child. That's not right: guide dogs are not supposed to do that sort of thing." I apologised, but she continued with her protest. I offered to pay for the roll, but she seemed to be determined to continue. I offered to accompany her to the bakery and replace the roll, but by then I had rather lost patience. My efforts to make restitution were ignored, and I concluded that there was nothing more I could do, so I continued with my journey.

Despite these minor mishaps, Stevie continued to be a joy to work with, and the most faithful friend anyone could ask for. In October 2004, we moved to a larger house located much closer to the children's school. They loved their new home, and also the fact that there were to be no more long walks in the rain or snow. It would only take us a couple of minutes to get to the playground. We all had much more space and settled in really well. Stevie learned some new routes, and enjoyed chasing the children around the nearby park. I have very fond memories of pushing them on the swings, catching them at the bottom of the slide and of all of us chasing each other through huge piles of leaves in autumn.

Five months after we moved, I noticed that Stevie seemed to be putting on weight. I wasn't overly concerned, and put it down to the fact that we were no longer walking several miles every day. I had a routine visit from a guide dog mobility instructor and mentioned this but didn't think it would be much of a problem. A couple of weeks later however, he still seemed to be gaining weight, and while on the bus one morning, I was worried about something else. When I found my seat, I took off Stevie's harness, and encouraged him to lie under my seat. As he obeyed my instruction, I heard him yelp as if in pain as he lay down.

It got to the point where I couldn't settle, I felt that there was something wrong, and so took Stevie to my local vet. I was reassured that there was probably nothing to worry about, but just to monitor the situation. I felt a distinct sense of uneasiness about my precious friend, and didn't really know what to do. Alarm bells definitely did start ringing two weeks later, when I presented Stevie with his breakfast, and he made no attempt to eat it.

A Labrador who won't eat its food, in my experience, certainly means that there is something wrong. One Friday evening, I walked with Stevie to the vet for his emergency appointment. I have to say, that my vet did sound very concerned as she informed me that it was best if I left him overnight, so that tests could be carried out. I knew just by feeling his tummy that there was no way he could have put on such a huge amount of weight in such a short time without there being something wrong. It is fair to say, however, that it would only have been apparent to someone who lived with the dog every day. As I took a taxi home, I sat with Stevie's harness in my hand, and had a very heavy heart. I desperately wanted my dog to be ok. Stevie was always such a happy boy. What I mean is, he just always got on with things, and nothing ever seemed to dampen his spirits. I lay awake that night, worrying about him. What if he had been in pain, and I hadn't known? What seemed worse, was that he had been faithfully working for me, and what if I'd made him work while he was hurting.

I had a very anxious time the following morning, pacing around, wondering what was happening with Stevie. There was no way however, that I could have prepared myself for the news that I was about to receive. The phone rang about twelve o'clock, and the vet's voice was very subdued. "Stevie is under anaesthetic. We have found a large tumour in his abdomen, and I think it would be kinder if we didn't allow him to come round, but give him an injection to put him to sleep." The voice was very sympathetic, and sensitive toward the situation, but I simply couldn't take in the news. I was completely horrified. I knew that in this situation, I needed to seek advice from GDBA before giving permission for any further procedure, and so told the vet that they were to do nothing until I had spoken to my instructor.

As I replaced the receiver, I found it impossible to contain my emotions. It took me a few minutes to get myself together, but I knew what I had to do, and immediately rang Pete Smith. Pete was the district team manager of GDBA. He had trained Stevie, and then trained the two of us together only a couple of years previous to this event. When Pete answered the phone, I tearfully spluttered and stammered out my situation. I don't remember much about the content of the conversation, except, that I was repeatedly pleading, "Please don't let them put Stevie down, Pete, please don't let them! There must be something we can do!"

Pete eventually managed to calm me down. He was very honest with me, and said, "If Stevie was an older dog, it would be kinder to let him go, but Stevie is only just four years old. I will speak with the vet, and if there is the remotest chance that anything can be done, we will try."

I trusted Pete, and I knew how much he loved Stevie. I wasn't aware at that time, but on that day, Pete was moving house. He didn't let me worry about that, however, but put Stevie first. Several minutes elapsed, and then suddenly the phone rang. Pete told me that it had been decided, bearing in mind Stevie's age, that an operation could be carried out within a couple of days. He couldn't make any promises about how things would work out, but Stevie would be given the best possible chance.

Stevie remained at the surgery, and forty-eight hours later, had his operation. It was a very complex and delicate procedure, during which there were two separate occasions when Stevie nearly died on the operating table. After several hours, with the dedicated expertise of the veterinary team, a tumour weighing ten pounds, was removed from Stevie's abdomen. Yes, it really did weigh ten pounds. Photographs were taken, and details recorded, and the case was used for trainee vets in other medical centres. I had been reassured that someone would call me when the procedure was completed, and true to their word, I was contacted at around six thirty that evening. Stevie had come around from the anaesthetic, and after only half an hour, was wagging his tail, and trying to stand up. Everyone had fallen in love with him, and was amazed and overwhelmed by his resilience.

For the next few days, I made regular calls to the vet every morning, and every evening to check on Stevie's progress. His condition continued to improve, and he got his appetite back. Finally, the day arrived when I was able to collect him from the vet's. I walked into the surgery, and spoke with the receptionist. I'll never forget what happened next. In the room behind her, was a row of kennels, where dogs were kept while waiting to be picked up by their owners. Stevie must have recognised my voice, because I suddenly heard him whining and then barking. I knew instinctively without a doubt that it was him, and once again, my eyes were filled with tears. I was asked to take a seat and wait for a few moments. When the vet had finished attending to his patient, he would collect Stevie and speak with me. As I took my seat, I could still hear Stevie; it seemed that he wanted to see me as much as I wanted to see him. Several minutes later, when Stevie refused to give up his whining, the veterinary nurse opened his kennel, and brought him over to me. I gently placed my hand on his head, and then ran my hand down his soft coat. I don't really know what I had been expecting, but what I found, once again made me cry. My dog had never been overweight before carrying the tumour, but now--now he was painfully thin. I was quite shocked, and my heart went out to him. I was, however, extremely grateful to the team of vets who had battled to save his life. In a situation like that, there are no words to express the depth of one's gratitude.

I returned home with my precious dog, and a huge tray of special food which Stevie would have to eat for the foreseeable future. He wore his special collar, the type that looks like a large lamp shade. He hated it, but it was absolutely necessary, to stop him tampering with the vast number of stitches he had. In the weeks that followed, I tried to do everything I could to make Stevie comfortable, and aid his recovery. There were many nights, when he would be in his bed beside me, and I would lay awake wondering if he was ok. Was he in any pain? Was there anything else he needed? And the one I remember the most, "Oh darling, I know you hate that collar, I wish I could take it off for you, but I really, really can't!"

Pete visited us several times to see how things were going. Frequently, he did a very good job of lightening the mood by commenting, "Ten pounds of tumour, that's the size of a cat!" For several years following, he regularly referred to Stevie as the dog who swallowed a cat. He also made us laugh by referring to Stevie as the pajama case. This was because when Stevie lay on his back, you could clearly see a long row of stitches right along his tummy which looked like a very long zip. Stevie however, took everything in his stride. One afternoon, he gave me cause for concern, because he began pacing back and forth in our living room. He stood at the door several times and whimpered. I had recently let him out for a wee, and was very worried in case he was in pain and there was something wrong. I opened the lounge door, and attempted to guide him over to his spending pen, but he just lay down on the patio. His tail started to wag and then he let out a rather low contented sigh. Suddenly it dawned on me. Poor Stevie had been stuck in doors, under strict instructions to rest, and not to have any exercise. All he wanted to do was relax out in the sunshine, bless him.

Despite devoting much of my time to Stevie, the daily routine had to carry on as normal. The children had been anxious about their dog, and I did all I could to alleviate their concerns. Getting around was more difficult for me. I had always been a competent white cane user, but having to go back to using one after partnering with Stevie, took some getting used to. The tap, tap of my cane seemed to take a whole lot more concentration than being with my dog. Also, I always felt so guilty about going out and leaving him. Stevie made it clear that he wasn't amused by following me to the door whenever he saw my cane, and making attempts to get out with me. As I closed the door, he would whine as if to say, "Why are you leaving me? Why can't I come too?"

Only six weeks after his operation, it became so difficult, that I rang Pete. I wanted to ask if I could begin taking Stevie out on very short walks. Pete agreed to visit us, and asked me to get Stevie's harness ready. That afternoon, I suddenly heard a knock at the door, and then a huge burst of laughter as I let Pete in the house. Our front window looks into our dining room. Pete had knocked on the door, and Stevie had run over to see who it was. When he saw Pete, Stevie had immediately run over to his harness and put his head through it, as if to say, "Thank goodness you're here, now let's get to work!" Pete couldn't believe how enthusiastic Stevie was. We trotted along as if nothing had happened to him. It was agreed that he could start having walks again, as long as it was only in short stints. Stevie was certainly much happier after that. His tail would wag vigorously. Did I mention Stevie's tail? Everyone used to comment about it. Not so much his actual tail, but the manner in which he used to express himself with it. Instead of wagging from side to side, his tail would go round in circles like a helicopter. It's a wonder he didn't actually lift himself off the ground at times. People found it hilarious. That though, was my Stevie!

In the next few months that followed, Stevie made several visits to veterinary hospital to receive further treatment. It was during a trip to collect him from a hospital in Hertfordshire that I learned something about him that I had never known before. An employee from GDBA drove me down to collect him, and as we sat waiting for him, the lady who had driven us sat eating a banana. As Stevie was brought out to us, his eyes immediately fixed on it. The look he gave her was so intense that she asked the vet if she was allowed to give Stevie a very small piece. Since his first operation, Stevie had been fed a specific special food to eat. He was no longer able to have his regular few treats, and I missed giving them to him. Now, he had been able to eat a tiny piece of banana.

The following day, Stevie had to attend a scheduled appointment at my local vet's surgery. I mentioned about Stevie's seeming need for banana. The vet started to laugh, and commented that Stevie's potassium levels had been very low in recent weeks. Bananas are high in potassium, and maybe that was why he wanted some. From then on, I was allowed to treat Stevie to a piece of banana a few times a week. He loved it. Actually it was more than that, he couldn't get enough, and I had to be really disciplined about how much I gave him. The situation became very comical, because we reached a stage where simply mentioning the word "banana" meant he would go bananas. If I said, "Ooh Stevie, would you like a piece of banana?" He would start to do a little dance, and then bark. On one occasion, I was having a conversation with a friend. Not having any prior knowledge, she mentioned something about banana bread. We were both taken aback, because Stevie was in his bed taking a rest, but suddenly he dashed across the room. At first I didn't twig, but then suddenly I realised what was going on. From that point on, we would have to spell the word during conversation, if we didn't want him to hear what we were saying. It was so funny, and he was just so amazingly lovable.

I'm pleased to say that Stevie made a full recovery. I had been told that there was a chance that the tumour could re-occur, but I decided to simply enjoy Stevie whatever the future held. I can't thank the guide dogs association enough for their on-going support, and the way in which they managed Stevie's recovery process. I am sure that Stevie is the most expensive guide dog in history, considering the extent of the treatment he required. As far as I'm concerned, he was worth every penny. Thank you to everyone involved at GDBA, your dedication to all the dogs and their owners is truly amazing.

Even though Stevie was required to stick to a special diet following his operation, it didn't stop him from trying to snatch the odd treat. I had just left a shopping centre one afternoon, and was making my way to the bus stop when I felt Stevie dive for something on the ground. I immediately said "no", and in a flash, reached forward and grabbed the item from his mouth. It turned out to be a ring doughnut. I looked down at him, and in a low stern voice said, "Leave it!" As I paused, wondering what I was going to actually do with the offending doughnut, I heard an irate voice behind me. A woman was shouting at me, telling me to leave that poor dog alone, and that she was going to report me to the guide dogs people for being cruel to my dog. I turned and said, "Madam, this dog has recently undergone major surgery. Eating anything he finds on the ground could seriously jeopardise his health." Despite my explanation, she walked off, still issuing her threat. With a weary sigh, I turned and continued with my journey. I was frustrated, but knew that if indeed she did speak with anyone from GDBA, the people that knew me well, would understand that I had done the right thing, and not done anything cruel.

There was also a time when Stevie was too quick for anyone and managed to get his fill. My Nanna Margaret sadly died in 2003. We made the trip up to Blackburn to attend her funeral. My sister was looking after Stevie during the service, as I was due to sing a solo. After the service was finished, we all made our way from the chapel, and into the dining area for food and refreshments. As Kirsten walked across the room with Stevie, someone walked past pushing a large metal trolley full of food. On the bottom shelf was a large dish of trifle. Before Kirsten could do anything, Stevie dashed forward, and plunged his face into the dish. We hadn't had much to smile about that day, but as the news spread around the room to the other guests, the place was suddenly filled with laughter. Thanks Stevie, I didn't approve of your actions, but you were always able to make us laugh.

One of my most memorable moments with Stevie occurred during a trip to John Lewis. I was scheduled to meet a friend in the coffee shop, and so we ventured into town. When we arrived in the store, it took quite some time to locate the lift, but eventually, we found it. As we entered, a young man followed us, and stood in the opposite corner of the lift. As we ascended to the first floor, He suddenly exclaimed, "You look like you're going to enjoy that Mr. Dog!" I looked toward him with a perplexed expression. He then said, "Did you know that your dog has a filled baguette in his mouth? Hmmm, it looks like chicken salad! He certainly looks very proud." As I put my hand to Stevie's mouth, indeed, there it was, a large filled baguette, each end of it sticking out of the side of his mouth. I have to admit, that it made me giggle. Strangely, he had not made any attempt to eat it, but just stood there and wagged his tail.

As I sipped my coffee, I mulled over two things. Firstly, where, and when had Stevie snaffled the offending item? I had walked across town, and around the shopping centre, and John Lewis, trying my best to look like a respectable citizen, while sneaky Stevie had been proudly displaying his stolen goods to all! And secondly, what about the person returning to their office or home, eagerly anticipating lunch, only to open their bag to find that their chosen chicken salad baguette was gone.

Stevie retired in July 2010. It didn't seem like he really wanted to, but together with the advice from people at GDBA, we decided that it was time for him to rest. He had done incredibly well, considering his medical history. Bearing in mind Stevie's personality, and his attitude toward his work, I knew I couldn't keep him at home with me. It was something that I had to consider and prepare for long before the day actually arrived. I would have been allowed to keep him, together with a new young working dog, but I considered that for Stevie to watch another dog take over his job would have made him unhappy. Some friends of my parents who lived up in Lancashire had recently lost their pet Labrador, and when my Dad mentioned the prospect of adopting Stevie, they couldn't have been more enthusiastic.

So, everything was arranged, and the day arrived when Brian and Kath travelled down to collect Stevie. It was one of those strange times. I felt so very sad, but knew that I was doing the right thing. I asked the rest of the family if Stevie and I could have some time together, and Gaz and the kids went to the park. Stevie and I sat together; I cuddled him and cried. I told him how much I loved him, and what a wonderful dog he was. I knew that Brian and Kath would love him and give him a fantastic retirement. When they arrived, Stevie seemed to be quite happy in their company. As they left, Brian gave the impression that I'd given him a cheque for a million pounds, rather than handing over my dog. I knew instinctively that everything would be fine. Also, I could visit Stevie whenever I went to see my parents. Kath and Brian did indeed treat Stevie like royalty. He lacked for nothing, getting their undivided attention, and frequently being taken to their caravan for holidays, where he would be treated to long walks. Unfortunately, Stevie only enjoyed eighteen months of his retirement. During a walk, he suddenly collapsed and was rushed to the vet's, where it was discovered that the tumour had returned. He was in a very bad way, and it was time to put him to sleep at the age of twelve.

It was a very sad day in February 2012 when I received the news. However, as I looked back I was so incredibly grateful to everyone who had helped Stevie and me through those difficult times when he was ill. The decision to operate when he was only four had paid off. He had worked until he was nearly ten years old, and enjoyed the time he had left in retirement. Thanks, Brian and Kath for looking after Stevie so well, we all miss him but have precious memories to treasure.

Stevie brought so much joy to everyone he came into contact with, that it wouldn't be right to end on a sad note, so I will tell you about another occasion which has made us laugh many times over the years. Stevie and I were out in our local shopping centre one morning. After selecting my shopping, we joined the short queue at the check-out to pay. A middle-aged well-spoken gentleman stood in front of me and placed his items on the counter. As he proceeded to make payment, I heard him say in a raised voice with a churlish expression, "I hope that the woman behind me isn't trying to look at my pin number!" I felt quite offended by both his suggestion and tone, but kept my cool. I put on my best smile and immediately retorted, "Absolutely not Sir, but I couldn't necessarily speak for my guide dog. He is very clever you know!"

34. Never work with children or animals

Having spent much of my time with young children and a guide dog, I disagree with the advice to actors, concerning children and animals. In my experience, it is often adults that can give you cause for frustration and exasperation. One afternoon, Rosie and I were walking home from school. Josh had been invited to play at a friend's house, and so I decided to take Rosie to a local café for a drink and a cake. My daughter was around five years old at the time, and was quite excited about our little trip after school, especially as it would just be the two of us. On arrival, I approached the counter, and Rosie made her choice. I decided to have a slice of toast, and enquired as to whether the toast would be already buttered or whether I could do that myself. My reason for asking was that I had been in establishments where I had received toast which had already been coated in margarine, and I prefer butter. The lady behind the counter, however, proceeded to say something which made my blood pressure rise. She leaned forward toward Rosanna and said, "No, it doesn't come already buttered, but you can help your Mum and do that for her, can't you!" I was not amused! I wanted to respond immediately by asking my daughter if she had enjoyed the carefully crafted soufflé, followed by the perfectly made baked Alaska we had eaten for dinner the previous evening. This however wasn't true, so with a grumpy expression, I chose the table closest to the offending person, and made sure that when my toast arrived, she could see me butter it for myself.

Sadly, there are times when the acts of young children can leave you lost for words. As I explained earlier, I used to pull Rosanna's pushchair beside me. She would be facing in the opposite direction, but as she was right there beside me, she was fine and didn't seem to mind. Rosie would have been around two years old when we were walking home one afternoon, and just passing our local park by the shopping centre when suddenly, an object flew past us. Josh immediately turned round and saw two boys around ten years old. We continued walking, but seconds later, a second object, a large stick, flew past Josh's shoulder. He turned to me and said, "Mummy, those boys are throwing things at us." Feeling a little uneasy, I quickened my pace. Suddenly I heard a scream, and Rosie began to cry. A large stone, the size of a doughnut had hit her on the knee, thrown by the two young boys behind us, who were now running across the cycle track at speed. I was completely shocked, and very, very upset.

Josh and I checked that there was no serious damage to Rosanna, and comforted her, before walking the short distance to our home. I held myself together for the sake of the children, but inside I was really shaken up. Once both of the children were happily eating a snack in front of the TV, I hid myself in the kitchen and rang the police. CCTV footage of the area was checked, but the culprits were never found. I know the two boys were only about ten years old at that time, but now that around 14 years have elapsed, I sometimes wonder if they remember their cruel actions, and ever feel some sense of remorse.

I consider myself to be quite a resilient person most of the time, but on that occasion, my confidence was seriously dented. If I was out on my own, I was ok most of the time, but when I was with the kids, I felt vulnerable. Parents always want to protect their children, but I had been unable to do that, and Rosie had been hurt. I kept thinking, "what if the stone had hit her head?" I was eternally grateful that it hadn't but did spend quite a lot of the time crying in the few days that followed, when the kids were not around.

Several days later, I needed to go to the shops. It was Sunday afternoon, and so I left the kids with Gaz. I was walking past the park on my journey home, when I heard something that made me distinctly uncomfortable. A group of teenagers were walking toward me, and I was filled with a sense of foreboding. Determined to face my fears, I carried on walking. As they walked alongside me, I was perturbed to find that their conversation ceased and there was silence. Not knowing what to expect, I was surprised but relieved at what I heard. A young person, I guess around thirteen suddenly said, "respect!" They carried on walking and resumed their conversation, as I, very relieved, continued to make my way home, reassured that not everyone was now going to be throwing stones at me.

Many shopping trips at the supermarket occasioned moments of laughter, frustration and poignancy. I was once standing at a checkout waiting to pay, when the member of staff admired my guide dog. She then immediately began complaining about another blind guide dog owner who had apparently just left the shop. For some reason, the lady didn't seem to approve of that particular dog and uttered in a disdainful tone, "I don't know why she brings that dog. Why can't she leave it at home?" For me, it was one of those weary moments I am confronted with regularly when I am left thinking, "Really, you just don't get it do you?" Feeling exasperated, but not wishing to appear hostile, I said gently, "Maybe it's because she needs the dog to help her get here in the first place."

We are all involved in the learning process, and I certainly learned something one afternoon in that same supermarket. Josh, Rosie and I had been doing various errands in the town centre, and I needed to collect a few food items before returning home. I told the children to go and choose a magazine while I found a member of staff to help me do my shopping. I was surprised when Josh turned and said, "We can help you Mum." Gaz and I have always had quite strong views with regard to parenting in our situation. We wanted our children to grow up and enjoy their childhood without feeling responsible for us. What Josh said next though, caused me to reflect and consider things from a different perspective. "Why won't you let us help, don't you trust us?" I felt terrible, and reassured him that I did trust both of them. I just didn't want either of them to feel like they had to help us all the time. We got a trolley, and the three of us had great fun choosing items and chucking them in the trolley. The only thing was that I ended up spending much more than I had planned on that day.

I am pleased and privileged to announce that my children have brought me far more pleasure than pain during their lives. Carrying on the Readfern tradition, we regularly enjoy times sitting around our dining table with great food and conversation. Josh and Rosie must have been around 11 and 8 respectively, when we were enjoying Sunday lunch together one afternoon. At that time, relating "blonde" jokes seemed to be a popular pastime. Josh and Gaz exchanged jokes avidly, as I uttered my disapproval, but what was to come next, made me laugh uncontrollably. As Josh finished his joke, and the guys fell about laughing, quick witted Rosanna announced, "You see, it all goes to show that two blondes don't make a bright!"

We have all often heard the phrase, "life begins at forty", and this was certainly true for me. Only three months before my fortieth birthday, I was somewhat surprised to find that I was going to have another baby. It wasn't something we'd planned, but once we got over the initial shock, and had a couple of large Jack Daniels—well at least for Gaz- we were both pleased and excited. I remember the day we told the children, who were then twelve and nine. They seemed surprised, and then spent the next few minutes giggling--I can't possibly think why! They were far more excited than we had anticipated, especially Rosanna who was now clearly revelling in the prospect of being a big sister. The pregnancy went well, without any

282

major problems, and in June 2009, Nathaniel was born weighing eight pounds and one ounce.

I only stayed in hospital for a couple of nights, but I must say that the care I received at all times was excellent. I had prepared as well as I could as my due date drew near, speaking with my consultant about my requirements, and what could be done to make life easier, such as being given a bed at the end of the ward, close to the door so I could get to the bathroom myself. Mum travelled down as soon as she knew that Nathaniel was on the way, and was waiting for me with a home-cooked meal when Gaz and I brought our little boy home for the first time. It seemed strange to be once again surrounded by nappies and baby grows, but Nathaniel was a brilliant baby, and settled very well.

Nathaniel has always been a fantastic fun-loving chap, but as he approached his first birthday, I learned that there was going to be one situation that was going to cause on-going stress and strife. Shopping absolutely brings out the worst in him! I am very lucky to have friends who help me get my weekly shop. As soon as Nathaniel was old enough to sit in the trolley seat, he quickly perfected the art of reaching out, grabbing random items from the shelves, and throwing them in the trolley. It took us twice as long to carry out our task, as we would have to spend time putting back the unwanted items. When he became tired of taking items from the shelves, he decided it was time for a change. His next trick was to constantly turn, pick items from the trolley, and throw them on the floor. When that's a bag of crisps, you're kind of ok, but when it's a tin, or a breakable item, then the problems begin. I often cringed, as I dreaded a smashing sound, or an unsuspecting shopper suddenly having to dodge a flying tin of baked beans or, even worse, being hit by one. My heart was often in my mouth, and I began to dislike those times as much as Nathaniel did.

Once he reached the "terrible two" stage, in addition to his trolley tricks, came the tantrums. As I was helping a friend pack my shopping one morning, Nathaniel decided that he'd had enough, and lay stretched out on the floor. After some firm but reasonable words from Mummy, he decided to remain defiant and stay where he was on the floor. I was determined not to make a scene so, as he started to cry, I boldly picked him up. He started to kick out, and scream. Without shouting or making a fuss, I simply tucked him under my arm on my hip, and marched out of the supermarket. On another occasion when my mum was staying with us, she decided that it would be a good idea to take Nathaniel into town with her, while I kept an appointment.

Mum suggested that, because Nathaniel was now walking well, she would leave the pushchair at home. I was suddenly filled with a sense of dread. This really wasn't a good idea. I tried to explain, that maybe it would be easier if she took him in the buggy, but Mum was sure everything would be ok. As we went our separate ways, a smile lit up my face, as I contemplated how their morning together would unfold.

Two hours later, I was beginning to think that I had misjudged the situation. Then my phone rang, and I heard Mum's voice full of panic. "Jane, have you finished your appointment? Can you meet me? I really need your help! I am in Waitrose and Nathaniel is having a tantrum. He is lying on the floor crying, and he has thrown his shoes across the floor. Neither I, nor the staff can get him to behave." Far from thinking "I told you so", I felt really bad, and wished I'd insisted on the buggy idea. I marched across town at speed, and by the time I reached my destination, Nathaniel was sitting on a bench outside the supermarket, in a much more jovial state of mind. Had the threat of "Mummy is coming to speak with you now!" changed his mind?

Let's face it, shopping can be really boring whatever age you are. So, I decided that compromise was required. As we left the house one morning, I told Nathaniel, that if he was good and helped us do the shopping nicely, after we had finished, we would take him to look at the toy section. I was amazed how smoothly our shopping trip went that week, and Nathaniel did get to look at the toys afterwards. I was so impressed at his patience, that I recall rewarding him with a colouring book and crayons.

The following week, as we got into the car, and I told Nathaniel about the plan, I felt rather more relaxed than normal. I didn't have any idea though, about my son's ideas. As we walked around the supermarket, I suddenly noticed that Nathaniel was once again selecting items from the shelves and placing them in the trolley. I kept saying, "No darling, we don't need that this week." However, he continued to throw things in the trolley. Suddenly everything became clear, Nathaniel shouted, "Mummy, is the trolley full now? Can we go and look at the toys?"

Nathaniel has always been a child who knows exactly what he wants. When he was three years old he approached Gaz. Josh was watching a film in the living room, but Nathaniel wanted to watch cartoons. Nathaniel told his Dad that he needed to watch TV instead of Josh. Gaz told Nathaniel he should share the TV, and he should go upstairs to Rosanna and watch TV with her, or ask her if he could watch a cartoon on her iPad. Instead of following this advice, Nathaniel went to Josh and said, "Josh, why don't you ask Rosie if you can watch telly with her, or borrow her iPad?"

I was walking to the shops with Nathaniel a few days later. We were only a few steps away from the entrance when I met a friend. We began a conversation, but neither of us was aware that Nathaniel had walked into the shop, helped himself to a bag of Randoms, and brought the packet of sweets outside to eat while we continued chatting. When I heard a rustling sound, and realized what had happened, I ended the conversation rather abruptly, to apologise to the shop owner and pay for the sweets. It's a good job they know me quite well in there! Gosh! Toddlers who help themselves to cartons of orange juice, Nathaniel helping himself to sweets, and a baguette swiping guide dog--it's a wonder that I've managed to keep on the right side of the law.

Actually, I've always said that someone should make a film all about a blind woman with a guide dog, and her children. It would be rather amusing if the dog and the kids could talk with each other, while the woman was completely unaware. Can you imagine the conversations?

Talking of guide dogs, shortly after Stevie retired, I learned that my new dog was going to be a Labrador/Retriever called Snoopy. I trained with him during the summer of 2011, and we bonded quickly. Snoopy (or Snoop Dog) as he is often called, just wants to get all the love he possibly can, and has a great character. We were still getting to know each other when, one morning, as we were sitting together, I heard the post drop through the letter box. My immediate thought was "Oh I'll get that later." But someone obviously had other plans. Moments later, I heard Snoopy walking toward me, and then felt his paw on my knee. I stretched a hand toward him, to find, much to my surprise, that he was carrying the letters in his mouth. Wow! I'd never had a dog before who collected the mail for me! It really made me laugh, my GDMI was amused when I told her. He had not been specifically trained to do that, but he did get a good deal of praise for his actions and initiative.

That wasn't the first time Snoopy had managed to surprise both me and my GDMI. During a training session, we had been walking through the town centre, when suddenly I felt Snoopy's lead suddenly tug me forward. I heard a gasp from my instructor behind me, and then felt her hand on my shoulder. I was completely unaware of what had happened, but my GDMI sounded quite shocked. Sounding rather flustered she asked me if I was ok, and if I wanted to sit down. I didn't have a clue what she was talking about, and was feeling rather perplexed. There wasn't anything wrong with me, I was fine, but why did she sound so shocked and concerned? It turned out that during our walk, Snoopy had noticed a pigeon and, uncharacteristically, had jumped straight up in the air in an attempt to get to the bird. I'm glad to say that it hasn't happened since, but I found the whole situation quite funny.

One afternoon, a visually impaired friend visited me for coffee. We had not seen each other for many years, since being at school, but she was attending a summer camp in the area, and so decided to call in. It was great to see her, especially as she brought her young daughter with her. I offered her a coffee, and while the kettle got on with its work, I introduced both of them to Snoopy. Once they had both got a drink, I brought out the biscuits. When I said they were Penguins, they enthusiastically accepted my offer. I handed one to my friend's daughter, and as we continued with the conversation, I handed another to her mother. Several minutes later, she tentatively exclaimed, "Do you have one of those biscuits? I'd really like one!" I was surprised, and immediately apologised, explaining that I thought she had already had one. The words were still on my lips as we both twigged, and said, "Snoopy!" As I approached my dog to investigate, I heard a tail wag, and found that for the last few minutes; Snoop had been proudly sitting there carrying the mystery biscuit in his mouth. We laughed, and I praised him for not actually eating the biscuit; but it went straight in the bin, sorry Snoop.

35. It all happens!

There are times in my life when I encounter situations which make me want to bang my head against a brick wall: times when I want to bury my head in my hands and say, "You just don't get it do you? You really just don't get it." There have been occasions when I have wanted to throw a plate across the room, others when I have thumped my hand on the table in total frustration, and sometimes, when alone, I have found a quiet corner, and cried tears of frustration. Several times I have contemplated the question of why does it have to be me who is blind? But there have been many more times when I have considered that whatever I am going through, there is always someone else who is experiencing something much worse than I, and been grateful for what I have. It is then that I dust myself down and carry on.

So many people have told me that they admire me so much and don't know how I cope. To me, the answer is simple; you have two choices, sink or swim. Get on with it, or don't. For me, I choose to get on with it in the best way I can, as do so many other visually impaired people. I often remember Mrs. Alexander, who used to run the local society for the blind when I was a child. She used to tell us, "Come on now kids, get on with it! You can do it, blindness is NOT a disability, it's just an inconvenience!" There are several choice words that I could use before the word "inconvenient" just to emphasise exactly how inconvenient it is to have a visual impairment, but I will refrain. I did, however, love her sentiment, and her attitude. If we wanted to go dry skiing, she took us dry skiing. If we wanted to go pony trekking, she took us, and if we wanted to go parachuting, she would arrange it; as long as she didn't have to participate.

In contrast, on many occasions, people's actions or words have made me giggle, even when unsuspecting members of the public end up seriously embarrassed when they realise their mistake. I cannot remember how many times I have been asked for my driving licence when identification was required. I recall being in a bank and opening an additional account, without a thought, the member of staff said, "I'm going to need some ID, do you have a birth certificate, and your driving licence. I looked down at my guide dog and exclaimed, "No not today, my dog hasn't finished his course of driving lessons yet!" A few more funny stories will give you a taste of every-day life.

I was once playing my flute in a band in a church which had around nine hundred people in its congregation. The stage was quite large, and I needed help to get to my position on the stage, and then to get off the stage and into the wings. When we had finished playing our set, I put down my instrument, and waited, as usual, for another member of the band to guide me. On this occasion, I waited, and then waited some more. As it became apparent that no one was coming to rescue me, and the preacher had made his way centre stage to speak, I began wondering what I should do. I was standing in front of the drum kit which was on a raised platform. Feeling rather awkward, I decided that the best thing to do would be to walk around the platform, and sit on the floor behind the drum kit, so that, hopefully, I would be out of sight. As I turned I heard a voice, and a friend of mine who had been sitting at the front had come on the stage to rescue me. Thanks Judy, you're a star!

In my opinion, severe sight loss plus no sense of humour equals a pretty miserable existence, so it is essential to develop one. One morning I was part of a social gathering of visually impaired people. We had brought with us a range of cakes to share during the course of the morning. As a few of us chatted together and waited for everyone to arrive, a member of staff from the same building approached and, noticing the cakes, said, "Ooh, you lot look after yourselves well. Mmm, carrot cake, that will help you see in the dark!" It was clear that the person in question hadn't realised the significance of what they had just said, and I quickly retorted to my friend, "Oh yes, Peter, we need plenty of that in our group don't we!" The person realising what they had said, disappeared in a flash and a fluster, as we laughed uncontrollably.

A classic "you don't get it" moment took place one morning as I sat in my local doctor's surgery. There was extensive building work being carried out in the vicinity, and getting around the area was problematic. Our library was due to be demolished, and I had been asking friends when the work would commence, so that I could learn an alternative route into the shopping centre. Suddenly, a man in a high vis jacket walked into the surgery, and began giving information about the work on the library, which was very close to the surgery. He told the details to the receptionist, and I listened avidly trying to gain some useful information for me, and other visually impaired friends. As the conversation came to a close, I stood up and approached the gentleman in order to gather some information for myself. As I began asking about an alternative route, and what was being done to assist the many other blind people who used the shopping centre, he quickly replied in his low cockney accent. "Don't worry, mate, you'll be ok, we'll put signs up." I gently told him we wouldn't be able to see the signs. His answer was, "Don't worry mate, we'll put Braille on 'em!" I tried my best to explain as clearly as I could that Braille signs would be ineffective, because, if people didn't know they existed, they wouldn't look for the information. Eventually, I walked back to my seat, feeling exasperated, and thinking to myself, "I'd stick a Braille sign on your blummin' brain if you had one!"

Let me try to explain the situation. If I am in a building, it is very helpful if someone informs me that several rooms actually have Braille signs, especially when I am anxious to ensure I don't want to mistakenly enter the men's toilets. However, if there is a Braille sign somewhere on a street, for example, I could walk along there every day for years, and be completely unaware of its existence.

I was given the task of checking out hotels in Cambridgeshire, and choosing one for a group of visually impaired friends to stay for a weekend. I had already pre-arranged with a member of staff to make a short visit to explore the facilities. On my arrival, accompanied by my guide dog, I met with the lady concerned, who was very friendly and began by showing me around downstairs. I had tried to explain that I had very limited vision, but this obviously had not sunk in. As we visited each area, her introduction began, "As you can see, over there is..." In the dining room, she suggested that we could have our own private dining area if we preferred, but recommended that we sat near the window, because there were some lovely views of the river... hmmm. My tour continued upstairs with the pointing and "as you can see over there," routine, and I was informed that the fire alarm flashed red for those who couldn't hear. "I'm sure that is a good thing, but we are visually impaired", I thought to myself.

Just before it was time for me to leave, I thanked the lady, and asked if she would mind guiding me across the car park, and over to the pavement. She was happy to assist me, and we chatted as we walked. Suddenly, she stopped by a car, thanked me for coming and said "Well, here is your car." I was suddenly hit with surprise, bemusement, and amusement. I gently explained that I hadn't arrived by car, but had travelled on the bus. At no time since I had met that lady, had I been accompanied by anyone else, so I have no idea why she thought I had come by car. She replied, "Oh, I'm sorry, I thought this was your car." We made our way to the pavement, and as I walked away to my nearest bus stop, I grinned. How I wished I could have actually had the keys to that car. If so, I would have opened the driver's door, sat Snoopy in the driving seat, and placed his front paws on the steering wheel. I would have then closed the door, and sat in the passenger seat. I would have turned, and given the lady in question a wave and shouted "goodbye". I am convinced that if I'd done so, she wouldn't have batted an eyelid. I really don't think that she would have given it another thought. Well, what's wrong with your guide dog driving you home? All together now: "You just don't get it do you?"

It's not only other people we laugh at, we laugh at ourselves! Gaz and I were having a meal together recently. As we ate, Gaz began pouring himself a glass of wine. Although I had put wine glasses on the table, the first one that Gaz found as he reached out was similar to a shorts glass. As he began pouring, Josh suddenly saw what was happening and told him to stop. In the middle of the table were two candles in glass holders. Unfortunately, they were a very similar size and shape to some of our drinking glasses. "Come on Gaz, you're supposed to use your wine glass not the candle. Are you blind?"

I can't possibly tell you just how many times I've been deceived by a simple every-day object. I can be walking along the road when I hear someone coming towards me, and I hear them say, "Hi there!" Instantly, I think to myself, "I don't recognise that voice, but I don't want to appear rude because they obviously know me." So, I smile and say, "Hello!" Then, as the person walks past me while talking, suddenly I become aware of what has happened. They were never talking to me, but using a mobile phone.

Conversely, I was once in my local convenience store buying a few items. As I finished paying for them and turned to make my way to the door I heard a voice saying "Hello". Having been caught out by the mobile phone thing many times, I figured that this greeting was not directed at me, because my name wasn't used. Still feeling unsure about the situation, as I opened the door I heard the same voice say, "She never said hello to me!" I then heard a female voice reply, "Maybe it's because she didn't know that it was her that you were talking to." If the person concerned is reading this, "Sorry!"

There are moments when one's disability can cause surprises. Gaz has a particular liking for an American jazz vocalist by the name of Kurt Elling. When I heard that he was doing a gig in London, I was very pleased. The concert took place within a few days of my husband's fortieth birthday, and I had been wondering what to buy for him. Once the tickets were booked, the planning began. Gaz's sister lived in London, and I phoned to see if we could stay with her for a couple of nights. It was difficult keeping it a secret, but a couple of days before we were due to travel, I did some internet grocery shopping and sent it to Gaz's sister ready for the big party the night before the concert.

Amazingly, everything went to plan, and during the party, Gaz was pleased to learn about the concert taking place the following day. On our arrival at the venue, we heard that there was to be a support artist before Kurt Elling. A British female jazz singer named Claire Martin opened the evening. I had never heard of her before, but I loved her voice and really enjoyed the songs. At the end of the evening, we decided to see if there were any CDs for sale. I was keen to find one by Claire Martin, but was somewhat disappointed when I couldn't find one. Feeling despondent, I followed Gaz, and we went to get his album. By this time, a very long line of fans had formed, waiting for Kurt Elling to sign CDs. He was extremely gracious, didn't rush people, and took the time to speak with each person in turn as he signed their albums. Gaz enjoyed a great conversation with him, and I was pleased. The evening had been a great success.

The building was very quiet and empty as we stood on the steps outside, waiting for a taxi. As we stood there,two other people joined us, and we began a conversation. Gaz explained that this was a surprise birthday present for him and he had been a fan of Kurt Elling for a while. I then chipped in, saying that I liked him too, but actually, I personally preferred the support artist, and was disappointed because I wanted to know more about her and to buy one of her CDs. There was then a gasp of delight, and a CD was thrust into my hand. I genuinely, hadn't realised that the person I had been talking to was actually Claire Martin. As my face turned rather red, we all laughed and chatted for a while longer until two taxis arrived to take us to our destinations. Claire was so unassuming, and naturally friendly. Thanks Claire, you are a joy to listen too, and it was an absolute pleasure to meet you. You made my evening!

You never know quite what is around the corner, and this was certainly the case for Gaz late one evening. He had been attending a band practice, and a friend was driving him home at around eleven o'clock that evening. As they drove down the sloping drive, Gaz knew that he was home. Gaz got out of the car, the friends said their goodbyes and he walked over to the door. He reached out his hand to touch the familiar metal door handle, but found that it was locked. Having no key with him, he knocked on the door. Suddenly he heard the familiar sound of Snoopy barking. But wait a minute, that's not Snoopy. When the door eventually opened, the voice he heard didn't sound like mine either. A rather surprised woman asked Gaz what he wanted.

Gaz's friend had dropped him off at the wrong house. A very embarrassed Gaz made his apologies, but was at a loss to know what to do. He didn't have a clue as to his whereabouts, and, not having a white cane with him, felt very much at sea. Luckily, the husband of the lady who had opened the door offered to walk him back home. I'm sure Gaz thanked you at the time, but thanks again to the gentleman who helped that evening.

Let me return to the subject of public transport. One very cold, wet day during December, my three children and I had taken a trip to a part of Peterborough I am not familiar with. I had learned of a shop that sold Jamaican patties, and wanted to buy a box for Gaz as a surprise. It was freezing and we all shivered at the bus stop, waiting to make our journey home. Little Nathaniel didn't seem to be enjoying himself, and spent a good deal of the time crying. Eventually, a bus drew up, and we eagerly got on. I offered the money to pay for the children, but the driver asked to see my ticket. I told him that I didn't have one, but wished to buy one each for the children, and showed my bus pass. He then said, "No, I need to see your ticket!" Feeling rather puzzled, I asked, "what ticket?" to which he replied, "The ticket from your car." I replied, "I don't have a car, look, I have a guide dog." He then said, "Well then, if you don't have a ticket, you can't ride on this bus. It's a park and ride bus so you'll have to get off." I pleaded my case, referencing the bad weather, the fact that I had a small baby who was clearly fed-up, and that I was happy to pay for all of our fares. My efforts were futile, however. This guy was driving the bus nowhere until we got off.

I was furious as once again, we all stood and shivered in the cold. It was also Sunday, so buses were not as frequent as during the rest of the week. I had no idea about park and ride buses, but assumed that this was a temporary service on the run up to Christmas. Christmas! Merry Christmas Mr Bus Driver! We had been standing for nearly an hour altogether when I heard a bus. I smiled, but then my heart sank when Josh announced that it was another park and ride bus, It stopped, and the driver asked if we were getting on. I explained our situation, and clearly, this bus driver had entered into the Christmas spirit, because he allowed us to get on and drove us into the town centre. Thank you, whoever you were. I haven't forgotten your kindness.

I am amazed at the number of people who enter into a conversation with me while travelling or waiting for a bus. Only recently, I approached a bus stop and enquired whether I was in the correct place. An elderly couple informed me that I was, and that my bus was approaching the stop. Despite the fact that I had just arrived, and they had been waiting, they insisted that I get on the bus first. I thanked them, and got on. As I was finding my seat, I heard the lady I had spoken to asking for the same stop as me. I sat down, and they both sat opposite me.

We had not travelled far, when I heard the lady ask her husband, "I wonder if that lady knows when to get off the bus?" Her husband hesitated and then said, "Uh, I don't know!" The question must have been praying on her mind, because a couple of minutes later she turned to him and said, "I wonder if the dog knows which stop to get off at?" I turned my head aside and grinned. I knew exactly when to get off, but it was nothing to do with my dog, more the result of my talking satnav, discretely placed in my top pocket, just loud enough for only me to hear.

Moments later, I could feel the tension in the air, and almost hear the lady's brain ticking over. It was difficult not to laugh out loud as I heard her next question, "I wonder if the dog will jump up and press the bell when it is her stop?" As we approached our stop, I got in quickly and pressed the bell before anyone else, I just couldn't resist. As I stepped on to the pavement, closely followed by the same couple, I wondered about the conversation they would now be having. "Snoop" I said, "that's given me an idea. Maybe I should teach you to press the bell on the bus. Imagine the fun we'd have!"

36. My Liverpool home revisited

Early in 2013, I promised myself that this would be the year when I would attend the annual reunion at St. Vincent's School. It had been twenty-one years since I had been to one, and it was about time I revisited to meet old friends. I had attempted to make the trip on many occasions, but other commitments had prevented it from happening. Several times the dates fell on the same weekend as I had committed to play my flute for a church event. The previous year, the weekend clashed with my youngest son's birthday. This time, I was determined that I would do everything to make sure I could attend. When I learned the date of the reunion, I immediately booked my overnight accommodation, and looked forward with great excitement. Each year, around twenty beds are made available in the school, so that past pupils who need to travel a considerable distance, can stay overnight. I didn't want to miss out, so made sure I rang to make my reservation. I was so pleased to learn that a space was available, and also hoped that there would be people attending from the time when I was at the school.

As the day drew closer, I learned that a small group of former pupils were planning to stay in a hotel in Liverpool on the Friday evening before the event on the Saturday, in order to extend the weekend. Two girls, Gemma and Edel, who had attended St. Vincent's at the same time as me would be there, so I needed no persuasion to book myself a room for that evening. By the time April came around, I had paid for my accommodation, and my rail tickets, and all that was left was to wait for my weekend of fun to arrive. I have to admit, that a couple of days before I was due to travel, a tinge of nerves hit me. I had loved the school, and made some precious friends, but would I feel the same? Would the people I'd got on so well with still like me? I began to worry whether, following my visit, would the bubble burst or would I leave with those same happy memories?

The week before my scheduled journey to Liverpool, Mum had visited me for a few days, and then returned to Lancashire taking with her my three year old son. I had decided that the two teenagers would be fine with their dad, and following my weekend, I was to travel to my parents' house to spend a week with them, while I was in the area. I awoke early on that Friday morning, but was too excited to get back to sleep. I had already started to pack my suitcase, so I chose to get up and finish the job. I paced around the house, grabbing items and throwing them into my case. It seemed to take me much longer than normal as I frequently referred to the list I had compiled. I didn't want to forget anything important. I made sure I had my mobile phone and charger, the prize I'd been asked to bring for the raffle, several pairs of shoes and, of course, my laptop: all the essentials I couldn't do without. An hour before my taxi was due to arrive to take me to the station, I tried to lift my suitcase, and immediately decided that I needed to leave some items at home. I had been given an idea of where in the building I would be staying, and when I imagined trying to carry my case up three flights of stairs I knew I wouldn't manage it. Now in a minor panic, I retrieved a smaller case from one of the bedrooms, and items started flying. It probably looked like a scene out of a comedy film, but about fifteen minutes later, I had completed my task. I zipped everything up, and then lifted my case. I couldn't take everything I wanted, but I was pretty sure that I could carry my load up at least two flights of stairs and, if needs be, drag it up the other.

Moments later my taxi arrived, and I was on my way. I wasn't particularly looking forward to the four hour train journey, but, as I sat on the platform at the station, I was pleasantly surprised to find that a friend of mine was also travelling to Liverpool to visit her son, so we sat together.

As the train snaked its way through the countryside, I found myself at times musing about how the weekend would go. I'd been looking forward to my trip for several weeks, but would it live up to my expectations? At four thirty that afternoon, I stepped from the train at Liverpool Lime Street. The weather was cold and blustery, but I was in high spirits. I was back in the place I loved, and excitedly looking forward to meeting everyone.

I arrived at my hotel, where I was greeted by very friendly staff, one of whom showed me to my room. I washed and changed, and as I left my room I suddenly heard a familiar voice. It was Michael, one of my friends from St. Vincent's and we chatted briefly before my phone rang. It was Josie, I told her I'd arrived safely, and only a few minutes later I heard a knock at my door, and there she was. As always, it was wonderful to see her again. Josie had left St. Vincent's in 1993, but had remained in Liverpool and regularly attended the reunion.

We walked to the restaurant nearby, where the rest of the group joined us, and we enjoyed a meal together. There were people I'd been looking forward to meeting such as Gemma and Edel. Others I hadn't met before, such as Kath and Mary, but it was great to get to know them. As we laughed and talked together, I felt happy and relaxed.

Although some of us hadn't seen each other for years, it felt as if we had been in regular contact. That is what I've always loved about St Vincent's people, the sense of unity, friendship and togetherness, all of us welcome in the St Vincent's family.

As the evening drew to a close, we all decided that it was time to get a good night's sleep before the big day. I went to my room, and was just about to get changed when there was a knock at my door. It was Gemma, carrying a bottle of wine, and she immediately walked over to the table and began filling the two mugs on my tray. I had never drunk wine out of a mug before, but what the heck, let the party continue! We laughed our way through the next couple of hours until the wine bottle was empty, and the clock said two a.m. Now it was really time for us to try and get some sleep.

As Gemma left my room, and I closed the door, I felt great. I had been so looking forward to meeting her again, and I was already having such a great time. I got into bed and lay there with my head full of thoughts. Gemma had reminded me about so many things I had forgotten, including one of the prayers that Josie taught us to say as we knelt around my bed every night. I hardly got any sleep, because my mind was in overdrive with all those memories, and the excitement about the following day.

The next morning, there were yawns, groans, and possibly a couple of headache tablets handed around, as we ate breakfast together. We'd had a brilliant evening, and now there was the reunion to look forward too. The school wasn't due to open until around one o'clock that day, so, after breakfast, I made my way back to my room. The time seemed to go very slowly. We met up again for a light lunch, but I wasn't very hungry, I was impatient for my taxi to arrive. Eventually, Edel and I got into a taxi, and were finally, on our way. As we turned into the long driveway, I was disappointed to find that instead of hearing that familiar crunching sound of the gravel, there was nothing. It had been replaced by tarmac. That would be the first of many changes I would find that day.

As we got out of the taxi, there was a small group of people chatting and laughing. I made my way through the door and into the front hall. There was time to register, and have a cup of tea before making our way down to the assembly hall for the AGM. Once the formalities were over, I joined a group of people who were looking around the building. Along the way, I met up with my friend Marie, and her husband Mark. Marie had been in Josie's group with me when

I had been at St Vincent's. It was lovely to meet up with her again, and we decided to go and look around our old classrooms in the junior department in Queens Wing. The room in which I had been on my very first day, and where I was taught by Mr. McCall, and next door where Mrs. Orpen had given me my first Braille lesson was now a cookery room. Next door, where Miss Kennan had taught me for a year, and Mrs. Cunliffe the following year, was now a music room. I located Mrs. Pope's old classroom where she had handed out those chocolate bars for the swimming gala, and the unforgettable birthday sweets. I walked down the small side corridor where I had had my singing lessons to find a recording studio. Impressive! I was also blessed to meet Sid Wilson along the way, and had a brief conversation with him. Marie kindly took a photograph of the two of us together, and Josie took one of me with Joe Lambton.

While I was exploring, I decided it was time to find the room where I would be sleeping that evening. I had been told that I would be staying in Bridgeman, the unit in which I had slept during my time at the school, and was feeling excited about revisiting that part of the school. Josie helped me locate my case in the front hall, and we walked up the front stairs together. As Josie opened the door to the corridor and I stepped inside, I was surprised. The whole wing had been renovated, and was completely unrecognisable to me. Inwardly, I felt a tinge of disappointment, but I pulled myself together, reminding myself that this was many years later. Anyway, the rooms seemed to be so much nicer now. When we couldn't locate my room number, we needed to find Michael to help us out. Eventually I found that I wasn't staying in Bridgeman, but in a wing of the school opposite to an area I remember as Sister Anne's group.

Earlier that day, I had made friends with a lady called Pauline. She had been sitting behind me in the assembly hall, and we had begun talking when the meeting was over. During the course of the afternoon we had a raffle. Pauline won a bottle of wine, and as she was presented with it, I said to her, "Ok Pauline, I'm sitting on your table this evening!" I knew where my room was and how to get back to it, even if I were to help Pauline drink that wine. By then, it was around five o'clock, and time to make my way back to the dining room ready for the main event of the evening.

On arrival, I found Pauline seated at a table with the wine bottle in front of her. Eager to get the party started, we opened it, and soon were joined by Gemma, Edel, Jo, and her husband Rob. We had a great evening; with food and entertainment and just a few more bottles of wine.

Later in the evening, as we all joined hands and sang "You'll never walk alone", it felt like I'd never been away. Two of the care staff, Sue and Marie, from my time as a pupil, who were still working at the school were enjoying the party with us and it felt great. It was around two thirty in the morning when I finally trudged to bed, and I slept very well.

Sue and Marie were amazing that weekend. Not only did they stay till the end of that very late night to clear up, but they were the first to get up the following day to make breakfast for us in the dining room. Thanks Sue and Marie. After breakfast, there were many hugs and goodbyes. We'd all had a great time, and were already making plans to return the following year. I made my way back to my room to collect my belongings, and then went down to the front hall to meet Josie. We had arranged to have coffee together before she dropped me off at the railway station to make the journey back to my parents' place. As Josie left me at the station at lunch time, I wished that the weekend could have carried on longer. My train journey would only take around an hour, but as I sat there, I mulled over my weekend. I felt very happy and contented. Everything had turned out just the way I wanted, and the bubble was still very much intact. As Michael W. Smith says in his song, "Friends are friends for ever." Well, all I can say is thank you so much to all the people who made my weekend so special: "St. Vincent's forever!"

Lightning Source UK Ltd.
Milton Keynes UK
UKOW03f1056291116
288779UK00002B/123/P